THE PRODUCT BOOK

THE PRODUCT BOOK

JOSH ANON
with
CARLOS GONZÁLEZ DE VILLAUMBROSIA

PUBLISHED BY

PRODUCT SCHOOL

ISBNS 978-0-9989738-0-7 PRINT
978-0-9989738-1-4 POD
978-0-9989738-2-1 EPUB
978-0-9989738-3-8 MOBI

BOOK DESIGN BY *The Frontispiece*

PUBLISHED BY Product School

TABLE OF CONTENTS

INTRODUCTION

Thank you for picking up this book! We know your time is valuable, and we will do our best to make this book worth your while.

One of the most important parts of being a product manager is knowing who your customers are and what they need. So, who do *we* believe *you* are, and what *need* will this book fill? Fundamentally, you are someone who'd like to know more about product management. Maybe you're a recent graduate trying to figure out if product management is the right career for you. Maybe you're an engineer actively transitioning into product management. Maybe you're a start-up founder figuring out how to build your product division. Or maybe you're already a product manager who naturally evolved into the role, seeking to fill gaps in your knowledge.

Furthermore, there's a lot of wisdom out there regarding best practices for product managers, but most of it focuses on parts of the product-development life cycle. This book will give you an end-to-end view of what goes into building a great product, as well as what product managers do each day.

The upcoming chapters will cover a mix of theory and practical advice to teach you how to identify an opportunity, and build a product successfully to address that opportunity, whether the result is a new product or a refinement of an existing product. Whether you are new to product management, or an experienced veteran, this book is here to help you learn the needed skills to be a successful and effective product leader.

A brief word of warning: Much like chess, poker, and Minecraft, product management is easy to learn, but can take a lifetime to master. If your goal is to be a product manager, consider this book the start of your journey. Becoming a truly effective product manager takes practice!

If after reading this book you still want to become a product manager, consider enrolling in Product School, the world's first tech business school. Product School offers product management classes taught by real-world product managers, working at renowned tech companies like Google, Facebook, Snapchat, Airbnb, LinkedIn, PayPal, and Netflix. Product School's classes are designed to fit into your work schedule, and the campuses are conveniently located in Silicon Valley, San Francisco, Los Angeles, Santa Monica, and New York.

Now, read on to begin your journey through the wide and fascinating world of product management.

CHAPTER ONE
WHAT IS PRODUCT MANAGEMENT?

"Nobody asked you to show up." Every experienced product manager has heard some version of those words at some point in their career. In this case, those painfully frustrating words are from Ken Norton, partner at Google Ventures, in a blog post titled "How to Hire a Product Manager." Think about a company for a second. Engineers build the product. Designers make sure it has a great user experience and looks good. Marketing makes sure customers know about the product. Sales gets potential customers to open their wallets to buy the product. What more does a company need? Where does a product manager fit into that mix?

Those simple questions are what cause not only the confusion, but also the opportunity that comes with product management. Heck, if you're transitioning into product management, these questions might make you worry that product managers are irrelevant. And if you are currently a product manager, you might feel a sudden need to justify your existence. Truthfully, without a product manager a company will continue to operate pretty well—to a point. Yet with a strong product manager a company can become great.

WHAT DO PRODUCT MANAGERS DO?

Put simply, a product manager (PM) represents the customer. No one buys a product because they want to give the company money. Customers buy and use products because the products address their needs. Done properly, the products let the customers be awesome. The end result of representing the customer is that a PM helps the customer be awesome.

There's a lot behind this simple definition, though. Adam Nash, CEO of Wealthfront and former VP of product at LinkedIn, summed up product management by saying, PMs figure out what game a company is playing, and how it keeps score (hint: it's not always about how much money the company makes).

Day to day, PMs must understand both business strategy and execution. They must first figure out who the customers are and what problems the customers have. They must know how to set a vision, finding the right opportunities in a sea of possibilities, by using both data and intuition. They must know how to define success, for the customer and the product, by prioritizing doing what is right over doing what is easy. They must know how to work with engineers and designers to get the right product built, keeping it as simple as possible. They must know how to work with marketing to explain to the customer how the product fills the customer's need better than a competitor's product. They must do whatever's needed to help ship the product, finding solutions rather than excuses. Sometimes, this even means a PM getting coffee for a team that's working long hours to show appreciation. By the way, PMs manage products, not people, so they must achieve everything using soft influence, effective communication, leadership, and trust—not orders.

Even though it's not always obvious what PMs do from the outside, they genuinely do a lot! PMs do so much that they're sometimes even called "Mini CEOs."

Ironically, the thing a PM does the most is say "no." Some people believe that product managers just dictate what features to build. Given everyone has lots of ideas for features, why bother with a PM? It's true that everyone has lots of ideas, some of them good, but most ideas people have are for things *they* want, not necessarily things *customers* want. For example, think of an engineer who spends her days using cryptic command-line tools—I'm sure you know someone like this! This engineer probably prefers keyboard shortcuts, dislikes GUIs, and favors using code to explicitly specify meaning. Now, imagine that engineer is part of a team working on an iPad word processor for senior citizens. Do you think the features the engineer would prioritize match what the customers need? A large part of a PM's job is to figure out the small number of key features to prioritize for the customer, and to lay the groundwork for long-term business viability by gracefully saying "no" to the numerous requests that don't fit the customer's needs.

Similar but Different

It's also worth looking at roles that are related to, but different from, product management. These jobs get confused with product management because in some companies a product manager will also handle these roles' responsibilities, even though they aren't the product manager's primary strengths. For example, remember how we said a good PM would do whatever it took to ship the product? Further confusing things, all of these related roles are abbreviated "PM."

Project managers are most often confused with product managers. While there are many subtle differences, they can be summed up by saying that a project manager owns the schedule and helps ensure the team is on track to meet any deadlines. The project manager will often work with the product manager, and a product manager will provide input on the schedule. Project managers are masters of schedules and Gantt charts, not of representing customers.

Program managers are usually a bit more similar to product managers, but program managers generally focus more on the "getting it built" side, working closely with Engineering and Operations. If you're building a wearable, for example, the program manager will likely be in touch with the manufacturing facility frequently, whereas a product manager will have limited direct interaction with them. Program managers tend to be masters of execution, sort of like a "super" project manager.

To further confuse things, the title that describes what a product manager does varies slightly from company to company. Microsoft, for example, calls its product managers "Program Managers." Apple generally splits the product manager role into the "Engineering Program Manager" (EPM), and the "Product Marketing Manager" (PMM), with the PMM being closer to our definition a product manager, and the EPM being closer to a project manager.

Product managers are like the conductor in an orchestra. The conductor never makes a sound but is responsible for making the orchestra as a whole sound awesome to deliver a great performance to the audience. Great conductors understand and engage with everyone in the orchestra, using the right vocabulary with each section, diplomatically moving everyone together toward the shared goal of a great performance.

Project managers help keep all the rehearsals organized so that the orchestra will be prepared for the concerts. Program managers are involved in planning the entire season's schedule for the concert hall, setting things up so that the project managers can make each performance successful.

BECOMING A PM

There's no obvious path to becoming a product manager. And if you're reviewing résumés for potential PM hires, especially if you're a start-up founder, it's not obvious what to look for. Most careers have a very clear-cut path—you go to school, study computer science, and then you're set to become an engineer. Product management isn't one of those careers.

Because product management is a relatively new discipline, it has a much less formalized training process than other careers. Given that the role often comes down to "doing whatever it takes to ship a product that customers will love and that achieves business goals," product managers should be smart, talented people who can figure things out on their own.

Beyond that, product managers commonly have an intersection of a technical background—not just engineering—such as industry expertise, and communication skills. The most common type of product manager is someone with an engineering/computer science background who became interested in business. PMs often start out as individually contributing engineers who then find themselves taking on more responsibilities: conducting customer interviews, working with Design to validate ideas, and possibly even collaborating with marketing to make sure what they're working on aligns with customer needs. They're not necessarily the best coders or the most definitive domain experts, but their mix of skills makes them unique. Sometimes PMs come from Design, Marketing, or even business school!

At Product School, we often talk about the Product Triangle (Figure 1-1). This is a simple way to visualize and understand where product management (ideally) sits in relation to other core departments:

Engineering (product development), Design, and Marketing. This diagram is helpful for two reasons. First, it visually emphasizes that product management is a generalist role and PMs need to be able to work with significantly different domains. Second, as you go through the process of building a product, you will shift your balance to different parts of the triangle—more on this shortly. Thinking about which leg of the triangle you're focusing on will let you think about the right way to communicate—you'll talk with Design differently than you do Engineering—and the right goals to set during each phase.

Figure 1-1. The Product Triangle, showing product management at the intersection of three core domains.

A common question about becoming a PM is, *how technical do PMs have to be?* They need to know enough that they can work effectively with engineers, participating in things like bug prioritization and scoping meetings, but they don't need a computer science or electrical engineering degree. Especially for software PMs, knowing how to code even a little will be beneficial, and if you want to become a PM but don't know how to code, we'd highly recommend learning the basics. Fortunately, there are plenty of resources to help you learn—you can enroll in a boot camp like Code School or Hack Reactor or take an online course from *lynda.com* or Udemy.

A big benefit to learning to code is that PMs frequently rely on a way of thinking common to coding—top-down design and bottom-up implementation. This means that you think about the big picture, break it down into small pieces, and then build those small pieces first. After building the small pieces, you combine them to get the big picture. Learning to code will give you consistent practice thinking this way.

Another common question is, *how business-oriented do PMs have to be?* PMs don't need an MBA—in fact, some tech companies prefer not to hire MBAs—nor do they need a sales background. They should understand the industry of the company they're interested in and be able to answer the following questions: Who are the customers? Who are the major players? What differentiates one company from another? How do the businesses make money? PMs should also understand basic financial concepts such as revenue vs. profit—revenue is how much money a company takes in, and profit is how much is left after expenses.

In general, when we're working with people who want to make the transition to being a product manager, we recommend they start with an industry/company they're already very familiar with. That makes for an easier transition because they likely know the answers to many of the questions above, even if they don't explicitly realize it! After you have a few years of product management experience, it's fairly easy to switch to a new domain, as you know the right questions to ask to be successful. If you're a founder looking to build your start-up's product team, we'd recommend focusing on finding the best product person possible, even if that person isn't familiar with your domain.

Types of Product Managers

While you will often hear people talk about product managers in the general sense, you will also hear about specialized product managers. Depending on your background, you might find one of these specializations a more appropriate career choice than the general role.

The most common specialization is *technical product management*. This refers to a PM who has a strong technical background, and who works on a technical product. For example, this person might work on a software API where the end customer is a software developer. Technical PMs won't be writing the code or performing technical tasks, but they need to understand the details of what goes into those tasks.

Another specialization is *strategic product management*. This role is the complement to a technical PM, and it's someone who has a strong business-oriented background.

Once in a while, you'll also see titles linked to specific verticals or tasks, such as *growth product manager* or *mobile product manager*. These roles are more focused than the general PM role, and a person in such a role will have a more specific set of skills, such as being an expert in all the different things you can do to grow a product—that is, get more customers using it.

HOW PRODUCT MANAGERS GET PRODUCTS BUILT

While sometimes it might seem like the CEO imagines a product in the shower, and then tells the engineering team to build it, any one who has been a CEO knows this is not the case. Product management is similarly misunderstood by the general public. On TV you're likely to see the guy get out of the shower and start hacking on a laptop with bright green text, occasionally solving a hard problem by drawing on glass. The real world doesn't work like that. So, how do products get built? What does a product manager really do, and how?

In reality, products continuously undergo a product-development life cycle, and a product manager shepherds the product through each phase, owning some phases and contributing to others. The product-development life cycle involves discrete steps, and each step emphasizes a different leg of the Product Triangle.

While the steps are well defined, there are multiple approaches to how these steps can be implemented. On one end of the spectrum there's the *lean* approach, based on Toyota's manufacturing methods and adapted to software/product development by Steve Blank and Eric Ries. The lean methodology focuses on very fast, iterative cycles where your goal is to make something small, release it, learn from it, and use that knowledge to figure out what to do next. Lean cycles might happen in just a few days. On the opposite end of the spectrum you have the *waterfall* approach, where you build something big in a very linear fashion—you spend a lot of time planning a product, and once you've decided what to do, that's what you're going to build and ship even if it takes a long time. The product moves through each process step by step and, like a waterfall, things flow one way, and—almost—never change once they're defined it. Waterfall cycles might take a year or more.

For software product development, larger and older companies tend to use a waterfall approach, whereas many start-ups use a lean approach. As you might expect intuitively—and there have been many studies to back this up—building products with a lean approach is more successful because you're not risking everything on a potentially long, slow-to-create project. Instead, you risk a little bit to build something small, learn from it, and iterate. For that reason, even larger and older companies are shifting towards a lean approach, moving away from waterfall.

The most common approach you'll encounter is a hybrid of waterfall and lean where the PM will plan a bit upfront to find the right opportunity, but then the teams will implement the product in an iterative way. This is nice because it lets you keep a big-picture goal in mind, but change course if needed such as if you find a significant technical obstacle or find that customers don't want the product you're building. We'll mainly focus on a hybrid approach in this book.

Hardware product development takes a more waterfall approach because it's harder to change things you're physically building. For example, hardware requires a lot more planning up front, and the iterative cycles during development to get new hardware builds are a lot longer than with software. However, the overall principles for building products are very similar to those for software, and the process is similar enough that the life cycle stages we'll teach you about apply for both hardware and software product management.

In future chapters we'll dig into each stage of the product-development life cycle in depth. For now, let's look at an overview of each stage, starting with the planning phase.

THE PRODUCT-DEVELOPMENT LIFE CYCLE

Every product goes through five key conceptual stages:

1. Finding and planning the right opportunity
2. Designing the solution
3. Building the solution
4. Sharing the solution
5. Assessing the solution

Put another way, this process involves figuring out what problem to work on, figuring out how to solve it, building the solution, getting it in customers' hands, and seeing if it worked for them. Sounds easy, right?

Conceptually, it is! The devil's in the details. To help you see how each stage connects, before we dive deep, let's look at a high-level overview of each stage.

Finding and Planning the Right Opportunity

The very first phase of the product-development life cycle is to find and clearly define the next opportunity to pursue. The world's a sea of possibilities! What should you build next? Usually, it's up to the product manager to create and sort through all the possibilities, picking the right one to focus on next.

This phase is a critical part of your job. Unlike the other phases, where other disciplines take the lead, this phase is where product leads, taking input from other disciplines. It's probably the most different from anything expected in another position. Because this is so core to your job, we'll cover finding the right opportunity in extreme depth, breaking it down into three parts: strategically understanding a company (Chapter 2), creating an opportunity hypothesis (Chapter 3), and validating that hypothesis (Chapter 4).

To a product manager, strategically understanding a company involves learning about aspects of the company that contribute to its product success including its target customers, its expertise, its competitive landscape, and more. Understanding these aspects, which we sometimes refer to as a company's context, will help you make the right product decisions, and start to find focus in the sea of possibilities. A simple example is CNN.com's team. They are great at building software products—including a website and mobile apps—that deliver the news quickly and efficiently to their customers. Because their PMs know they have software and not hardware expertise, they are—probably—not encouraging CNN.com to build a news-focused smart watch, or other hardware product.

Clearly identifying the company's goals, another strategic element, will help you narrow down and prioritize the possibilities. At a high level, company goals fall into three categories: growth, revenue, and customer satisfaction. Specifically, does the company want to get more users for the product, increase its revenue from the current customers, or make its current customers happier? If the goal is revenue, how does the company currently monetize their product, and how can you increase the value for customers to make them more willing to pay for the product? If the goal is growth, what's stopping new customers from using the product? If the goal is to delight their customers, what can you deliver that they would love, but wouldn't expect? By understanding the current goals you can think strategically, and make sure the products you're building align with those goals, helping the company be successful.

In addition to these, there are some other strategic company context questions you should know the answer to: What is the company building now? What does it excel at compared to its competitors? Who are the key customers you aim to solve a problem for? What's the company's vision, and—more fundamentally—why does the company exist?

With the company's context in mind, the next step, which we'll cover in Chapter 3, is to create an opportunity hypothesis. What do you believe is the right thing to work on next? It could be something as small as fixing a bug that's been in your backlog for a while, or something as large as building an entirely new product.

These opportunity hypotheses come from many different places. Looking at how existing customers use your product is a common source of new opportunities, allowing you to find ways to better serve your customers—and your company's goals. A *metric* is a measurement of a task a customer does with your product. Collectively, your metrics can provide some great insight! From metrics, you might find an opportunity, such as wanting to get higher engagement with a component of your product.

For example, CNN.com likely keeps track of what headlines visitors click on, how many people start watching each video, how many finish watching each video, how many scroll down and read each article, and more. They might then use this data to pull out conclusions, such as, "We should prioritize video content instead of text because people tend to watch videos to completion and see each ad, whereas very few people read articles to completion."

After thinking about the company's context and goals, talking with users, analyzing usage data, looking at existing bug reports and feature requests, and using other approaches we'll cover in Chapter 3, you'll have an idea about what to do next. But before you start to build a feature, you should do some type of validation work to ensure this is the right opportunity to pursue, and that it actually will help you achieve your goals. You have limited time and resources, and spending a little bit of time validating an opportunity hypothesis can often save you significant time and money by keeping you focused on the best opportunities. Chapter 4 goes into depth about how to validate an idea.

Once you've validated your idea, you'll need to develop it into something your teams can implement. An important part of the product-planning phase in the product-development life cycle is scoping the opportunity. *Scoping* means clearly defining the opportunity and the customers you want to target, along with the requirements for the solution. If you're building a pen, do you need it to work in space? Underwater? Upside down? You'll want to clearly define these situations to help everyone understand what the product will need to do when it's finished.

When working in lean or hybrid environments, you'll often hear the phrase *minimum viable product* (MVP). This is a term from lean methodology that simply means, "What's the most minimally featured thing you can build that will address the opportunity well for most of your target customers and validate your opportunity?" In other words, if you were to think about the core function you're trying to let customers accomplish, what's the simplest product you can build that lets them achieve that goal?

Continuing our CNN example, if you went back in time and were working on the first version of CNN's mobile app, what's the simplest app you could build that would provide value to your customers? It might be something with a list of news headlines and a refresh button, and when you tap on each, you see the video for the story. Again, the key to identifying the MVP is that you're focused on the core functionality it provides to the user—news, in this case—rather than focusing on all the possible features you might build in addition to that core function.

Identifying the MVP is a key part of scoping a product because it helps you identify the most important thing to build first—we'll cover tips on how to do that in Chapter 5. This lets you focus your design and development efforts to create a—hopefully—useful product that you can deliver to customers quickly, whether as shipped software or software tested in house. Testing the MVP with real customers will help you figure out what other features will be in and out of scope, as you quickly will get real feedback about what customers like and don't like.

Note that an MVP doesn't mean the product is bad or poorly built. In fact, quite the opposite—it should be very good at what it does, but it should focus on doing only a few key tasks.

Contrast this with non-MVP-based approaches to product development, which are especially common in waterfall development. In that world, you end up spending lots of time trying to build the "perfect" product with every feature you can imagine, it takes forever to build, and once it's out in the real world you discover that customers don't use half the features you thought they would.

A key differentiator between lean and waterfall is that lean leverages MVPs. With a lean approach, you build the simplest thing you can, gather data about how customers use it, and then refine the product if needed. This will let you work quite effectively, building only the features customers want and will use rather than wasting time building things customers don't care about.

Spending lots of time iterating internally and building features without releasing a product can be quite harmful to your business. With our hypothetical CNN app example, if we didn't take an MVP-based approach, we might decide to replicate the website completely, including features like comments, user-submitted video, and customized news streams. Building all those features could delay our launch by months, and who knows how much of our customer base would use those features on their phones. Yes, we could use metrics from the website to prioritize these features, but hopefully you get the point. Additionally, while we were taking lots of time and building features for our unreleased app, our customers wanted a mobile news app and turned to Fox News or another competitor that built its app using an MVP-based approach. The customers cared about the core function—getting news on the go—not about all the extra features. And it's hard to get customers back after they've turned to a competitor!

Most companies using a hybrid model never build a true MVP, but rather an MVP with some extra key features they believe will make the product more enticing. If you know for certain customers will want those key features, incorporating them from the start will help shorten the iteration cycle.

To be fair, hardware development often requires you to try to build more than an MVP because releasing a hardware update is much more complex than a software update. But keeping the MVP in mind, even with hardware, will help you prioritize your development efforts.

Sometimes, as we'll discuss in Chapter 4, your very first MVP will be human-powered rather than automated. For example, if you're a PM at Yelp and want to add a restaurant-recommendation feature, eventually you'll create a fully automated algorithm to generate recommendations. But you could build an initial MVP that makes it appear that the user is getting automated recommendations when it actually has a human making and sending these lists. If many people like and use this feature, then great, you'll build the automation engine. If no one uses it, then this very lightweight MVP saved you the time and effort of building the full feature.

Just as important as scoping the problem is defining your success metrics. What are your goals with the product, and how do you keep score to see if you're achieving them?

Going back to CNN.com, its ultimate goal might be to become the place people go to for news. This means its success metrics include the number of views on a piece of content, the percentage of people who consume each piece of content, the number of articles read or videos watched in a session, and how often the person comes back to CNN.com. The reason we don't solely use page views on a piece of content is because a person might click on an article but never read it. That means that person is not actually getting news/consuming content from CNN.com.

Product managers create a document that encompasses the entire planning phase, called a *product requirements document* (PRD), collecting all this planning information in one spot. A PRD contains the explanation for why you're pursuing this opportunity, the scoped problem definition, the success metrics, and more. But you don't create the PRD in isolation—you'll work with your team, your boss, and other product stakeholders to make sure the opportunity and requirements are clear and the goals are achievable.

One of the biggest reasons that other stakeholders, such as design and engineering leads, are involved in the PRD is that it will be up to them—not the product manager—to figure out the right solution for this opportunity. After all, the design and engineering teams are the experts in their domains, and the product manager is not, even if she started her career in one of those domains!

PRDs gained a bad reputation from waterfall development because they were huge dictating documents that people disliked reading. In fact, the lean model largely doesn't use PRDs. In the hybrid model, the PRD is treated as a great communications tool to get everyone on the same page and as a living—not dictating—document. Over the product-development life cycle, the PRD will expand to contain more information, but it starts by clearly stating the problem and why we're working on it. When the product's built, the PRD provides a great reference for the sales and support teams to understand what's in the product and why. We'll go over how to effectively write and use a PRD in Chapter 5.

Once we have this first draft of a PRD—clearly identifying the opportunity/problem and success metrics—and all stakeholders have agreed on the right problem to focus on next, we'll move on to the next phase of the product-development life cycle.

Designing the Solution

During this phase, covered in depth in Chapter 6, we'll figure out a feasible solution to the problem we've identified.

Here, PMs will primarily work with the design team, but the engineering team will offer input as well, to help gauge feasibility. For example, a CNN.com PM might have found that her readers complete a lot more articles when a virtual reality 360° video is included, meaning better success metrics, and the PM wants to integrate 360° videos into more content. The design team might then create designs where every breaking news story has a live-streaming 360° video to put viewers right there with the reporter, but the engineering team might not be able to build a live-streaming solution. This means the design team needs to come up with another solution that the engineering team can implement.

Even though the PM won't be coming up with the solution herself, she'll stay actively involved in this phase. She'll likely work closely with design to conduct user research, looking at people's current behavior. She'll also help communicate with Engineering to ensure Design isn't working in isolation—that everyone is working together to solve the customer's problems.

Contrary to popular belief, design doesn't just mean what the solution looks like. Design involves aspects like information architecture (In what order are things presented to the user?), wireframes (Where should the information live on the screen?), and pixels (How does it look?). It's uncommon to find a designer who's an expert on every one of these aspects, and a PM will likely be working with a design team rather than with just one designer to figure out how the product should function and look.

If possible, you'll want the design team to produce prototypes of the solutions that they can test with customers to validate the design. These prototypes could be printouts that you swap in when the customer clicks on something, clickable mockups working with fake data, etc. The key is to have something that accurately represents the solution, but that you can mock up without having to actually build the solution.

Design is done when you have validated a prototype as a suitable solution, Engineering has agreed to the viability of the solution, and you've defined the look and feel of the solution that all stakeholders have agreed to.

Building the Solution

Once you've defined the problem and designed a solution, it's time to build it.

Companies have different approaches to implementing solutions, depending on their history, the product, and their desires. For example, if you're working on a mobile app, it's very easy to release a new version to customers every week, and development is likely focused on smaller but more frequent releases—lean development is very common with mobile and web apps. If you're building hardware, there is a long time between the product's design and when its hardware is ready for mass production. Hardware-engineering companies generally have fewer but very high-quality releases. After all, it's difficult to release a hardware update to fix a bug!

In Chapter 7, we'll cover some of the most common software-development methodologies, along with tips for working with engineers. Suffice it to say the PM will stay involved throughout development, helping to prioritize bugs (backlog grooming), test software, and do whatever's needed to help the product ship.

A note of caution if you're currently an engineer who wants to transition to product management—development might turn out to be the most frustrating phase to you because you are not an engineer anymore. You will not be writing code for the product, or telling people what code to write. Your job is to stand aside, and let the people who are still engineers write the code. You help them however else you can, even if it's getting them coffee, but don't tell them what to do unless they ask for your help.

Furthermore, as a PM, you'll be put into positions where you have to negotiate taking on technical debt, meaning you need to ask Engineering to write kludgey code that isn't sustainable in the long term to get something done in the short term.

Engineers hate taking on technical debt—they want to write a complete answer from the outset. If you come from an engineering background, taking on technical debt can be hard. As a PM, you'll often have to make hard tradeoff decisions, accepting short-term debt to provide customer value faster. The opposite is true as well, which is hard for PMs from a non-technical background. You'll have to pay off that debt later—cleaning up the code—otherwise the code can get unwieldy, and it can become very hard to iterate on the project.

Also, although we're presenting the product-development life cycle in a very linear fashion, it's a lot more iterative in real life, especially between designing and building the solution. For example, while Design will have figured out the most common use cases in the prototyping stage, there are likely many edge cases that will come up while Engineering's building the product. Product, Design, and Engineering will work together to address these needs and questions that arise while working on the product.

During the development phase a PM should try to find effective opportunities to share prototypes of the product with customers or people inside the company, so that you can get early feedback about the product. Does it address the customer's need effectively, or is there a big tradeoff you didn't anticipate? If you prioritize building the minimum viable product you previously identified, then you can start testing the core product once the MVP's ready. It's important to ask for this feedback at the right times—if you wait until right before you release to get feedback, you might not have time to act on what you learn.

New information that affects the product's scope might come up during development, too. Going back to our example of 360° live-streaming on CNN.com, maybe a third-party company released a tool that makes it very easy to live-stream these videos. That'd make it simple for CNN.com's engineers to add on-the-scene 360° video to breaking news stories, which was originally deemed out of scope because of the technical challenge.

In the product-development approach we're presenting in this book, it's always best to do more investigation up front, so that you don't waste resources designing a solution and then have to change large parts of it. But the best product managers are ones who know they can't define everything perfectly up front, and that it's generally impractical to spend months trying to do so. Instead they do their best to plan, but also seek out new information to help the product get better, and react to any needed changes with open arms.

The development phase of the product-development life cycle is done when a working product that has been thoroughly tested is ready for release.

Sharing the Solution

As much as we'd like to believe that if we build it, they will come, the world doesn't work that way. Product marketing (Chapter 8)—in fact, marketing in general—is an incredibly important part of the product-development life cycle, and really begins after we've built the solution. This phase of the life cycle is where we launch our product, sharing it with the world and letting our customers know how our product will help them.

Effectively telling the world about our product is so important that some companies even create a separate position, the *product marketing manager*. A PMM is very similar to a PM, but a PM tends to be more internally focused—getting the product built—while a PMM is externally focused—working with customers to understand their needs and to communicate the product's value.

Early in the first stage of the product-development life cycle, even before scoping the opportunity, it should be clear what this product will do for the customer. This isn't a list of what features it has or what the product does, but rather what problem it will solve. In the product marketing phase of the product-development life cycle, you figure out how to succinctly and effectively communicate how the product solves that problem and makes the customer awesome. It's essentially storytelling, and we call it "messaging."

For example, going back to CNN.com's 360° VR video streaming feature, if we promoted the feature itself, "Live 360° VR video streaming," most customers wouldn't know what that meant—or care. Instead of talking about the specific feature, we can focus on the value and the benefit this feature provides: "Be on the scene with our reporters." We might then go on to say what the feature is and how to use it, but we've led with a clear message about why a customer should care.

This phase of the product-development life cycle is more than just messaging, though. We'll also plan for the product's release. Release might involve planning a beta test, creating marketing assets for a website or ad, working with key partners before release, briefing the press, or planning a launch event. The exact needs will vary from launch to launch.

Broadly, this phase of the product-development life cycle is done when the product is launched, but there will likely be many marketing campaigns and tasks to help achieve the product's success metrics beyond the launch. Marketing will continue even while the team, internally, has moved on to the next version of the product, or to a completely different product.

Assessing the Solution

The last phase of the product-development life cycle is to assess how the just-completed iteration of the cycle went, see if you're on track to achieve your success metrics, and come up with a recommendation for what to do in the next iteration. As you might guess, that recommendation feeds into the initial planning phase of the next iteration.

During this phase, you will meet with the team that you built the product with and assess how it went. Did everyone get so burned out that half the team quit? Was the team very happy with the process and excited to work on the next project? What was the team's overall competitive strength, and what could they improve at? Use this feedback to determine what went well, and what you should do differently the next time around.

Now that the product's released, you should start seeing real data about how people are using it. Is it in line with your expectations, or is something far off? And most importantly, does it look like you're on track to achieve your success metrics? For example, CNN.com could look at how many people are watching its new 360° broadcasts and whether the overall number of people getting their content from CNN has increased after the release of this new feature. If the number of people watching these broadcasts and seeking out more content on CNN improved, then your product was a success. If it's unchanged, then you should evaluate why this strategy didn't work how you expected—why don't customers like it?

Once you've had a chance to see how your new product was received by your customers, you'll put together a recommendation for what's next: should you iterate more on this feature/product, move on to something else, or end-of-life this feature/product? This recommendation will help inform the next iteration through the product-development life cycle, and we'll explain how to create a good recommendation in Chapter 9.

As you can see, there's a lot to product management and the product-development life cycle! But don't worry, the following chapters will break each step down into more detail and help you understand how to be a great product manager who makes awesome products that customers love.

CHAPTER TWO
STRATEGICALLY UNDERSTANDING A COMPANY

One of the first things a great product manager should do before even thinking about a product is to understand the company that makes it. Every company is a little bit different, and they have different priorities, values, strengths, and weaknesses. Knowing these details about a company—understanding the full context of its current situation—is the starting point to find and evaluate product opportunities and make strategic product decisions. We'll build upon how to leverage these details in the following chapters.

Analyzing a company breaks down into three main categories: What product are we building? How do we know if our product's good? What else has been, is being, and will be built?

WHAT PRODUCT ARE WE BUILDING?

This category of analysis is focused on the company's current product. This might be an existing product that you're tasked with improving, or it might be the next new product that you want to build.

Why Does the Company Exist?

The most fundamental thing to understand about a company is why it exists. What's its mission statement or, even more importantly, its core belief: the value it adds to the world that differentiates it from other companies?

Simon Sinek has a great TED talk called "How Great Leaders Inspire Action" and a book on the same topic, *Start With Why*. In both, he advocates for what he calls the Golden Circle (Figure 2-1). Specifically, he says that the "why" of a company is what people actually care about and buy into. How you deliver that value and the products you create will build on top of this core value. From a product point of view that "why" is your guiding light—it will help you figure out what fits with the company's reason to exist and what doesn't. Put another way, the products you build are a means to an end. That "end" is the bigger picture and what customers buy into/want to achieve when they buy your products.

Think about storytelling—the "why" is the theme. What's this story about? What specific viewpoint does the writer want to share with the world that led to her writing the story? Themes in movies are often obvious: love conquers all, revenge doesn't lead to happiness, etc. A company's theme can be a little harder to decipher. Often its theme is expressed as a value within the company's mission statement, which you can usually find on the website. But even if a company has a clear mission statement with a clear theme, it may forget about it when making decisions, leading to mixed results.

Let's look at Sinek's example of Apple. If Apple started with the "what," which many companies do, Sinek asserts its messaging would read, "We make great computers. They're user-friendly, beautifully designed, and easy to use. Want to buy one?" That's fine, but it sounds pretty generic. Many other PC manufacturers even make the same claim!

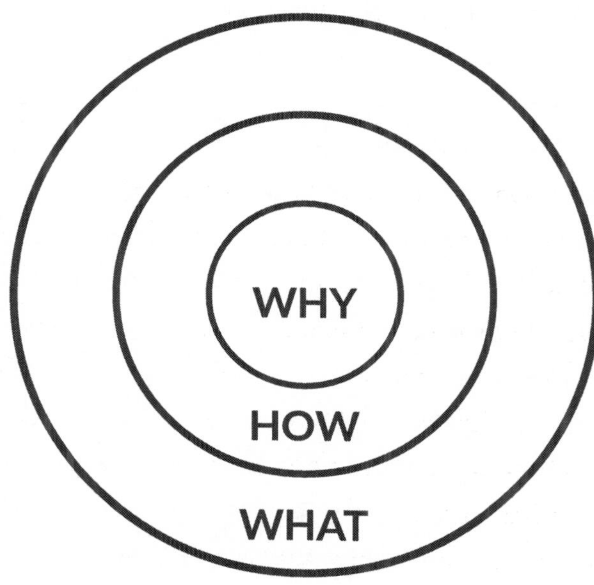

Figure 2-1. Simon Sinek's Golden Circle, starting with "why" as the most important aspect of a company.

Instead, recall the Think Different campaign Apple ran in the late '90s, which talked about Apple's "why" without even mentioning the products: "Here's to the crazy ones." Starting from that mission statement, Sinek says a more realistic marketing message from Apple would be, "With everything we do, we aim to challenge the status quo. We aim to think differently. Our products are user-friendly, beautifully designed, and easy to use. We just happen to make great computers. Want to buy one?"

That version starts with the "why" (challenging the status quo), then moves into the "how" (being user-friendly, etc.), and finally the "what" (selling great computers). It's way more compelling than the first version, and it also says a lot more about what Apple represents, and who they are as a company.

"Why" is at the core of the Golden Circle because it's the most fundamental thing you need to understand about a company. Everything a company does, from the products it builds to the feature decisions it makes for those products, should emerge from that value. If it doesn't, there's a good chance that decision isn't working well for the company.

Google writes its mission statement as, "To organize the world's information and make it universally accessible and useful." There's an implicit value proposition of driving the human race forward, which Google does, primarily with data. It's unlikely to make a toaster oven, even a Wi-Fi-connected one, because that doesn't organize the world's information, make it accessible, or drive us forward. However, Google did purchase Nest, which made appliance-like devices, including a thermostat and a smoke detector. Nest's products involve organizing information about your home and applying computer science to that information to make your home function better. The Nest Thermostat learns you behavior and automatically adapts how it heats and cools your house to save energy—thereby saving you money—while still keeping you comfortable.

It's worth noting that every company whose fundamental mission is "to make money" rather than focusing on what value it can add to customers' lives has failed. Sinek discusses this in detail in his talk. If your company functions well and customers want the products you're making, you'll make money. Revenue is be validation that a company is doing the right thing for its customers—revenue should not be a company's reason for existing. This isn't true for only socially conscious companies like TOMS, the shoe company, but for all companies. Customers will pay for your product because it makes their lives better, not because they want to give you money.

Similarly, companies that start without a mission, but rather with some invention that they're trying to find a use for, often fail. Specifically, if your company started because someone said, "This is a cool idea—can we sell it?" rather than "This invention would make people's lives better because…," you have a solution looking for a problem. An engineering innovation by itself doesn't make a product—products are solutions to problems people encounter. You'll often hear startups talk about "pivoting" because they found customers didn't want the product they made, and the startup is trying to repurpose what it built to something customers will use.

Some companies are moderately successful without having a clear mission statement. But they struggle to grow because it's be unclear to their leadership why their product was successful and how to expand the product line. The result is a product portfolio that feels very disconnected. Misfit, which was purchased by Fossil, achieved success with its Shine wearable activity tracker, but it didn't have a clear mission. Its follow-up products included a smart light bulb and sleep sensor, and they failed to gain much attention. Misfit appears to be aware of this problem and has tried to fix it, though, as it's now focused on making wearables a natural part of your life, with fashion-conscious activity trackers, and smart headphones with a built-in activity tracker. The implicit value proposition is that Misfit wants you to live a better life, and it achieves that by enabling you to analyze your life, especially your health.

As a product manager, keeping the company's core value proposition in mind will help you understand the company's vision. Understanding the vision will let you understand the company's goals, which lets you understand its product roadmap. We're getting ahead of ourselves here! Suffice it to say, your first task when looking at a company from a product point of view needs to be understanding its "why."

Customers and Personas

The most fundamental part of a company, after why it exists, is who it's solving problems for. Essentially, who are the customers for your product, and why are they buying your product? You will optimize your products for these people.

Let's imagine we're building a camera accessory that plugs into the iPhone, like the DxO ONE. Your customers are likely people who enjoy shooting with their smartphones, but want better image quality than the built-in camera provides. Since we're iPhone-specific, we won't care about people with Android phones. And, since we're building an accessory that people need to pay extra for, we will ignore people who are happy with the built-in camera.

But even amongst all the customers we do care about, there's a lot of variability. Maybe one loves taking photos of his dogs while another takes photos of her ferrets. Dealing with lots of real people and their variability can make for complex discussions—our camera accessory has to work with cats, dogs, ferrets, rabbits, etc. Instead, it would be easier if we just abstracted things and said, "Our customers take photos of their pets."

We can take the various common traits we care about in our potential customers and abstract them out into a persona. A persona is a fictional, typical customer, and defining key personas lets you segment your customers by highlighting the things your customers care about that are relevant to your product. Personas are tools to help you understand your customers, they are not actual end customers. A great way to think about the difference is that Facebook and Snapchat have many of the same customers, but their internal personas—how they segment those customers and what aspects of the product they care about—are different.

You've likely already talked about a persona without realizing it. When someone asks, "Can my mom use it?" they don't mean their actual mom, she might be a rocket scientist. Instead, they mean the "mom" persona of a middle-aged person who is never the first to buy new technology, and will break many gadgets simply by turning them on. When we say, "Can my mom use it?" we're actually asking if the product is user-friendly enough that someone in the "mom" persona can use the product to achieve a goal without breaking it and without asking for help.

Good personas will have a picture and a fictional name. They will include any relevant details about the person's life such as demographics, outside activities, and common tasks, as well as what problems the person is looking to solve. Think of a full persona as a way to bring a typical customer to life—you want enough detail that you can imagine yourself in the persona's shoes. Roman Pichler put this into a template you can fill out to start crafting your own personas (Figure 2-2).

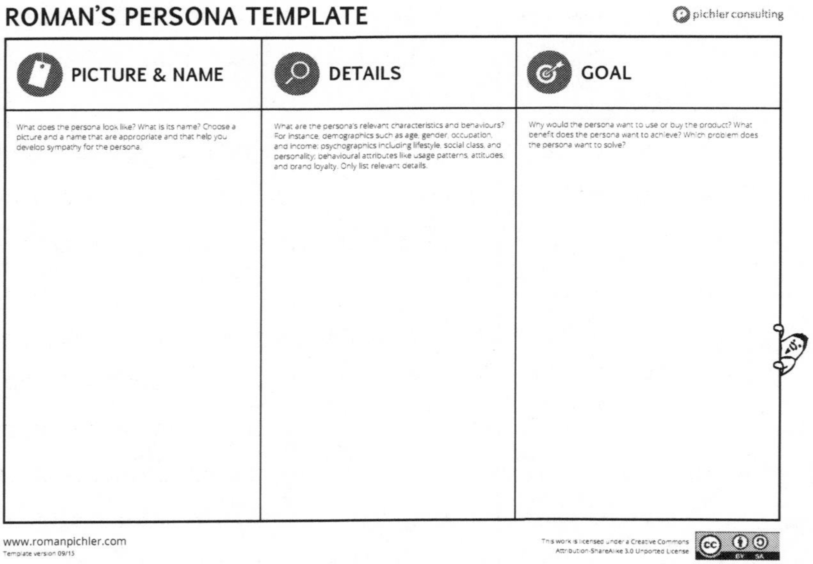

ROMAN'S PERSONA TEMPLATE

pichler consulting

PICTURE & NAME	DETAILS	GOAL
What does the persona look like? What is its name? Choose a picture and a name that are appropriate and that help you develop sympathy for the persona.	What are the persona's relevant characteristics and behaviours? For instance, demographics such as age, gender, occupation, and income; psychographics including lifestyle, social class, and personality; behavioural attributes like usage patterns, attitudes, and brand loyalty. Only list relevant details.	Why would the persona want to use or buy the product? What benefit does the persona want to achieve? Which problem does the persona want to solve?

www.romanpichler.com
Template version 09/15

Figure 2-2. Roman Pichler's persona-building template, available at *www.romanpichler.com* and included under the Creative Commons Attribution-ShareAlike 3.0 Unported (CC BY-SA 3.0) license, *https://creativecommons.org/licenses/by-sa/3.0*.

While it's tempting to make your personas very detailed, describing every aspect of the person's life, they can quickly become overwhelmed with lots of irrelevant details. Keep them as sparse as possible overall, but with enough detail that they're believable and represent a real target market. If you're wondering how to do this, write a detailed persona, and for every statement you make about the person, if it's not relevant to your product, delete it.

The key things you're looking for are this person's priorities, related to your product/area of expertise. What is the persona "IT Tech Tom" trying to do that's significant and what's actually insignificant: What extreme pain points does he have and what pain points are insignificant? What are the things he must have from any solution you create? For example, IT Tech Tom might be very busy his entire workday with customer support tickets. He would likely favor a new automated machine deployment system over one that involves lots of manual intervention.

A way to envision these customer's priorities is to imagine the customer's journey. What problem is a given persona trying to solve, what does he do when he tries to solve it, and what happens as a result? Tell us a story about the customer.

Don't forget about the social or emotional side. Dental headgear can solve orthodontic problems—a significant pain point—but do you want to be the kid on the playground who has to wear headgear for two years? Other factors, like which distribution channels reach the various personas, and whether they're willing to pay for different parts of the product, can help differentiate personas.

Personas contain demographic information only if it's relevant. For example, Airbnb's "host" personas probably don't include how much each person makes per year, but they likely do include why a persona is interested in renting her place out. A young urban host might be renting a couch or second bedroom to help pay for his condo. In fact, he might have to do so, meaning he cares most about maximizing how much he gets for his space vs. having someone there all the time. A retired couple who are snowbirds, flying from Pennsylvania to Florida each winter, might want to rent out their vacation home when they're not using it, to supplement their income. They'll likely prefer Airbnb guests who stay for longer periods of time, and treat the home like their own, even if it means their vacation home is empty periodically.

This might be counter to what you know about typical marketing theory, where demographics are key. Again and again, product theory and practice have shown that focusing on a common problem, pain, or desire yields better segmentation than demographics.

Harvard Business School professor Clayton Christensen has been working on a customer-segmentation approach he calls "jobs to be done" for over a decade. Thinking this way helps build great personas. The example Christensen gives is that when a fast-food company tried to improve its milkshake sales, it first did traditional demographic segmentation and asked each persona (e.g., the 18–35-year-old milkshake drinker) about her ideal shake and implemented changes. Sales were stagnant.

But when the fast-food company focused on who bought milkshakes, when they bought them, and where they drank them, it found a different way to segment its customers. One segment bought milkshakes in the morning to keep them feeling full until lunch. As an added benefit, the morning milkshake gave them something to occupy their free hand while driving during a boring commute. That group wants a milkshake that takes a while to drink so that it lets them feel full longer and lasts for the commute. Now consider another segment: customers buying milkshakes as a special treat for young children. Kids likely just want a tasty treat and don't have the patience to drink a milkshake for 30 minutes. Using pains and goals instead of just demographics will help you segment your customers into useful personas.

It's possible your product has multiple personas. For example, the people who read and write reviews on Yelp are customers, but the businesses these people review are also Yelp's customers. Create multiple personas if needed, and identify the primary one you want to satisfy.

Sometimes the customer and the buyer—the person using the product and the person actually purchasing it—aren't the same, such as parents buying a swing set for their kids. This is common with enterprise software, and you'll need to create separate personas for these cases.

Ultimately your goal with each persona is to have enough information and detail about that category of customer that you can imagine yourself in this person's shoes. This will help you empathize with that customer, understand his pain points, and think about ways your product can solve that pain (we'll go into this in depth in Chapter 3).

Because personas help you understand what a group of customers is like, a key piece of a persona is to be authentic—if you find your persona is incredibly busy, working 80+ hours/week, how much time do you think he'll have to learn how to use your product? If you fail to note how much your persona works, you could make the wrong product decisions, errantly assuming this persona has time to watch a long onboarding video tutorial.

Whenever you start working on a new product or at a new company, find out as soon as possible who the relevant personas are. Make sure they're clearly written down in the Name/Picture/Details/Goals format. Many companies use Word or Google Docs files with their persona data, and there are specialized tools that explicitly manage your personas and organize the research that goes into each one (As of the time of writing, the landscape of persona tools is so in flux that we've elected to leave it up to you to search and find what's current).

If there's nothing written down, it's still likely the company has a rough idea of who its customers are. Use that knowledge to write down a first draft of the persona, you will revise it over time.

It's not mandatory to have pre-existing customer knowledge to build a persona. Just make your personas rough at first, and as you learn more about your customers, refine the personas, perhaps dividing them up and creating a new persona when key differences appear. You might even find as you talk with customers and show them prototypes of your product/feature that someone you thought was a certain persona really isn't.

Take Airbnb, for example. Even though business travelers travel frequently, they might not be the best persona for Airbnb to focus on because they expense their hotel rooms, meaning they're not price sensitive, they care more about service than connecting with the host, and they often have rewards cards that let them accumulate free stays for personal travel. Airbnb focuses on making interactions with your host and other locals part of your travel experience. Business travelers, however, are there to work, not to feel like a local. All of that means they're currently better served by regular hotels, and Airbnb might choose not to spend lots of time targeting that persona right now.

You'll also want to ensure your personas align with what your product does. If you're building payroll software for a small to medium-size business, your personas should be based on coffee shops and doctor's offices, not a stay-at-home dad. Stay-at-home dads won't have any reason to buy your software, and you want to spend your time making decisions based on the customers who will buy and use your software.

Note that "everyone" is not a persona, as "everyone" is too vague to help you make decisions. Many people think that big companies like Google, Facebook, and Apple target "everyone," but they don't and are quite forward about it. Facebook started off targeted at one persona, college students. Over time Facebook grew, adding high-school students and beyond, and its current customer base is very diverse. Facebook likely has many internal personas, but when it releases new features, they're still targeted at specific personas. A "Henrietta High-School Student" persona doesn't care about the reviews feature on business pages, but a business that created a Facebook page certainly does!

Another great attribute to consider about your personas is where on the adoption curve they fall. Not everyone buys/starts using something new at the same time. There's a general theory of adoption—which can refer to a new product or a new feature—that says there's a tiny group of early adopters that have to be the first to have new things—think of the first person you know to own a smartwatch. Then, there's a slightly larger group of people who like being one of the first—but not necessarily *the* first—to have something new—think of the first person you know who bought an Apple Watch but didn't own a previous smartwatch.

Unfortunately, there's a gap (see Figure 2-3) before you get to the next group of people. If your product's awesome and delivers on a value proposition your customers care about, you'll continue on to the next step, mass-market adoption, when the bulk of potential customers buy/use your product. Eventually, even the late adopters—the people who always seem to be years behind everyone else technology-wise—will start using your product. Considering where your various personas fit into this curve will help you understand when they're likely to adopt your new product or feature. This will help prioritize features. Early adopters will tolerate missing features that laggards might require, for example.

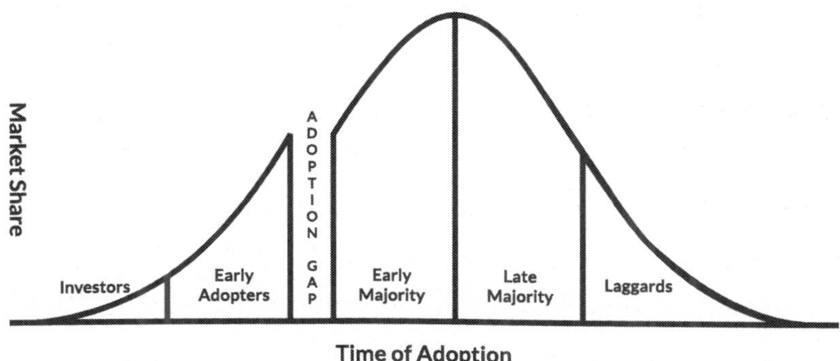

Figure 2-3. The adoption curve where the x-axis represents the groups of customers that will potentially purchase your product over time. The y-axis represents the approximate market share of each group.

But if your product isn't awesome, when you hit the chasm before mass-market adoption, your growth will stop because your product doesn't provide enough value to most people's lives. The mass market won't adopt it.

Whenever you think about how to make a product better, your first thoughts should be about who the target personas are and what needs they have that aren't currently being met by the product. This gives you a great immediate filter to make sure you're making strategic decisions about what to do next.

CHAPTER TWO TIP

Throughout this book, to give you an additional perspective, we've asked experienced product managers to share their best advice about each chapter's topic.

Our first tip comes from Jeremy Toeman, vice president of products at CNET. Jeremy runs CNET's audience development, engagement, and social media teams, and he's responsible for building CNET's multichannel products, including web, mobile, and apps. Jeremy has more than 20 years of experience, including being VP of product management at Sling Media; working on Dropcam, Sonos, and Sphero; and founding multiple companies that had successful exits. In other words, he knows what he's talking about! Here's what he has to say about personas.

MAKING PERSONAS REAL WITH EMPATHY

With ~20 years under my belt, I've noticed the consistent trend is for product managers to define personas with 90% demographics, and 10% wants/needs/emotions. Maybe less. For example, it's easy to create Jill—a 23-year-old in a major metro who has a roommate, loves travel, and is very into the DJ scene. Jill is thinking about buying her first car. That's a great starting point. But it's barely the tip of the iceberg.

Does Jill care about what the car says about her, or does she care about fuel efficiency? Is Jill focused on saving money, or on resale value? Does Jill care about the car tech, or just that it gets her places? Further, does Jill enjoy the research process, or does she just want to be pointed in the right direction? Is she going to make a little comparison spreadsheet for herself, or just wing it?

Far too often products are coming to market without considering the needs of the individual, as opposed to pure demographic fit. All of the above scenarios are valid to a product manager who is designing a site/app to cater to car buyers. But a simple review of car-buying websites shows a distinct lack of consideration for emotional needs versus purely practical ones.

When the TV industry tried to bring 3D technology into the house, they showed a distinct lack of empathy. Sure, 3D movies were performing well in theaters, so it made logical sense to bring that kind of tech into the home. But an empathic product manager could have easily predicted the poor reception: movie theaters are primarily solitary (though shared) experiences, whereas family/living rooms are primarily social experiences. And no family wants to sit on the couch wearing a bunch of goofy glasses (not a problem in a darkened theater).

Great product managers can put themselves into the mindset of the persona, and really get into his/her skin to understand the wants and needs and, most importantly, the emotional triggers of their users. And truly great product managers will cycle through many different personas as they consider the product's core needs. This process determines the subtle differences that can take good products and transform them into exceptional ones.

Use Cases

Use cases are simply how a company expects each persona to use the company's product to achieve a goal. They provide the context to let you understand the link between your personas and your products.

Day to day, a PM will need to think about what use cases they want to support for their product, which helps in finding and prioritizing opportunities. The use cases will affect everything from what features you prioritize to solve your customers' problems to what customers you'll market your product to.

For example, a key use case for an iPhone is checking your email on the go. Apple will make product decisions for the iPhone that help you know when you have new mail, and let you reply to mail, compose new mail, etc. Conversely, the iPhone isn't designed to help you press cloves of garlic, although you could theoretically use it to do so—we'd recommend buying a garlic press instead. Apple cares about the former, not the latter. The choices it makes will be focused on improving email on the go, even if it means a future iPhone is no good for cooking with garlic.

That example is pretty drastic and obvious, so let's look at a more subtle example companies often face. One major category of company is called enterprise or B2B (business to business), which applies to companies that create tools to address other companies' work-related needs. B2B companies will frequently pick a size of customer company to focus on—small, medium, or large—and then further focus on select industry verticals.

Gusto, formerly ZenPayroll, is an HR-solutions company for small businesses. It realized that small businesses have a wide range of fairly complex "*run the business*" (RTB) needs such as HR, accounting, and office-administration. One person usually can't do all of those tasks, small businesses don't have the resources to hire many people to do those tasks, and existing tools like ADP are overkill for small businesses.

Gusto's initial persona was likely a small-business owner—we'll call her "Suzanne Small Business Owner." The Gusto website lists instances of this persona, including in her repertoire tech startups, coffee shops, auto shops, creative agencies, law firms, and restaurants. Those are the customers Gusto targets.

Let's pretend Suzanne owns a coffee shop. Put yourself in her shoes for a second—what are the RTB tasks she has to deal with? The simplest ones are around payroll: she wants a way to collect W2-related information (US-government-required work forms) for her employees, she wants an easy way to pay employees, and she wants an automated way to provide them with tax information. These situations she wants to address—problems she wants to solve—are use cases she might want to use Gusto for, and Gusto will likely build features to solve these problems.

At the top of Gusto's website is a Payroll link. When you click on it you'll see that Gusto specifically states how it has employee self-onboarding for W2s and more, payroll solutions, and automated taxes. It has built features into its product to enable it to work in these use cases that its target persona, Suzanne Small Business Owner, has.

Gusto initially focused on one use main use case: payroll management. But over time it has expanded to cover more use cases, such as health insurance. Over time, Gusto will likely continue to help small businesses simplify their RTB tasks. They'll be addressing more use cases that Suzanne Small Business Owner deals with.

However, if a large business tried to use Gusto, the business would find features it needed lacking because its requirements are more complex than those of the small businesses that Gusto targets. Gusto doesn't handle all the use cases for a large business, but a more complex product like ADP does handle those use cases.

Down the road, Gusto could choose to expand to support another customer, a large business. To address that customer, Gusto would create personas to represent the different types of large-business customers, like "Multinational Matt." Gusto would then add features to the product to address the use cases large business have but small businesses don't, like dealing with multiple international offices. This would be one way to grow and to gain more customers. However, supporting large businesses and their use cases isn't currently a priority for Gusto, so it hasn't built features to address these needs.

By focusing on specific use cases for specific personas, you can ensure that your product addresses the needs of those personas effectively, which makes your end customers happy. Adding features to support new use cases or making it easier to achieve current use cases is a common source of product opportunities.

Enterprise vs. Consumer Companies

Related to use cases and personas is knowing if the company is developing enterprise (B2B) or consumer (also called business-to-consumer or B2C) products. This simply means asking whether end customers are using the product in their personal lives, or at work. You likely don't need payroll software at home, and you likely don't need a smartphone-connected sous vide device at work.

The primary difference in how these companies function is that B2B involves more decision makers, and the people who decide to buy the product are often not the ones using it—e.g., a CTO will approve buying software for HR, but it's HR who uses it day to day. B2B companies often have larger sales forces with specialized roles such as sales engineers who help integrate the product into the customer's environment, and customer-training roles. You're unlikely to just start using SalesForce out of the box, for example, nor are you expected to.

B2B software also historically emphasized utility over usability: that is, as long as it solved your problem, it's OK if it's really painful to use. However, B2B technology has shifted to focus more on the end customer rather than just the decision maker. As we've seen with Slack, Gusto, and more, B2B companies are acting more like B2C companies, creating software with intuitive design that you can use out of the box with little training, just like you don't need training to use Facebook.

The tools and techniques you'll learn in this book will apply to both styles of companies. You'll build personas and break down use cases regardless of whether you're building B2B or B2C products. Just be aware that you'll have to do extra legwork to account for the additional decision makers and their personas in a B2B company. B2B software is also more likely to be subject to legal compliance requirements and to need to function in a multi-user environment, which creates additional fundamental product requirements that B2C software doesn't have.

HOW DO WE KNOW IF OUR PRODUCT'S GOOD?

In Chapter 1, we mentioned that a big part of product management is knowing how we keep score. Metrics, in particular success metrics, are how we measure that score.

Metrics are the measurement of different aspects of your product. These might include things within your product, like how many people complete a task, or things affected by your product, like how much revenue you're making. Success metrics, sometimes called *key performance indicators* (KPIs), are the key metrics that define how we keep score, like how many goals you scored in a soccer game.

Success metrics are useful because they help us validate if our current strategy is working, and if it's not we can dig into the overall metrics to come up with a hypothesis for how we could make changes to achieve our success metrics (more on this in Chapter 3). While product management sometimes feels like more of an art than a science, metrics provide the data-driven, scientific backbone to product management.

Your success metrics are defined by your current strategy and goals. Overall company success metrics come from the company's short- and long-term strategy goals, with long-term metrics being defined by the company's core values—the "why" we talked about earlier. If part of your company's mission is that you want your customers to love your products, then a key ongoing, long-term strategy company success metric will be how satisfied your customers are with each product.

You will have additional success metrics that change over time based on your short-term goals. For example, it's common to see companies switching their short-term goal from growth (people are using our product) to revenue (people like our product enough to pay for it). When goals change, what was a success metric one week might just be considered a regular metric the next week.

Generally, you'll have separate company and product success metrics, and the product success metrics will support the company metrics. Maybe your current company success metric is brand awareness, a common initial success metric for startups. In that case, your product success metrics will include number of downloads of your app, visits to your website, and so on: metrics that indicate people are aware of your company and products.

Later on, your strategy might shift to making your app part of people's lives, in which case your success metrics will focus on engagement: *Of those who downloaded the app, how many complete a core task? How many customers do that task each day/week/month?* As your strategy and success metrics change, your product plan and the features you choose to work on will similarly shift—you want to make sure what you're working on supports your goals and success metrics.

It's critical to compare these metrics over time, allowing you to see if your strategy is working. You might be using revenue as a success metric—getting people to open their wallets is a sign they value your product—and perhaps you have $1 million in revenue right now. That seems great until you realize you had $10 million in revenue last month.

A common question PMs deal with is, *how do we pick the right goals and supporting success metrics to focus on?* In general, it depends on your company. But Sarah Tavel, who was Pinterest's founding PM for search and discovery and is now a partner at Greylock, noticed a trend in the success metrics of successful consumer-focused internet startups, and she wrote up her findings in a blog post entitled "The Hierarchy of Engagement."

Tavel noted that there are three distinct strategy phases startups, and by extension new products, go through: engagement, retention, and self-perpetuating. Startups that go through all three tend to turn into multibillion-dollar companies, whereas startups that get stuck in one phase commonly fail.

The goal of the first phase is to get customers using your product and completing the core action, like posting a photo to Instagram. This is a sign they're engaged with your product, and we could say that completing the core action is a success metric that supports an engagement goal.

Pinterest's core action is pinning something. In 2011, when Pinterest was growing well, over 50% of its weekly users were still pinning things. Compare this to Viddy, a video-sharing startup that became popular in 2012. When Facebook started featuring Viddy content on April 24, Viddy's growth skyrocketed to about 35 million users, as you see in Figure 2-4. But the daily active users and the people actually posting content was much lower, peaking around 5 million users, or around 14% of all users. Even though Viddy appeared to be doing well, with lots of people signing up, very few completed that core action. Viddy shut down in late 2014.

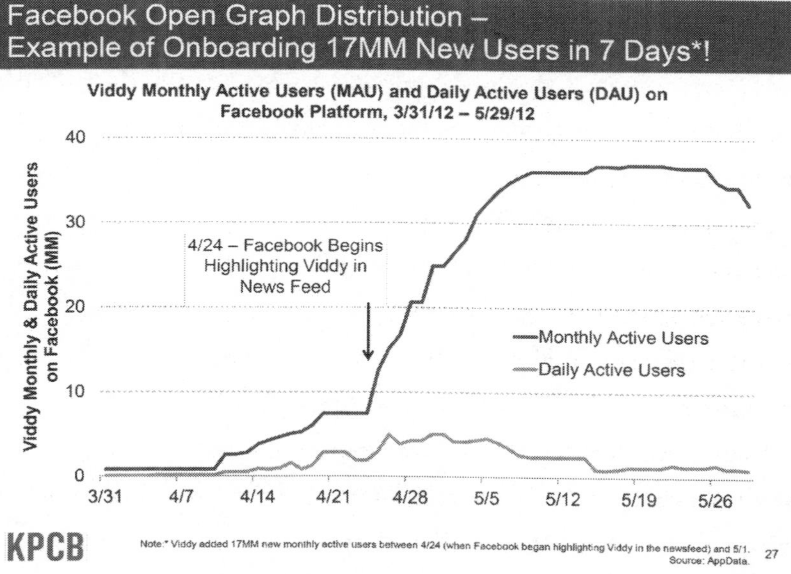

Figure 2-4. A graph of Viddy's monthly active users (top line) vs. daily active users (bottom line) for April/May 2012, from KPCB/Mary Meeker's Internet Trends report.

Now let's look at the second of Tavel's three phases, retention. After companies saw good engagement—what "good" means varies—they'd shift towards retaining users with success metrics around how frequently those customers use the product in a given time period. The idea is that if the product gets better for users over time, they will keep using it and they'll miss out if they leave. In fact, it's better to have slightly slower growth but a higher percentage of customers continuously using the product than constant growth but low retention because you'll end up with more customers over time.

A simple example of this is frequent-flier points on airlines: The more you fly, the more status you achieve and the more pleasant flying becomes. In software, think about social networks. The bigger the audience you've built up on Twitter, the more you'd have to lose by stopping using Twitter and trying to rebuild your audience on another network. Products that don't encourage customers to continuously use them are easily replaceable. Lyft and Uber are the same for an end customer whether you've ridden once or a hundred times. You likely just request a ride from whichever service has the shortest wait time. And if a new competitor comes around that offers an incentive, such as ride 10 times and get $10 in credit, you lose nothing by deleting the Uber app and using the competitor instead.

The final phase that Tavel describes is when your goal is self-perpetuation. This means your product has various loops that keep the customer engaged, and encourage other customers to get engaged. Your success metrics will be around how often people complete these loops. Pinterest gets better when more people post pins because this leads to better discovery of new, relevant things to pin. And sharing notifications (which we'll look at more in Chapter 3 with the Hook Canvas) encourage both new customers to pin something and existing users to return to the product.

Tavel goes on to describe cohort performance as the ultimate success metric your company should look at over time, encompassing all three of these stages. Specifically, look at the number of weekly users completing the core action and the percentage of weekly active users completing the core action over time. This shows growth from the size of the cohort, engagement from the ratio of users completing the core action, and retention from your performance over time.

While these stages don't apply directly to some products, like a B2B product a company mandates its employees use, the principles are still applicable. You want your customers to be able to complete the core tasks in your product smoothly and repeatedly, and as long as those core tasks align with use cases your customers care about, your product is off to a good start.

Vanity vs. Actionable Metrics

As product managers, we see a lot of metrics. Some are more helpful to us than others, and we often talk about two categories of metrics: vanity and actionable. *Vanity metrics* are those that sound useful, and might be great for some other business need, but don't help us measure product performance. *Actionable metrics* are real data we can use to make decisions.

Let's look at an example, using Tavel's first phase, engagement. When you're launching a new product, say an app, as a product manager your goal is to have people completing the core task. Maybe 1 million people downloaded your app on the first day—congrats! That sounds awesome, right? While getting someone to be aware of and download your app is the first step, it doesn't mean they actually opened and used your app—things look very different if only 10 people actually completed your app's core task.

Numbers like page views and downloads are vanity metrics because they sound useful. They might be useful in investor pitch decks, negotiating display-ad prices,*1 million people look at our pages each day!*, and for other company needs. But from a product management point of view, they don't help us measure if our product is successful.

Instead, product managers need to focus on actionable metrics that let us make decisions. Now that we know only 10 people completed our product's core task, we can look at other metrics to try and figure out why so few people were engaged with the app.

How to Measure Metrics

The most common way you'll measure metrics is by adding bits of code into your product to measure customer behavior, and to automatically collect the individual measurements into an analytics tool, like Google Analytics.

Usually these measurements are very simple: *How many people uploaded a file? How many people clicked this button? How much time did a person spend looking at a web page or a screen in an app?* Early on when planning a product, you'll want to think about what metrics you want to capture and work with your development team to capture those metrics (Chapter 5). For legal reasons, customers often have to opt in to providing this analytics data, which is why you frequently see disclosures in usage term sheets or pop-ups in software alerting customers that you're collecting usage data for a product.

However, not every metric gets captured automatically. It's tough to know from an automated tool whether customers like your product or swear at it multiple times a day when they use it. If your long-term goal is for customers to love your product, what should you do? Companies frequently use surveys and interviews to sample groups of customers and gauge these higher-level metrics. Sometimes these surveys are automated, such as a pop-up asking how you like the app on a scale from 1 to 10.

Net Promoter Score®

The Net Promoter Score (NPS) is a metric developed by Satmetrix, Bain & Co., and Fred Reichheld. It's a high-level way to gauge overall customer satisfaction with your product by seeing how likely customers are to recommend it to others, on a scale from –100 to 100. The idea is that if customers love your product, they'll tell others about it. If they're ambivalent, they could switch to a competitor. And if they dislike it, they might tell others to stay away and cost you business.

NPS is measured by asking customers, "On a scale of 1–10, how likely is it that you would recommend [brand] to a friend or colleague?" *Promoters* rank your brand 9 or 10 and are "loyal enthusiasts who will keep buying and refer others, fueling growth." These are the people you want! *Passives* will rank you 7 or 8 and are "satisfied but unenthusiastic customers who are vulnerable to competitive offerings." *Detractors* score you from 0 to 6 and "are unhappy customers who can damage your brand and impede growth through negative word-of-mouth."

From those replies, the NPS is the percentage of promoters minus the percentage of detractors, giving you a score from −100 to 100. Reichheld, in his 2003 article about NPS, entitled "The One Number You Need to Grow," found that many companies' NPS were low, with a median being 16 across 400 companies, showing that a lot of companies have work to do to improve customer satisfaction!

Measuring NPS over time is a way to see how customers are reacting to the product changes you make (or don't make). If your company's goal is customer satisfaction, with NPS as your success metric, and your NPS is lower than you'd like, then your immediate product goals will be around improving your customers' happiness. We'll dig into how to figure out what changes to make to improve customer satisfaction in Chapters 3 and 4.

Whew—for such a simple concept, there's sure a lot to success metrics. But they are incredibly important to product managers, as they let us figure out if our product and the strategy we're taking are meeting our short- and long-term goals.

WHAT ELSE HAS BEEN, IS BEING, AND WILL BE BUILT?

Unfortunately you can't look at a product or a company in complete isolation around this moment in time. What the company did in the past likely has an impact on where it is now. Microsoft completely missed the start of the mobile era, and that has led to its drive now to be "mobile-first, cloud-first."

It's also worth thinking about where a product might go next. While sometimes you'll build a product by releasing it to customers, getting feedback, and reacting to customer demand, you'll also often need to think about the long term to support overall company strategic initiatives. What do you want to do in three months, in six months, or in two years that you need to lay the groundwork for today? Maybe your product is free right now but your company wants to add a subscription payment system—your customers aren't asking to pay you each month, but your company needs to generate revenue to survive. You'll need to do work now so that you can handle billing information later.

Roadmap

Companies generally collect their product plans into a roadmap. A *roadmap* is a document that shows what the company/product is doing now, what the company/product plans to do over the next *N* months, what the company/product plans to do later, roughly how much effort each high-level task will take, what products the company will create, and what features they will have, etc. It's a valuable tool to help people communicate about the company, both internally by helping employees understand what projects you're working on next, and externally by helping partners anticipate your needs or plan for products you're releasing, a situation common with hardware-component providers.

Roadmaps are often fairly detailed in the short term—short term being

3 to 6 months for most software, 6 to 12 months for large software projects, and 12 to 18 months for hardware—and become more vague over the long term. This happens over the long term because priorities can change, and it's not worth planning out details for things that might not happen. Just knowing you want to work on something at a high level is sufficient.

Companies and products will have related roadmaps. The company-level one defines how all the products come together, and the product one—obviously—focuses on each specific product. Company roadmaps are generally determined by senior executives at a company, such as the CEO or the head of product. Product roadmaps are created by the product's PMs, and are often influenced by *and* exert influence over the company roadmap.

The factors we discussed at the very beginning of this chapter, in the "What Product Are We Building?" section, affect the roadmap, too. The best roadmaps are ones where the company has set goals to achieve and then planned projects that will help it achieve those goals. These roadmaps will also provide the sense of the ownership needed for each project, and determine the order in which the projects should happen. The next chapters will cover how we find opportunities and how items end up on the roadmap, but for now simply know that roadmaps are not arbitrary.

Roadmaps take many forms. Sometimes they're a spreadsheet using colors to show all the scheduled projects, their timeframes, and what goal each project supports. Other times companies use a special tool like Aha! (*http://aha.io*) that has additional features, such as bug-tracking integration with Jira so that you can dig into specific details like how each bug relates to the roadmap. It doesn't matter what tool you use to create your roadmap—it matters that you *have* a roadmap.

There's one major risk with roadmaps—you don't know the future, and if your plans change someone might ask you later on why you didn't deliver an item on the roadmap. Keeping roadmaps up to date and keeping items further out intentionally vague—even if you have more accurate timing estimates—can help alleviate this issue.

Competition and Climate

The last element to think about when trying to understand a company is what's going on around that company: *What are other people building? Who are the company's main competitors? How are their target use cases, personas, and end customers different? How are their products different? How are they winning or losing compared to another company? Are you aware of who's out there?*

At Product School, we had a student who cofounded a service focused on helping schools book their facilities for other events. Originally, he and his company were not aware of any other competitors. However, while the student was in class and working on his final project, he discovered that another company had pivoted from focusing on broader booking services to focusing specifically on schools. While this was validation that there's an opportunity with the use cases his company was targeting and it focused on delivering a better product than its competitors, it stressed him out knowing that his company wasn't the only one playing in that space anymore!

Beyond competition, what's going on in the industry in general? Has some broader invention or change caused every company to drastically alter its plans? For example, as smartwatches become popular, many companies are racing to create their own watches or versions of their apps for watches. And with Google Chrome now blocking Flash ads, ad tech companies are forced to adjust their plans to deal with this change.

Broader world changes can impact a company, too. China devalued its currency in August 2015, possibly to keep its manufacturing rates attractive, and that has had an impact on revenue for companies that sell in China. It also might have had an influence any company looking to build its products in Vietnam.

The world, and especially technology, doesn't stand still! A great PM will stay on top of the news to make sure that her company doesn't fall by the wayside because it missed a broader force that changed!

A 5C ANALYSIS

If you've ever talked with consultants or MBAs, you probably heard them name-drop a framework or seven. There is a variety of "standard" frameworks in the business world—we say "standard" because there are many similar frameworks, and different companies pick different standards. We'll cover some common ones in this book, but we will always prioritize presenting things with a product focus, even if it means we don't use a framework.

There's a framework called 5C that's similar to the areas we just covered. It's a *situational framework*, meaning it helps you understand a company's current situation so that you can create an opportunity hypothesis. The 5C structure is generic—useful to product, marketing, and more—whereas the way we presented the sections in this chapter is very focused on product management. It's good to know what the "C"s stand for because you'll likely hear 5C mentioned. Plus if you need to do a situational analysis on your feet in a meeting or interview, it's relatively easy to remember.

Company: This refers to the company's experience, technology, culture, goals, and more. It's similar to the material we covered in the "Why Does the Company Exist?," "How Do We Know If Our Product's Good?," and "What Else Has Been, Is Being, and Will Be Built?" sections.

Customers: Who are the people buying this product? What are the market segments? How big are they? What are people's goals with buying this product? How do they make buying decisions? Where do they buy this type or product? This is similar to what we covered in the "Customers and Personas" and "Use Cases" sections.

Collaborators: Who are the external people who make the product possible, including distributors, suppliers, logistical operators, groundwork support personnel, and so on?

Competitors: Who is competing for your customers' money? This includes actual and potential competitors. You should look at how they position their product, the market size they address, their strengths and weaknesses, and more.

Climate: These are the macro-environmental factors, like cultural, regulatory, or technological trends and innovations.

Sometimes product managers add a "P" to the 5C structure for "product," and specifically call out the product(s) the company makes. This is a mix of what we covered in the "What Else Has Been, Is Being, and Will Be Built?," "How Do We Know If Our Product's Good?," and "Use Cases" sections.

INTRODUCING MOOVER.IO

Throughout this book, we'll use a fictional company, Moover.io, as a case study. Let's look at its company context using the principles in this chapter.

Moover was started about a year ago to help people save time—its "why"—initially focusing on making it easy to get estimates and book a move. Currently, Moover has an iOS app where you enter some very basic details about your move: zip codes to and from, date you want to move, packing needs, number of rooms, number of stairs, and any other special notes. You click "Submit", and over the next few days, moving companies return bids. If you see one you like, you can tap "Book", and Moover sends a note to the moving company, which follows up with a phone call to confirm any needed information. Moover charges a small, fixed fee of $10 when you click "Book," using Apple Pay or PayPal. There's also a simple web dashboard app for the moving companies, where they can see outstanding bids with the basic information about the potential customer's home, along with whether a customer accepted or rejected the bid.

Moover's target use case is moving from and within bigger cities, as it's worked with only moving companies in San Francisco, New York, Los Angles, and Chicago to set up the service.

Moover has two key personas. The first is the moving company, Ant Moving. Ant is a mid-sized moving company with about 10 crews that has someone in the office who gives estimates over the phone full-time. Ant doesn't have a full online booking system set up because it's easier and cheaper to do things by hand. The second persona is Really Busy Rob. Rob's a busy person who likes using app services to handle the mundane details in life. He prefers Lyft to owning a car, orders dinner from Postmates, and more. Rob doesn't mind paying a small fee for these services, as he feels his time outweighs the fee. Rob works a lot, and having to arrange a move is the last thing on his mind! Moover also learned from interviewing lots of potential "Robs" that Rob could easily be "Roberta" because gender doesn't matter. Rob's likely been out of school for a few years and has accumulated enough stuff that his possessions don't fit into his car anymore, and we won't find Rob on a college campus.

Moover has two current business goals: to find ways to improve customer satisfaction, and to grow the business. Moovers currently experiencing limitations that prevent it from reaching this goal, for example, right now that follow-up phone call to plan details is annoying, especially if the moving company has to come on-site, and Moover has no way to handle special cases, like a piano. The people at Moover, however, aren't sure what they should focus on next, nor are they sure if they're missing an opportunity.

Right now, moving tech isn't exactly a hot market, and Moover's main competitors are specific companies' booking systems and people willing to make a few phone calls—or use a service like Fiverr to have someone make the phone calls for him.

Moover just raised $1 million and hired its second product manager: you! Throughout this book, we're going to help Moover figure out what feature to build next and walk through how to build it.

CHAPTER THREE

CREATING AN OPPORTUNITY HYPOTHESIS

A key part of your role as a product manager is understanding your customers and their problems and needs, and making sure what you're building next is right for them, be it a feature or a new product. At the end of the day, very few companies fail because their technology doesn't work. Companies fail for lack of customers.

Here's a dirty secret: everyone thinks they know what their customers need. But like we mentioned in Chapter 1, most people—even your boss's boss—really have no idea what customers need until they've done some work! Every company has a different approach to figuring out what customers want, and there are tweets, blog posts, books, and epic operas about how to do so—well, maybe not operas, yet.

We're going to take an approach modeled on the scientific method—come up with a hypothesis about your customer needs and how you can address them, then validate or invalidate it. This chapter will cover different ways to generate a hypothesis. Chapter 4 will discuss how to validate it, and Chapter 5 will help you transition from ideation to execution.

Keep in mind what we're teaching you is just one way to approach figuring out what to do next, albeit it is a good one. A lot of the content in this chapter is a bit chicken-and-egg—some of the material we taught in Chapter 2 comes into play here, as does future material from the Customer Development section of Chapter 4. Customer development can influence your personas, use cases can inform opportunities, and so on. Rather than debate ad nauseam where to start, we've chosen an approach. We encourage you to keep a similar mental model, based on the scientific method, no matter where you start, so that you're always making informed decisions about what to do next.

YOU HAVE OPINIONS, NOT FACTS

There's some bad news you should know up front. Generally, less than 50% of ideas you'll execute—even awesome ideas—improve the metrics they're supposed to improve. Amazon tests all its new ideas and has data to back up this 50% figure. Yammer follows a similar practice and has seen similar numbers. As a product manager, you want to find ways to spend your time on features that matter. This starts with accepting that your ideas start off as opinions and not facts.

It's sometimes very hard for product managers to grasp that their opinions are not necessarily truth. We like being right, and we're taught in school that it's bad to be wrong. The real world—and building products—isn't like that. It's OK to be wrong, but we want to figure out if we're wrong as soon as possible and course-correct before we put lots of resources into our incorrect opinions. If you're wrong but insist you're right, the product will fail. But if you're wrong, realize it quickly, and adjust accordingly, you're much more likely to succeed.

How often has someone said to you, "I have a million-dollar idea for a product that does *x*," and the voice inside your head answers, "I wouldn't buy it." Lots of people have opinions about what product or feature to build. Everyone assumes they're average, and that if they want something, lots of other people do, too. Because of this, many people go immediately from an idea right to building it, never once seeing if others would actually buy the product. Early-stage startups frequently have this problem—these are also often the startups that eschew product management. Unfortunately, these companies end up in trouble because after spending lots of money to build a product, they find out no one wants it. As a result, bad things happen, ranging from their abandoning the product without recouping their investment to going out of business.

Wouldn't it be great if you could limit these disaster scenarios in a cost-effective way? The approach we're going to teach you, focused on creating and validating an idea, will let you quickly and cheaply filter out ideas that won't help you. Note we're not talking about "bad" ideas—an idea could be good but just not help you or your customers.

Steve Blank, a tech entrepreneur, worked with a number of startups and noticed a trend in the ones that failed. Specifically, these startups would focus on their business plans and go right to product development, skipping any validation of their fundamental idea—sound familiar? By the time a startup would get feedback from customers, it would be so far down a path that it'd be tough to make changes. Blank noticed that startups failed mainly due to lack of customers and a profitable business model, and the ones he worked with and their investors didn't see value in taking time to figure out if people really wanted what they were building. Ironically, this disconnect was especially an issue for the startups' founders, who created the initial hypothesis the company was founded on. They quickly became isolated from direct customer feedback, as they hired people such as marketers to interact with customers for them.

Blank's work led him to conclude that "in a startup no facts exist inside the building; only opinions." He then created the idea of customer development, which essentially says that whatever you come up with at first is an opinion; you might be wrong, and you need to interact with real potential customers to learn the truth ASAP. This chapter is about forming a good opinion. Chapter 4 is about how to find out the truth about your opinion.

Customer development became a core part of lean methodology, which we briefly mentioned in Chapter 1. Lean Startup is a business that applies a product developmental methodology, adapted by Steve Blank and Eric Ries from Toyota's revolutionary manufacturing pipeline, to product/software development. Lean Startup is focused on helping companies be successful by quickly and iteratively determining what customers want, building something that fills only that need, validating the solution, and repeating.

Customer development is a key part of Lean Startup because it's a way to quickly increase your learning, so as to avoid wasting time. We believe this approach is useful both in startups trying to develop their initial product and in established companies improving existing products. After all, a great PM needs to help the customer be awesome, and you want to focus your time on building things they need!

With this in mind, how do you create the best possible hypothesis about what your customers want?

WHAT'S YOUR GOAL AND HOW DO YOU WANT TO ACHIEVE IT?

The very first thing to establish is your goal for this product development life cycle iteration. Is your company focused on acquiring new users? Does it want to improve revenue? There's no silver bullet to pick the right goal to focus on—if you've achieved a core set of engaged customers who continuously use your product, perhaps your next goal will be revenue, followed by growth. Your main priority is to pick a specific goal. What you pick to work on next will be in service of this goal, and this is the core of how PMs strategically choose what to work on next.

Next, you need to think about how to achieve that high-level goal with an actual product. How do you want to achieve that goal at a high level? Do you want to iterate on an existing product, finding ways to improve it? Do you want to build something completely new—a blue-sky opportunity,also sometimes called blue water or ocean? In making this decision you can focus your thinking so that you can determine the details about what to build to achieve your goal.

Let's look at iteration first. Start by translating your higher-level business goal into a product goal, then focus on what changes we can make to a product to help meet that goal. For example, the company might want improved customer satisfaction, which could translate into "getting customers to read more articles" because that's a sign customers like the content.

Another example of using iteration to achieve a goal is when Facebook changed the Like button to have different types of reactions, such as love, sadness, and anger. Facebook's goal might have been to get more engagement, and the Facebook PMs implicitly knew they wanted to improve the core product rather than build something new. They decided to provide users with more post-feedback reactions—liking a post about someone's dog dying never seemed like the right reaction, and some users probably chose to post nothing rather than like the post. The sad reaction now provides an easy way to give the poster feedback, leading to more engagement on posts.

Iterations aren't just small changes, though. An iteration might be a complete overhaul or rewrite of the app or a feature, like when Gmail redid its "Compose" interface or when Apple switched from skeuomorphism to flat design in iOS 7. The key definition of an iterative change is that you're taking an existing product and making it better.

Iteration is incredibly important, as the first version of a product is never perfect for all customers, and it's through iteration that a product evolves to become something customers love. If you don't have product/market fit yet, we'd recommend focusing on achieving it before trying to focus on revenue or growth goals. What is also nice about iteration is that you already have information about how the customers are using the product, and your hypothesis about what to do next might come from quantitative sources (like how many users complain about a bug), or qualitative sources (like ideas the support team has).

The downside to iteration is that you can get stuck finding the "local maxima." This means that you've optimized something really well, but you focused so much on optimization that you missed a bigger shift that happened. Think about Blockbuster Video. Blockbuster could've spent lots of time iterating and come up with the ideal balance of price and rental days/late fees. It might have also iterated on the overall store experience, aiming to optimize number of rentals per customer, and come up with an in-store recommendation tool to optimize customer satisfaction, ensuring that every customer walked out with a movie. However, it still would've gone out of business because it missed the global change where customers switched to streaming video. This is where blue-sky thinking comes into play.

A blue-sky opportunity is something totally new. The biggest blue-sky examples occur when you believe the market/world is changing in a certain way, and you need to make a big transformation to address ght not exist yet but you believe will exist in the future. ou could make changes to your existing product to address rtunity, this new opportunity is different enough that it's be d by building something new, designing from the ground vantage of that opportunity. Blue-sky opportunities also you see a new opportunity to expand your business into sn't serve right now because you believe those areas will value.

it simply, blue-sky opportunities are about skating to where will be, not where it is now. Sometimes blue-sky opportunities thinking more broadly or reframing how you're approaching a m: Blockbuster saw its business as "video stores" and was locked handing customers tapes and DVDs. Netflix focused on "content very," and it didn't matter if that content came from the mail or reaming video. By thinking about how to let customers watch movies and TV shows in a different way, Netflix saw a means to exceed ckbuster's local maxima and find a new global maxima.

example of reframing to find a blue-sky opportunity is the e company MetLife. The company made an app, Infinity, to igital legacy by curating your memories. Digital legacies are becoming far more of an issue than they were even 10 years ago. Your life-insurance company is the one business that knows for sure if you're alive, so who better to trust with the key to passing on your photos, documents, and more when you die?

Sometimes, new technology and trends, like cloud computing, change how we solve problems, creating new opportunities. Looking at photo management; we've moved from physical albums to digital tools such as iPhoto. But even after iPhoto had been out for about 15 years—an eternity for technology—Apple decided the future of photo management was in the cloud. Rather than try to make iPhoto capable of managing a cloud-based photo library, Apple deprecated iPhoto in favor of an entirely new product, Photos. Unlike iPhoto, Photos was built from the ground up for iOS, since most people take their photos with a smartphone rather than a digital camera.

Another example of new technology creating blue-sky opportunities is when Facebook, recognizing the potential of virtual reality (VR), spent $2 billion to purchase Oculus, believing that the future value of Oculus' VR and its metaverse, to connect everyone together, would be huge and more than justify that price.

The downside to blue-sky thinking is the potential risk. Blue-sky thinking always requires a guess—even if it's a well-educated one—about what is going to happen, and developing blue-sky products takes resources away from iterating on existing products with real customers. New products almost always lose money at first because in addition to taking resources to develop, you must convince customers to use this new tool, causing key metrics will be lower at first.

This risk factor is where the "innovator's dilemma" comes from. It's hard for incumbent companies to justify trying to build the next big thing when they could be spending their money growing their current product, finding the local maxima. This leads companies to focus too much on their short-term goals, missing larger opportunities because of the short-term drop in profits that would result. After all, their current business is doing well: why change? For this reason, private startups that can find a new opportunity stand a chance of disrupting an incumbent—did anyone expect taxis to be as disrupted as they have been by the smartphone-app-based business model and the sharing economy?

Of course, big companies don't want to be disrupted, so they're also often trying to find blue-sky opportunities. Alphabet is a great example of how a big company can address the innovator's dilemma—most of Alphabet's revenue comes from Google search ads. If the company just sat around, optimizing that revenue, it'd have a few really great years. But Alphabet knows that business model won't last forever, and it would rather find the next big thing before someone else does. Alphabet is constantly trying to come up with the next big thing, and some of its work—such as self-driving cars—looks promising but hasn't paid off yet, whereas other investments didn't work out as well as Alphabet hoped—like buying Boston Dynamics. Unfortunately, if you follow Alphabet stock, you'll see that investors don't like all these experimental bets—they want to see choices that give immediate returns.

If you have an existing product, it's totally reasonable if your first opportunity hypothesis focuses on iteration rather than blue-sky improvements. But as you work to validate your hypothesis, you might realize the best way to achieve your goals and address your customers' needs is by building something new.

Thus far, you should have established a high-level company goal, translated that goal to a product goal with key success metrics (*why* you're making this change), and thought about if you want to accomplish your goal by changing your existing product or building something new (*how* you're going to accomplish your goal). Now let's look at how we come up with *what* specifically we can do to accomplish our goal.

QUANTITATIVELY FINDING AN OPPORTUNITY HYPOTHESIS

There are two major ways to determine what we want to do to achieve our goal: qualitative reasoning, and quantitative reasoning. *Quantitative reasoning* involves looking at data, interpreting it, and using that analysis to determine what to do next. *Qualitative reasoning* involves more abstract concepts like looking at your overall product vision or your intuition based on your knowledge of your customers in determining the next step to take. We'll look at quantitative reasoning first because it's the most common way PMs determine what to build next.

Quantitative sources are important because they allow us to collect data on how people actually use our product, to use that data to find insights, and then to apply those insights to determine what to do next. For example, perhaps Lyft wants to increase customer retention by getting people to use Lyft instead of Uber. We can turn that into a specific product goal by focusing on how to decrease the number of rides cancelled—fewer cancellations means more passengers served and happier drivers, which means more payment. This will also come by tweaking the current product, rather than building something new. When you cancel a ride in Lyft, you need to specify a reason. A PM at Lyft could look at the responses and come up with ideas about how to mitigate those reasons. Maybe he notices that midday the number of people cancelling their rides due to wait times skyrockets compared to the morning or evening. As a result, perhaps he'd find ways to incentivize drivers to be on the road midday, decreasing wait times, decreasing cancellations, and ultimately keeping customers in a Lyft rather than an Uber.

Quantitative sources are also nice because, after we've come up with and implemented our idea, we can compare the data before and after the change, and determine if it was successful. Our Lyft PM would compare the percentage of rides being cancelled and the reasons why to see if his change decreased the number of cancellations.

It's worth noting that quantitative sources are useful for both iterative and blue-sky opportunities, as are qualitative sources. Data on how customers use your current product might yield ways you can iterate the current product, or they could point out a trend that reveals an opportunity for a blue-sky project.

Metrics and Analytics

How do you know what to do if you don't know what your customers are doing? As we've discussed before, metrics are measurements of different tasks users do within your product. Metrics are the most common source of quantitative data about your product and your customers.

Metrics take many forms, from "How many people do you swipe right or left on per session in this app?" to "How many people who came to your site via a specific affiliate's link completed a purchase?" In Chapters 1 and 2 we talked about success metrics, which are the key indicators of if you're achieving your goals and if your customers are winning. When working with metrics, start by asking yourself if you're happy with where your success metric is—is it at the right level to effectively achieve your product goal, and if not, how can you improve this success metric?

Not every metric is a success metric. For example, our key success metric might be how many people complete a purchase, but we'll also measure how many people add items to a cart and how many people tap the checkout button.

Put together, these metrics give us a sense of what's going on comprehensively with the product. If lots of people tap the checkout button but very few actually complete a purchase, then we might have an opportunity to improve the checkout workflow so that more people complete a purchase. Workflows are often called *funnels*, and are great sources of opportunity hypotheses—we'll cover them shortly.

We call the process of gathering and analyzing these metrics collectively *analytics*. Analytics let you understand the state of your product, giving you a much better idea about what your customers are doing and how your product's working for them. Analytics make metrics useful by giving them context, allowing you to discover insights about what to do next.

Think about metrics as individual data points, such as a car's position, how fast it's traveling, the number of passengers, etc. In addition to seeing a success metric, like "the user turned the car off after driving for a while," analytics put those data points together to help you realize the family's taking their weekly drive to Grandma's house. Analytics also let you see if the family made it to Grandma's or if they ran out of gas. If the family constantly runs out of gas before achieving their goal of getting to Grandma's, you as a PM will look for ways to help them not run out of gas. OK, this metaphor's run out of gas. Let's move on.

Analytics and metrics are useful for several reasons. The first is that people often aren't aware of exactly what they do, and numerous studies have shown that self-reporting usage is unreliable. Automatically recording their actions lets us see what people are really doing with our product and how they got there.

If your product is very large, analytics can reveal a problem on one specific section that you might not find manually. Imagine if you were a PM at Amazon, and you wanted to watch how many people bought each product. If people stop buying various products, that's a warning you should look at the product to see what's up. If you asked everyone what they bought, you'd have an impossible task because of the customer volume. If you randomly surveyed people, you'd likely miss many niche products. Automated analytics, however, could easily find a product where the number purchased suddenly dropped from an average of five per day to zero.

Finally, when you look at analytics over time, you can get a gauge for where you're going. Perhaps your growth rate has leveled off. If you're unhappy with your trajectory, you'll dig into the component metrics to find the problem, and determining a way to address that problem will form your opportunity hypothesis. Again, after you've implemented the solution, you can re-evaluate these metrics to see if your strategy worked.

There are many analytics tools, with Google Analytics (Figure 3-1) and Mixpanel being two of the most popular for web and mobile apps. Adding these tools to your product is fairly straightforward and just requires a bit of tracking code and annotations so that you can track specific things, such as how many times a user clicks Play on a video. Physical products often require completely different analytics techniques, but as more physical products become connected, it's possible to collect similar usage data.

Figure 3-1. A sample screen from Google Analytics showing how often various events, the metrics we're analyzing, occur over time.

It's worth noting that analytics data isn't always perfect, and those imperfections can skew your analysis. If your app supports multiple platforms, the event might accidentally be tagged as "eventA" on Android and "event A" on iOS. This means you won't see the total times Event A happens unless you notice the problem and account for it.

Other times, there are inherent issues in your analytics tools. Google Analytics only samples a subset of your traffic for its reports, but for high-traffic websites that sample might not accurately represent your real data. If the data doesn't correctly represent what your customers are doing, you might make the wrong decisions.

Let's dig into how to use analytics to look at specific metrics and find opportunities.

Breaking Down Analytics

The first part of analytics is to make sure we're capturing the right metrics. Identify the key success metric supporting your goal and the metrics that support that goal. If your success metric is how engaged your customers are, you should track how often they complete the core "success" action and the steps that lead to it. If the right metrics aren't there, then your first task for this iteration of the product-development life cycle is to implement analytics for those metrics.

One common problem when you inherit an existing project is that a previous, well-meaning PM has been recording every single possible metric. This leads to data overload, and it can be very hard to sort out the useful metrics from the irrelevant ones. If you find yourself in that situation, we recommend doing an analytics audit and reassessing what data points you're recording—removing the irrelevant ones—before using the data to make decisions.

The next part is how we group metrics together so that we can spot trends and opportunities. There are three key ways: segmentation, cohort analysis, and funnels.

Analytics track every customer equally and report the average behavior. For example, a new customer will use an app's first-use tutorial—some might skip it—but a returning customer won't even see the first-use tutorial. If you simply looked at how often a customer views the tutorial out of how many times people use the app, it'd look like very few people use the tutorial overall. It's up to you to *segment* your data, which means grouping it by common characteristics.

Analytics tools often provide multiple ways to segment data. Common choices range from technical grouping (OS, browser, etc.) to behavioral (new/returning user) to demographics (country/language are common). After segmenting data, we can look at each metric, focusing on our key success metric and the supporting metrics, and see if it's in line with our baseline expectation. If it's not, we'll flag this as a metric to focus on.

You might find something surprising for a metric unrelated to what you're working on right now. Feel free to note it for later, but don't worry about it initially. There are lots of metrics for a product, and PMs can always find surprises. We're focused on a specific success metric and the supporting metrics that lead to that success metric.

Another way of grouping data is *cohort analysis*. This is very similar to segmentation, but it uses a point in time as a key characteristic of the group and is often used to look at behavior over time. For example, imagine your product's featured on TV's *Shark Tank—Dragon's Den* in the UK—where hopeful entrepreneurs pitch their idea to investors. You might want to compare how users who signed up before *Shark Tank* aired use the product compared to people who sign up later. And you'd also ask how those cohorts' usage compares after two months, after six months, etc. Or, more practically, what's customer engagement like over time with customers from before you created the first-use tutorial compared to customers who signed up after you implemented the tutorial? If you see a substantial difference in behavior at a certain point, flag that metric.

The last common method of grouping data is a *funnel*. This is when you measure key steps along a user's journey towards some task and group them together, in journey order. Typically a lot of people complete the first step and far fewer complete the last; e.g., many people might go to an Amazon product page, a smaller number click Add to Cart, and a smaller number still complete the checkout. "Leakage" is when a customer stops moving forward in the funnel.

Nearly any sequential-action group of metrics (workflow) can form a funnel, and your goal is always to look at how a user goes from initiating to completing an action. Not every customer enters your product the same way (e.g., tapping an app on the home screen to open it the first time, opening the app for the tenth time with a restored state, tapping a link that opens the app, etc.). Your analytics tool likely has a behavior flow report to see how users enter the funnel and where they go. Any place there's a substantial undesired falloff is a potential opportunity, and you should flag that particular metric.

Dave McClure, the well-known venture capitalist who founded 500 Startups, put together a talk called "Startup Metrics for Pirates," where he came up with a general approach to metrics for an entire product, called AARRR metrics—although he put it together for startups, where the success of a company depends on one product, it's useful for any product. The acronym stands for the following:

- **Acquisition:** How the user comes to your product.
- **Activation:** The user's first visit to your product and her first happy experience.
- **Retention:** The user liked your product enough to use it again (and hopefully again and again…).
- **Referral:** The user likes it enough to tell someone about it.

- **Revenue:** The user finds your product valuable enough that she pays for it.

McClure suggests breaking down the key behavioral steps for your product into these buckets (each bucket might have more than one metric within it) and using this funnel to see how users go from discovering your product to being willing to pay. Each large dip is a potential opportunity and a metric to flag, and the ones towards the top of the funnel are the ones to address first.

Note that the part(s) of the funnel you focus on will depend on your company and product goals. If your current goal is growth, you'd focus on the activation step rather than the revenue step.

It's also important to note that not every dip in a funnel is bad. For example, the Nigerian spam emails asking you to provide your bank account to a prince (or something similar) have only a 0.1% click-through rate—meaning only 0.1% of the people who receive it click the Send Money link. But this turns out to be an excellent filter for gullible customers, as 70% of the people who click the link actually send money. If they optimized the click-through rate and 90% of people clicked the link, it's more likely that the site would be reported or taken down, and the spammer would make less money overall.

It's also reasonable to combine segmentation and cohort analysis and funnels. For example, you might want to look at a funnel with cohort analysis if your product were featured on *Shark Tank*. You could track how many people went from clicking the checkout button to completing the purchase before you went on *Shark Tank*, compared to how many people complete the checkout funnel after you were on TV.

Ultimately, no matter how you look at your analytics, your goal is to find a metric you believe is worth improving in order to achieve your product and company goals.

CHAPTER THREE TIP

This tip is from Beatriz Datangel. Beatriz has worn several hats in the startup world. She's used her analyst experiences to land product management positions where she drives decisions from data and insights. Her focus at Product School is on how to use data and communicate metrics effectively. You can reach out to her via Twitter @bzdata.

WHAT ARE THE KEY DIFFERENCES BETWEEN VANITY AND SUCCESS METRICS?

If you ask what makes a great product manager, many will say it's an understanding of what goes where and how—not as simple when you're toggling between Excel spreadsheets, SQL queries, and visualized infographics. We live in a time when data lives everywhere. A product manager should know how to *extract insight* from the *right* place. Let's look at how to do so, using Amazon as an example.

Start by understanding the product's and the company's overall value proposition. For Amazon, the value proposition to customers is the convenience of buying anything and getting it quickly.

As a PM, you will need to think from the customer's perspective. If they chose your product/company out of all the competition for the key value proposition, you will need to know how parts of the product are performing to make sure the value proposition stays intact. What metrics do customers care about that support the value proposition? These include:

- Inventory of every item
- Number of items stocked with inventory compared to top lists/holiday shopping guides

- Percent of items ordered and arriving within an Amazon Prime shipping window (~48 hours)
- Average load speed of the website
- Average wait time between submission of a service ticket and resolution

If a website were slow or deliveries weren't on time, customers wouldn't necessarily think Amazon is convenient. If we fail to deliver on the above metrics, we wouldn't deliver on our value proposition to customers, and they'd shop elsewhere. Conversely, when we deliver on these metrics, customers are happy. This means these are success metrics we should focus on.

Well, what are vanity metrics, then? Eric Ries first spoke of vanity metrics in 2009, defining them as metrics often spoken of at a top-level view. They also are often referred to in acronyms:

- Pageviews
- Number of installs
- Daily/monthly users (DAU)
- Growth in users, installs, page views

It's great if lots of people look at Amazon each day and go to Amazon first, but if they don't complete their transactions on Amazon, then Amazon isn't winning. In other words, these metrics don't tell us if we're making our customers happy or not.

Vanity numbers are great for a quick headline. However, success comes with context. Be sure to look for metrics that matter towards a successful experience for the customer.

Turning Metrics into Opportunities by Asking Why

The challenge with quantitative sources like metrics is that they tell you what is happening but not why. Once you've identified a metric—or two—that you want to improve, how do you figure out what to do? There are a few ways to figure out what you should do, and one of the easiest is by asking "why." Specifically, ask yourself why you think the metric isn't where you want it to be. And if the answer isn't a hypothesis that you can test somehow, continue to ask yourself why until you get to a specific hypothesis. Your goal is to get to the core problem, the root of the deeper issue. You want to solve problems, not address symptoms. Asking why can help you find that core problem, leading you to the potential opportunity to focus on validating.

Here are a few ideas to help you. First, many people only focus on the end result of the funnel. They might say, "Not enough customers complete a purchase." If this is the case, ask yourself why. Look back up through the funnel and see where the leakage occurs. Then, ask why it's occurring there. You might need to go to that particular part of the product to see what might be blocking a user.

Segmenting your audience and focusing in on how each segment behaves can lead to a better hypothesis. For example, perhaps your site's conversion rate looks low overall, but when you segment it by browser, you see the conversion rate for Safari customers is much higher than for Chrome customers. Given there are more Chrome customers than Safari ones, the overall average conversion rate appears low. As you ask yourself why and try using the site in Chrome yourself, maybe you'll find a bug where a JavaScript error appears when you click Checkout in Chrome. Your opportunity hypothesis is that fixing this bug will improve acquisition for the shopping cart page, and eventually increase revenue.

Here are a few common, interesting opportunities you'll find for mobile and web apps in metrics:

- A low time on a screen and a high bounce rate—people who leave after viewing this content—on a page that's supposed to be important likely indicates a mismatch between expectations and reality. The content wasn't what the customers expected, so they left.
- A long time on a screen and a high bounce rate could be fine if the page is a long article, but if it's a page with very little content but lots of links, it could indicate the screen is unclear.
- A high number of screen views could indicate that this part of the app is important, therefore you need to optimize it well.
- A low number of views could mean this section is hard to find.

Intercom's Feature Audit

A company called Intercom, which makes tools to let product owners see who's using their product and communicate with them, has put together a number of great resources on its blog, Inside Intercom, at *blog.intercom.io*. One of the techniques Intercom shares is a way to look at your metrics and spot opportunities, called a feature audit.

In a feature audit, you start by creating a graph of *how many* people use a feature on the x-axis vs. *how often* they use it (See Table 3-1). When doing this, make sure to exclude "administrative" features such as password recovery, as they'll skew the result. The core value of your product, the reason it exists and people buy it, should be at the top right (Feature C) because everyone should use it all the time.

	Few people	Some people	Most people	All people
All the time	Feature A			Feature C
Most of the time			Feature B	
Some of the time				Feature D
Very little of the time	Feature E			

Table 3-1. A sample Intercom feature audit table.

There are four sources of opportunity:

1. Features on the top left of the graph are poorly adopted (Feature A in Table 3-1): very few people use them a lot. Sometimes that's OK—for example, if it's a niche feature for one key customer in an enterprise product that only that company uses—but often, you'll want to improve adoption of these features.
2. The second source is a feature that all the people use occasionally (Feature D): is it something you want people to use more often?
3. The third is that perhaps you should kill a feature if it's something in the bottom left that very few people use, and then only infrequently (Feature E).
4. Last, you might choose to improve a key feature that many people use frequently (Features B & C).

This view also shows a possible warning sign: if your product has only one feature that people use frequently, you're easily replaceable in their workflow. Ideally you'll have a few key features that people use frequently so that you're not a throwaway product when something better in one area comes along.

If there's an important feature you believe is for all customers but only some customers use, you'll want to improve its adoption. To do so, focus on asking why, just like we discussed before. Note that you want to be very explicit—don't just say, "customers don't see its value." Keep asking why until you get to the root cause. Why don't they see its value? The feature doesn't save them time. Why doesn't it save them time? There are too many steps to use the feature. Why are there too many steps? Eventually, you'll come up with a list of issues preventing customers from adopting the feature (e.g., time saving might be only one of many reasons a customer doesn't see a feature's value). Once you've done this you can focus on resolving those issues. Not all opportunities will be code changes, either. It's possible different marketing or design will help adoption.

If there's a feature that many customers use infrequently but you think would be beneficial if they used it more, it's possible users aren't clear how it works, which you can check via a funnel. You can also check the value, with the help of Marketing. To motivate users to use it more, you can use the Hook Canvas, by Nir Eyal, author of *Hooked*, to help create habits in your software.

Seen in Figure 3-2, the Hook Canvas has four elements. First is the trigger—what happens to get the user to the product? Second—what's the absolute simplest thing you can get a customer to do that will give them the reward? Third—what reward can you provide that's fulfilling and makes the user want more and invest in the product? Last, what tiny bit of action can you get the customer to invest in doing that will lead to more triggers and get them to return?

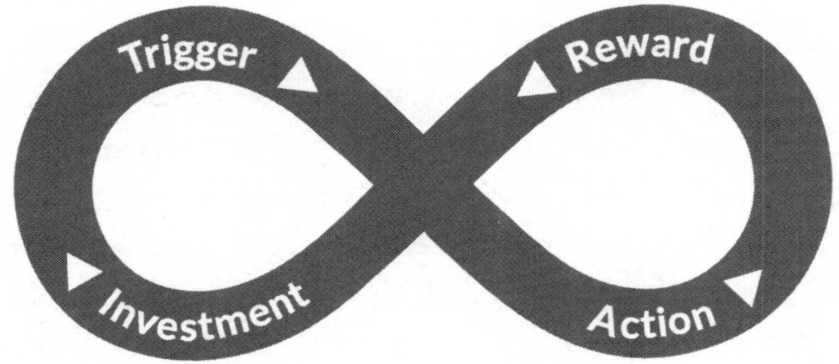

Figure 3-2. Nir Eyal's Hook Canvas and its four phases.

If you've heard of *gamification*, which involves adding gaming mechanisms to non-game products, you've seen the Hook Canvas in action. You might get an email from an airline saying you'll get bonus points if you sign up for a credit card. You fill out the simplest form the airline can give you, and—assuming you're approved—you get enough points for a free domestic trip. That makes you want to earn more points to get more free trips.

Eyal uses Pinterest as an example in Figure 3-3.

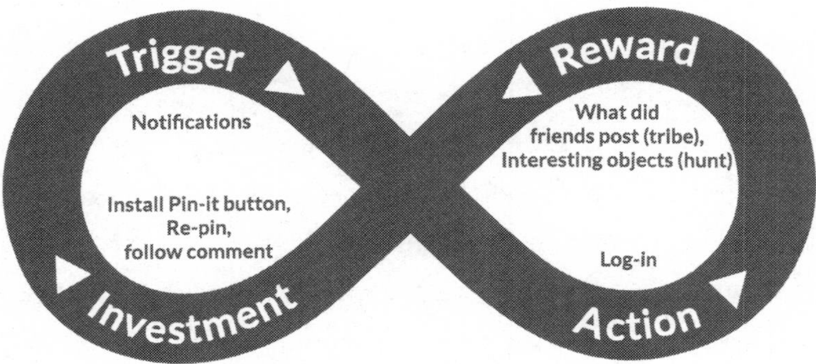

Figure 3-3. Pinterest's Hook Canvas, by Nir Eyal.

Surveys

Another way of gathering data to find opportunities is by sending out surveys, trying to gauge user satisfaction with different parts of your product amongst statistically significant parts of your user base. In Chapter 2 we discussed the most common high-level approach to determining satisfaction, a Net Promoter Score (NPS). Again, it's simply the question, "on a scale of 1–10, how likely is it that you would recommend [brand] to a friend or colleague?" Higher scores mean customers are happy and lower scores mean they're likely to be neutral or tell people not to buy your product.

It's good to dive in beyond a general NPS and ask how satisfied customers are with specific parts of your product. If they're less than a 10, have an open-ended question for feedback about how the product isn't meeting their needs and expectations. As you make changes to the product, you can resurvey to see how satisfaction changes over time.

Some products now are integrating this satisfaction survey into the product. For example, random Twitter customers will see a tweet in their timeline saying they've been selected for a survey, and tools like Intercom (*http://intercom.io*), Delighted (*http://delighted.com*), and UserVoice (*http://uservoice.com*) can be easily integrated and allow customers to provide feedback continuously.

Surveys can be used to gather more specific data, and we'll cover crafting good ones in more depth in Chapter 4, when we look at how to use them to validate our hypothesis.

Obviously, if a customer isn't satisfied and tells you why, that's a potential source of an opportunity hypothesis. But there are other ways to use survey data to find an opportunity, especially creating an importance vs. satisfaction graph.

Internally, you should have a sense of how important each feature is to the product. The features that are core to the product and used most often are likely the most important. For each feature, if you create a graph (See Figure 3-4) with customer satisfaction on the y-axis, increasing feature importance on the x-axis, and an y=x line, you'll easily spot opportunities. An important feature that has low satisfaction will appear below the line, and it should be your first priority to improve.

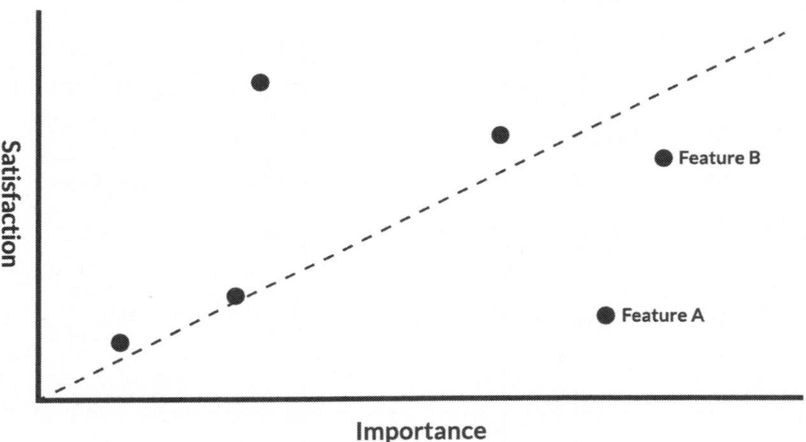

Figure 3-4. A graph showing satisfaction, with values gathered via survey, vs. feature importance, as determined internally. Feature A, with a very low satisfaction, will likely be the first place to focus, instead of Feature B, which is more important but has a moderate satisfaction.

Generally, you'll trade off importance vs. how unsatisfied customers are, so you might work on something that's fairly important with very low satisfaction (Feature A in Figure 3-4) before focusing on a feature that's very important with moderate satisfaction (Feature B). Also, it's fine if less important features have lower overall satisfaction; they're not critical to the product. Should those features become more important, then you should focus on improving them so that the user satisfaction stays above the x=y line.

What About Customer Interviews?

It's possible that while you're talking to customers, for example, while user testing another feature, they might say something that sparks an idea in your mind. However, we believe that customer interviews should not be the source of your first opportunity hypothesis. If you start customer interviews without even a vague sense of what you're looking to learn, the interviews will be unfocused and not useful, and you're unlikely to find a good hypothesis.

Instead, we believe you should start with an opportunity hypothesis, even if it's vague, and then do customer interviews to validate it. It's possible that while doing those interviews, you'll come up with a new hypothesis, and that's fine.

QUALITATIVELY FINDING AN EDUCATED OPPORTUNITY HYPOTHESIS

Not every opportunity arises from something that can be quantified and measured. As Henry Ford supposedly said, "If I had asked people what they wanted, they would've said a faster horse." Someone else once said that "data-driven optimization taken to its extreme just leads to porn."

You can pull from a wide range of qualitative sources to find opportunities. The biggest challenge is that these will take more work to validate than quantitatively found opportunities, as they don't come directly from data: you'll have to find data to support them.

Known Bugs and Sugs

The simplest qualitative iterative opportunity (which is also arguably quantitative) to look for is how a bug might be blocking customers from succeeding. For example, if you're trying to improve revenue and the QA team discovers that when customers in Europe try to pay, your app crashes while handling the US-dollar-to-euro rate conversion, then the next thing you might choose to work on is fixing that crashing bug.

The main way you'll validate a bug-related opportunity hypothesis is by looking for data about how big of an issue the bug is—i.e., how often does it occur and what impact does it have on the success metric? Maybe that conversion bug hasn't been reported by any actual users, and it's really something in the QA team's setup causing it. Or, if only a tiny portion of your customers are in Europe, then there are likely other ways to improve revenue you should focus on first.

It might seem silly to explicitly list bugs as an opportunity to explore—if you're an engineer, you'd likely prefer to have no bugs—but one of a PM's challenges is to weigh the overall value of fixing a bug against that of not fixing the bug and doing something else instead. Quality's always important, but not every bug is a high enough priority to go fix immediately.

Similarly, there might be existing "sugs" or feature requests in your backlog, which become the basis for your hypothesis. These might have come from a variety of places, ranging from random ideas people have had to data-driven sources like customer support tickets and insights from usability studies— i.e., studies where you test how real customers interact with the existing product/feature and note what they do well and what stumbling blocks they encounter.

Related to this is paying off "technical debt." Sometimes engineering has to make internal changes that essentially "do the dishes" in the code. It's important to periodically prioritize this engineering work because if you don't, it will become harder and harder to implement new features down the road. Unfortunately, when you work on these projects, from a customer perspective nothing changes. To validate this opportunity, you'll want to make sure that this is a good time to work on an internal cleanup rather than to deliver something new to customers, and that this internal cleanup will provide value to your team down the road, such as making it easier to implement another opportunity on the roadmap.

Intuition

How many times have you heard someone say, "I've got an idea for an app! Do you know anyone who can build it for me?" Sometimes there are good ideas, like being able to use an app to easily hail a car at an attractive price. Other times someone wants to build an app to help match their socks to their trousers. Clearly, no one has good ideas all the time, not even Steve Jobs—remember the iPod Sock?

A common source of opportunity hypotheses is existing hypotheses you or your company might already have based on your experience/prior knowledge. This is a great place to start because you likely do have a strong idea of what to build for your customers from your experience, but it's also potentially dangerous because this type of hypothesis often doesn't get validated properly. Many times, people are afraid of someone stealing their idea—which rarely actually happens—or they just don't want to find out that no one actually wants their idea.

Unfortunately, the second step for many first-time product builders isn't to validate their idea but rather to jump immediately into building it. People like to assume that if they have a problem, many other people do too, and these people will want their solution. This is risky because it might be very costly to build the product, and no one knows for sure if anyone else experiences this same problem or is interested in the same solution as they are.

The best way to come up with an idea on your own is not to think about what you the individual want but to really empathize with your target personas, combining your knowledge of your customers' pain points with your knowledge of what you could build and the overall goals and success metrics that matter to the product and the company. As a PM, you're in a unique position to know what the major pain points for customers are, how they're reacting to your product, what the technical issues are with your product, and what technical innovations have occurred within your engineering team. We'll show you a tool, shortly, called the Business Model Canvas, to make the synthesis of this idea more concrete. A great PM will also be paying attention to the broader tech world, thinking about how innovations elsewhere might apply to his product and customers.

Here's a simple example of an intuition-derived hypothesis for Moover. They want to make booking a move as easy as calling an Uber, so that means making it simple for moving companies to provide accurate estimates. Photos could help moving companies make accurate estimates, but people likely don't know how to take useful photos to show a space for moving companies. What if they added a feature where we had the customer stand in the middle of each room, slowly moving their camera up/down as the customer spun around, generating a 360° photo on screen? That way every customer takes a good photo of the space in question.

We can hypothesize that the result will make it easier for moving companies to give an accurate estimate. The next step would be to validate that photos, especially 360° ones, make it substantially easier for moving companies to make accurate estimates. This could be done by using an existing 360° app to take photos of a space and send both them and regular photos of a space to various moving companies, asking for their feedback.

Vision

You, your boss, your company, etc., likely have an overall vision for your products and the company that you want to achieve on a longer time horizon. Specifically, it's an image of the future version of the company you're trying to create. For Walt Disney, this meant looking at some land in Florida and having a vision of Disney World, knowing that everything he wanted to do next would be about building Cinderella's castle. For you, maybe you want to migrate from a locally deployed-at-clients solution to a cloud-based one. You'll need to take steps along the way to achieve this long-term vision, and you might choose to make one of these steps your next opportunity. As an aside, hopefully someone has done some validation on the overall vision!

The challenge with these opportunities is assessing whether you can provide an immediate value to customers or if it's delayed gratification. If you believe this opportunity will have an immediate benefit, validate it like any other opportunity. But if it's something that will take longer for customers to benefit from, you might only do some internal validation to ensure it makes sense to work on this project right now since it takes resources away from other projects.

Team Ideas

One of a PM's biggest challenges is a soft skill, soft power. No one reports to a PM: you can't tell people what to do. Instead you need to earn people's trust, and a great way to do that is to look at building a product as a team sport and not departments working in silos. No, it's not a democracy, and at the end of the day you'll often be the one making calls about a product. But if other people know you listened to and acted upon their input, they'll feel included in the decision-making process and happier with your decisions.

A great place to include other teams is in this ideation step. There are likely other teams that work closely with the customers, such as Design, Customer Support, Business Development, and Sales. Reach out to people on those teams and see what thoughts they've had based on their experience with customers and the product. Support teams especially appreciate this, as they spend all day working with actual customers, and they have great visibility into what the customers are doing with the product and saying about it. They often can provide data like support tickets to back up their ideas.

Beyond talking directly with other teams, you can organize a group brainstorming session. There are pros and cons to these sessions. A big pro is that many people feel included, and one idea might inspire someone else to build upon it with a different idea. For example, the sales team might make one feature request that they think would help the product sell better, and the support team might mention there are a lot of tickets around that entire feature set, so perhaps it should be completely redone.

A big downside to group brainstorming is that people often fixate on a few ideas or ways of thinking, missing other opportunities. As the group facilitator, you need to help get the creative juices flowing. One way to do that is to have everyone share the worst ideas they can think of, then figure out ways to make those ideas even worse. After you've done that, flip over and focus on how to make the product better.

Make sure to keep these sessions at least a little focused by listing your current product goals and success metrics. If you want to brainstorm ideas to increase engagement, for example, you're not going to want to talk about putting more ads in the product.

R&D

Related to teamwork, sometimes there are new inventions that a brilliant engineer, or team of engineers, creates. What's nice about these inventions is that there's usually a prototype of some form so that you can see it in action. Adding these inventions to the product—called *productizing*—is often how products are pushed into the next generation, and they can be a major source of customer delight because the customer didn't expect or ask for them.

However, it can often be a rocky road from prototype to product, and the initial product might have significant tradeoffs or limitations. If you choose to pursue an opportunity like this, make sure to work closely with Engineering to understand all the challenges you'll need to solve to make this prototype useful to customers in their daily lives.

The Competition

Stravinsky, Faulkner, Picasso...regardless of who said it, you might have heard the quote, "Good artists copy. Great artists steal." Sometimes your competition has a great idea, and stealing it—and making it better—is your opportunity.

Be careful with this source. "Because the other guy did it" is never a valid reason alone to create a feature—that's just copying. First of all, how do you know the competition is smart, and isn't making a mistake with this feature? You'll also want to make sure this feature/product fits within your company's context. Furthermore, you want to think about where the puck's going to be, rather than where it is right now. If you're always stealing, you'll never be ahead. But the benefit to this source is that you can see how the feature works in real life, how customers react to it, and what you'd like to do differently.

Here's a simple example: For years, many PC manufacturers made stripped-down, slow, small-keyboard, low-cost "netbooks," and many analysts kept calling for Apple to make one. Yet Apple prefers high-quality, high-margin products, and instead of doing what everyone else was doing and what analysts thought Apple should do, it created the MacBook Air (which was incredibly small yet had a full-sized keyboard) and eventually the iPad. Both leveraged Apple's strengths, both were loved by customers, and both had the margins Apple aims to keep. As of writing, netbooks are dead, and many PC manufacturers have created their own MacBook Air and iPad knockoffs.

Business Model and Value Proposition Canvases

Another way to create an opportunity hypothesis is to explicitly analyze how a product fits into a business and how the product provides value for the customer. Alexander Osterwalder and Yves Pigneur created two tools to help you determine those elements, the Business Model Canvas, and the newer Value Proposition Canvas, respectively. They also have two books, with the same titles as the tools themselves, that do a great job explaining these tools in more depth than we cover. Using these tools to look at your product, you might see a missing link that lets you think up an opportunity.

Business Model Canvas

The Business Model Canvas provides a way to look at all aspects of your company with a different framing than we showed in Chapter 2. It's very focused on people, values, and revenue, and filling it out requires you to list facts and hypotheses (e.g., "We believe these people will be distribution partners"). This tool was originally developed for a startup with one product, but it works for a product within a large company, too. Figure 3-5 shows this canvas, and you can find a version to print and fill out at *http://strategyzer.com*.

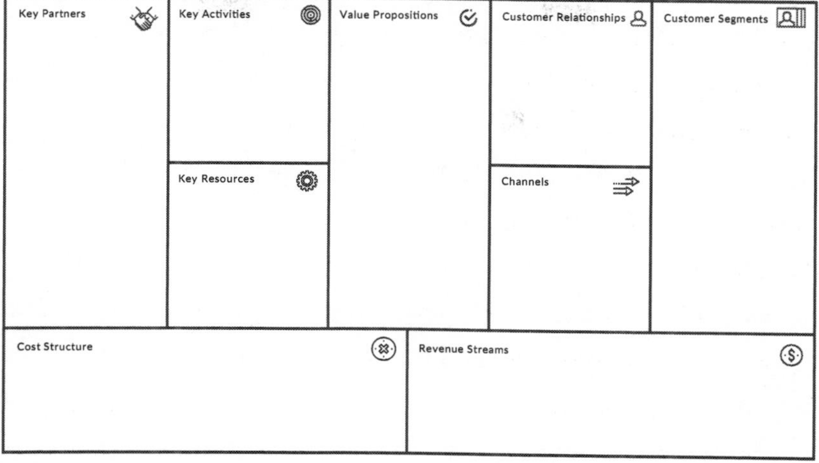

Figure 3-5. The Business Model Canvas provides a way to look at all aspects of your product.

Here's what each block covers:

Key partners: *Who are the people outside the company, from suppliers to contractors, who make the business model work? What key resources do we get from them and what key activities do they perform?* Companies rarely do everything themselves, and working with partners lets you reduce risk and optimize your activities. There are generally three types of partnerships: alliances between non-competitors, strategic partnerships between competitors, and joint ventures to build something new.

Key activities: *What are the tasks a company must do well to deliver on its value?* For example, Apple owns a number of key activities: software development, supply-chain management, store management/distribution, and more. Samsung's phone unit is focused more on supply-chain management and software development.

Key resources: *What are the most important physical, financial, intellectual (patents, copyrights, etc.), or human resources the company needs to succeed?* They can be owned or leased. For many companies making hardware, human and intellectual resources are key, whereas manufacturing is outsourced to an Asian partner.

Value propositions: *What's the benefit/value that a certain group of your products or services provides for a given persona? What customer pain points are you solving?* The Value Proposition Canvas will dig into this more, too.

Customer relationships: *What type of relationship, from personal to automated, do you want to establish with each persona?* For example, a high-value customer might have a direct email for an account manager whereas the average customer might only have online support forums available. Also consider what each segment expects, what you have now, how costly each relationship is, and how you expect to maintain each relationship.

Channels: *How does the company reach each persona to deliver the value, including marketing, communication, distribution, sales, and support? How are you reaching them now? What works best?* How are the channels integrated, for example, are sales only via your website?

Customer segments: *Who are the key personas the company/product will serve?* These are the most important personas that you believe you'll create the most value for, and they're who you want to prioritize opportunities for. The Value Proposition Canvas will dive into this more.

Cost structure: *Where do your costs come from?* This breaks down into fixed costs (salaries, rents, utilities) and variable costs (equipment purchases). For many companies, human resources are the greatest expense because people are needed to do key activities so that the businesses can deliver your value to their personas.

Revenue streams: This represents the company's incoming cash—revenue minus costs is the company's earnings. A company might have multiple revenue streams, depending on its customer segments, and asking what value you deliver that each customer segment will pay for, what they currently pay, and how they'd prefer to pay—e.g., lower recurring fee vs. higher one-time fee—helps you determine how to monetize each segment. For example, some companies offer discounted "Home" editions of their products, which lack features that matter at work such as document collaboration that aren't useful in an average household. The "Home" edition is one revenue stream and the regular version is another.

The Business Model Canvas is great because it lets us write down all of our hypotheses, from opportunity to distribution, in one place. Using the Business Model Canvas alone, it takes some deep thought to find a great opportunity hypothesis. Fortunately, the Canvas's authors have developed a newer tool, the Value Proposition Canvas (Figure 3-6), also available at *http://strategyzer.com*, which drills down into the Value Propositions and Customer Segments blocks to really identify how the product is or isn't providing value to the customers, and what the customers' needs are.

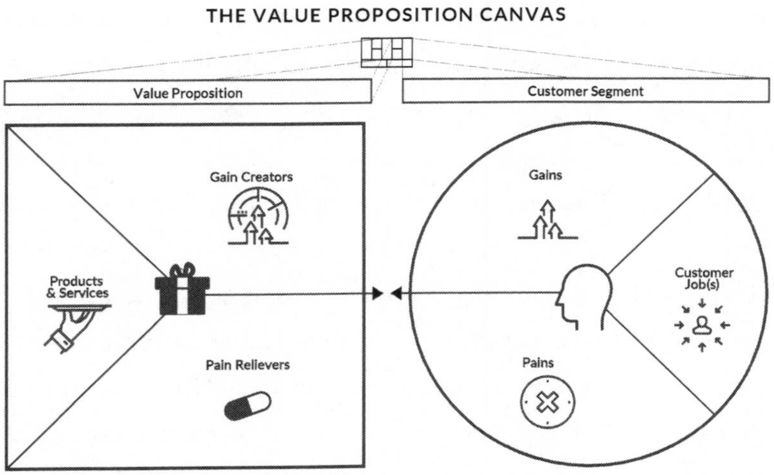

Figure 3-6. The Value Proposition Canvas is focused on the interaction between the customer and the product, and poorly met or unmet customer needs are a possible product opportunity.

The goal of the Value Proposition Canvas is to help you achieve product/market fit. This phrase simply means that "a good number of customers want what you're selling." This concept is especially important to startups building their initial product, as startups need to find customers as soon as possible. If they fail to find customers, they either need to pivot the business to focus on new customers, possibly even with a new product, or they need to close the business. This also applies to new features in existing products. After all, you want to build a feature a good number of customers will use.

The first part of the Value Proposition Canvas is diving into the customer—completing this part of the canvas can help you refine your personas! There are three key aspects to the Customer side: jobs, gains, and pains.

Customer jobs are simply the things the customers are trying to get done, in their own words, be it a task they're trying to perform, a problem they're trying to solve, or a need they want to satisfy. For example, an Apple Watch owner is likely interested in easily tracking her fitness—a task—and looking stylish—a need. Customers might have multiple jobs, and not all jobs have the same weight. If you ever heard someone say, "Fashion over function," that person's choosing a social job—looking trendy—over the actual task. Customer jobs align nicely with product use cases.

Gains are the outcomes the customer wants to achieve, in his own words. They might be expected, and either required or desired, or surprising, ideally in a positive way. Gains aren't just from functional utility: they might provide social value (*This makes me look cool!*), illicit positive emotions (*I love this product!*), or save money (*This is 1/10th the price!*). When talking with customers about the gains they want, make things as concrete as possible. If the customer says, "It needs to be fast" find out what "fast" means. 1 second? 10 seconds? 10 minutes?

Last, we have pains. These describe the obstacles preventing the customer from completing the jobs, along with possible bad outcomes and risks. Just like gains, try to make these concrete. If the customer says waiting for a taxi is a waste, ask how many minutes it takes until it feels like it's a waste. Also try to gauge how bad each pain actually is. Waiting 10 minutes for a taxi is a pain, but does it stop you from trying to hail a cab or getting in once it arrives?

The second piece of the Value Proposition Canvas is your product(s), and it also has three aspects: products and services, gain creators, and pain relievers.

Products and services are fairly straightforward: *What are the products and services available for each persona/customer segment?*

Gain creators refers to how your products and services create benefits and outcomes the customer wants, whether those are required, desired, or surprising. Again, these gains might be functional, problem solving, or social (including cost savings).

Pain relievers are how your product addresses the customer's top pains. You don't have to address every pain, but it should be clear in the Canvas how your product addresses the key pains.

Pain relievers and gain creators are the parts of your product that create value for the customer segment. The goal of the Value Proposition Canvas is to make these two categories—to make this value creation—explicit. If it's unclear or a piece is missing, you likely have a great opportunity to improve your product.

At the end of the day, product/market fit or feature/market fit comes down to addressing the key customer gains and pains successfully. If the customer wants important gains that you don't provide or has a big pain point you don't address, those mismatches create a very good opportunity for you to improve your product.

Also note that some products, especially B2B products, might have multiple personas, so you will need multiple Value Proposition Canvases, one for each persona.

As you work to validate your opportunity and learn more, redo your Business Model and Value Proposition Canvases to incorporate the new information. You might even want to specifically call out what's validated and what's still a hypothesis.

External Factors

While all of the ways to create an opportunity hypothesis so far give us educated, good hypotheses, sometimes there are external factors—shall we say—that force an opportunity.

The simplest and most understandable one is when a good business opportunity arises. For example, maybe a partner offers a large contract if a certain feature is added to the product within a given timeframe. It's likely still up to the PM to make sure this feature's worth it—usually by measuring the cost of adding the feature vs. the value of the contract—but this type of arrangement will often take priority over the previous plans.

Next, sometimes in regulated industries, regulations change and you have to prioritize complying with those regulations or your product might be pulled from sale.

The last qualitative method is also the most frustrating. It's when your boss or someone above you says, "Just do this." A good leader will have a reasoning behind the demand or even be willing to change her mind if you provide proof it's an invalid opportunity, but not every leader is rational, and not all rational leads are able to explain their thinking all the time. Sometimes you just have to prioritize what your boss wants, even if it's not the best opportunity.

USING THE KANO MODEL TO FIND OPPORTUNITIES

In the 1980s, Professor Noriaki Kano created a framework to help teams uncover and classify three categories of customer needs/attributes. Looking at where your product falls can help you uncover opportunities to work on next based on unaddressed or unspoken needs. Furthermore, it helps you assess if investing in your opportunity will provide a worthwhile return, helping you transition into prioritizing your opportunities.

The Kano model defines three principles that a product needs to achieve to be successful over time:

1. Value attracts customers.
2. Quality keeps customers and builds loyalty.
3. Innovation differentiates your product from others and keeps you competitive.

Then it maps these principles into feature categories.

Basic features. These are the things customers expect in a product, usually mapping to the value principle, and customers will be very unhappy if they are poorly executed or missing. Unfortunately, doing these really well won't make your users happy—it will just minimize their unhappiness. If your press the gas pedal in your car all the way and the car barely moves, you'll be unhappy. If your car is missing the break pedal, you'll be very unhappy. If an app you have to log in to is missing a password-recovery feature, you'll be very unhappy when you need it. If you have the fastest, most nicely designed password-recovery feature of any app, your customers will not be significantly happier than if you had a basic recovery feature. Basic features can be hard to identify when talking with customers, as customers expect them to be there and won't explicitly mention them. How often do you look for "toilet paper included" when booking an Airbnb? Generally you find out about a lack of basic features from complaint systems, lost-customer surveys, and attrition analysis.

Performance features (satisfiers). These are the things customers are often judging your app by and the things they look for before purchasing. Your customer's satisfaction with these features will be proportional to how well you execute them. These are fairly easy to find information about by talking with customers, be it through interviews or surveys, because they're things a customer will often explicitly ask for, compliment, or complain about. For example, faster performance in an app leads to greater satisfaction. Having fewer steps to achieve a goal also increases satisfaction.

Excitement features (delighters). These are the unexpected "wow" features that become product differentiators, innovations, and unique selling points, such as the iPhone's capacitive touch screen, Android's notification panel, or Wi-Fi on an airplane midflight. When you do these well they create significant excitement and delight. If they're missing, customers stay neutral: they don't know what they're missing. These features are the hardest to discover and really require an understanding of customer need. They're often found only qualitatively.

These three feature categories are commonly graphed together (Figure 3-7) to show how customer satisfaction compares to your level of investment/execution. It's a useful way to help judge how much effort you should spend on various features, along with evaluating what feature categories are worth focusing on next.

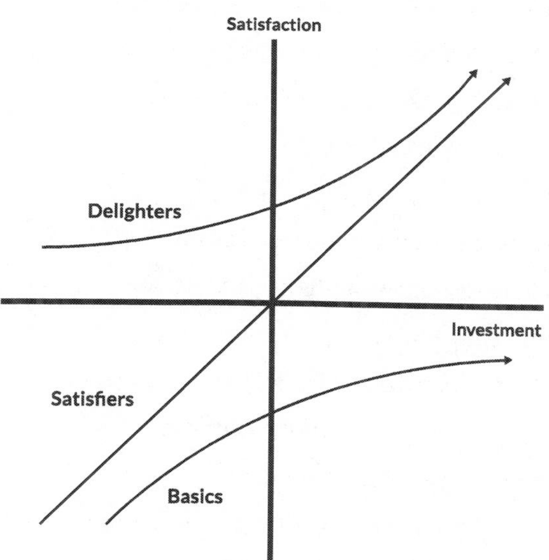

Figure 3-7. The Kano model provides a way to consider how much satisfaction each feature provides compared to what type of feature it is and how well it's executed.

Over time, each feature moves "down" in its category. Excitement features become performance features, and performance features become basic needs. The first time you had Wi-Fi on a flight, you were likely delighted to check your email while flying. Now you likely expect planes to have Wi-Fi and are disappointed when there's a poor signal or no Wi-Fi.

In general, the first version of your product needs to cover the basic features. Each successive generation should focus on a mix of satisfiers and delighters, along with making sure you're continuing to cover the basic features.

To find feature opportunities using the Kano model, map your product and its features against the model. What features are about meeting basic expectations? Are they meeting expectations? Have you covered all the basics? If so, move on to a satisfier or a delighter.

A big frustration for product managers is that basic features can require a significant investment to even get to a reasonable level. While you want to spend your time working on the satisfiers and delighters, skipping the basic features or doing them poorly will often lead to less customer satisfaction even if you have a great delighter feature.

If you're working on a new version of an existing product, consider what features started as excitement features but are now expected and something the competition has, too. Or similarly, what's something the competition added that your customers now also expect? How does that affect your feature mapping/opportunity hypothesis? Touch ID started as a delighter feature on the iPhone, and now fingerprint unlocking is fairly common and expected on smartphones. What new delighters can you find to achieve significant customer satisfaction?

MOOVER.IO'S HYPOTHESIS

Back in Chapter 2, we mentioned that when you book a move with Moover, the moving company does a follow-up call to plan details. Based on customer-satisfaction surveys, it has been found that this is the thing that current customers who give the company a lower NPS complain the most about. Being a young business, Moover has to balance growing the business against customer satisfaction.

The team did get together and brainstorm ideas, and the other possibility that emerged was some type of referral program to help with growth. But given how infrequently moves happen overall, the team's decided to focus on making customers happier first. The idea is that happy customers will naturally provide good word-of-mouth referrals, and later on if Moover doesn't have good enough growth they can try various growth techniques.

After looking at the satisfaction-survey results and the product workflow, this is what they came up with:

- **Company goal:** Improve customer satisfaction.
- **Product goal:** Reduce friction in the current workflow.
- **Opportunity hypothesis:** We can improve satisfaction for Really Busy Rob if we eliminate phone calls with the moving companies and consolidate communication into an in-app messaging tool.
- **Success metrics:** Since customer satisfaction is our main goal, we can measure it by tracking our NPS.
- **Other key metrics:** Other key factors that indicate if customers are achieving their goals and using this feature are the percentage of customers who complete the bid-to-completed-move funnel and the number of messages sent per customer.

At this point, as we did with Moover, you should have a hypothesis about the unmet customer need you want to address for your personas, an idea about why you fall short right now, the key metrics you want to improve, and, possibly, an idea of what you want to do to try to address this problem. All of these elements should have some supporting evidence, even for blue-sky opportunities. Read on to learn about how to validate these opportunities and see if they're worth pursuing.

CHAPTER FOUR

VALIDATING YOUR HYPOTHESIS

Now that we have an idea, we need to make sure it's the right thing to do next. Every idea has an opportunity cost. Working on Feature A means you're not building Feature B. The hallmark of an effective product manager is being able to sort out the great ideas from the merely good ones.

Continuing our scientific method analogy, now that we have a hypothesis about what to do next, we need to design and run an experiment to prove or disprove our hypothesis. In other words, we want to validate whether our idea—no matter how big or small—will really help us achieve our goals.

The ideal experiment to validate our hypothesis would be to build the full product and see how our success metrics change. Sometimes this is the right thing to do, such as if your hypothesis is that fixing a bug or adding a small feature will help you achieve your goals. But often, building the full product is a big investment in both time and cost. This means it's very risky to always build the full product to see if it achieves its goals. Instead, companies have started adopting the lean principles we've discussed, finding less expensive ways to validate an idea before building the product.

These validation approaches take many forms. Some ideas need only internal validation by looking at existing data like analytics and having a discussion with key stakeholders about the cost/benefit of this opportunity before you decide to pursue it or not.

With other ideas, especially for new products or major new features, you'll want to talk with real customers, both current and potential, directly via interviews and indirectly via surveys. This approach, called *customer development*, will help you understand your customers' pain points and goals more thoroughly so that you can validate if your idea will address their needs. You might even discover that a different idea many customers complain about is worth pursuing instead of your original hypothesis.

The last idea-validation method we'll cover is to run an actual experiment and seeing how your metrics change. For a new product or feature, you might choose to build a low-cost minimum viable product (MVP, covered briefly in Chapter 1). Don't confuse building an MVP with building the full product—as we'll cover later, MVPs might even be human-powered. Alternatively, if your idea is centered on changing a workflow, you might run an A/B test, which lets you compare two versions of something—like two different sign-up workflows—to see which one achieves better success metrics.

The right way to validate your opportunity hypothesis depends on your specific situation. In general, for each new idea you'll want to have objective data, anecdotal data, and cost/benefit data to be able to fully assess it. This means you'll have to do multiple types of validation. You might run an A/B test to gather analytics data, determine the cost by talking with the engineering lead, and then have an internal discussion with key stakeholders about the cost/benefit. Just showing that the idea will achieve its goals, which an A/B test can do, doesn't mean it's the right thing to do if the product is very expensive to build.

Last, once you've found and validated an idea, you need to assess where it fits on the roadmap. Just because you've found a great opportunity doesn't mean it's the best thing for the company to work on next.

Putting these ideas together with Moover, how might you validate your idea about how to improve customer satisfaction by building an in-app messaging tool? You already have data from an NPS survey, so focus your energy on doing customer development, interviewing real and potential clients to gather anecdotal data and ensure you truly understand their needs and pain points/how to make them more satisfied with Moover. If those interviews indicate messaging really is the biggest pain point, then talk with Engineering and Design about what it will take to build an MVP of this feature, and if the team agrees this will give the biggest business value for the cost, go build it.

Let's dig into each of these validation methods in more detail.

SWOT ANALYSIS

A *SWOT analysis* is a common method for looking at how an opportunity hypothesis fits in. SWOT stands for strengths, weaknesses, opportunities, and threats. This framework helps you identify the most important internal and external elements of achieving your goals.

To do a SWOT analysis, first identify your key goals and success metrics. Then create a two-by-two table like Table 4-1. The top row will be your internal elements—the strengths and weaknesses for the product/company around achieving your goals. The bottom row will look at external elements—the opportunities and threats, including things like cultural, governmental, and technological trends.

Strengths: Internally focused view of what you excel at	Weaknesses: Internally focused view of where you fall short
Opportunities: Externally-focused view of what you're positioned well to go after	Weaknesses: Internally focused view of where you fall short

Table 4-1. SWOT analysis provides a good way to put an opportunity in context at a high level, looking at both internal and external elements.

If your opportunity helps improve a specific strength, take advantage of an opportunity. Or conversely if an opportunity limits or converts a weakness or threat, it's likely worth pursuing even more. If it doesn't factor in or doesn't address one of the top-priority items, it's likely not worth doing now.

INTERNAL VALIDATION

As a PM, you'll find that there's no shortage of good ideas for what to do next. In an ideal world, we'd do a comprehensive validation of each idea, but this is rather impractical. Instead, we can do some preliminary internal validation to see if an idea is worth pursuing.

Here's a checklist of questions that will help you start validating an opportunity. If the answer to any of these is negative, then you should most likely not pursue this opportunity.

- *Is this opportunity in line with our vision?*
- *Does it support the product's vision and core function?*
- *Can we do it well with our capabilities (or is it feasible and desirable to expand our capabilities to meet the opportunity)?*
- *How does it contribute to our key metrics?*
- *Do we have any data, be it from analytics, surveys, or bug reports, to support this opportunity?*

- *Is it required to meet a critical business initiative?*
- *How does it contribute to our users' winning?*
- *Is it on our roadmap for this year, even indirectly as part of something else?*
- *Will it matter in two years?* (It's OK if the feature is to address an immediate need, but you'll want to limit those, as you want to prioritize things that have a higher value over time.)
- *Will everyone benefit? If it only helps a niche set of customers, is it worth the cost?*
- *If it succeeds, can we support it?*

Our friends at Intercom (introduced in Chapter 3) also suggest looking at your return on development investment to validate an opportunity. Create a two-by-two grid like Figure 4-1, looking at development effort (high/low) vs. how users value the feature/product (high/low), and figure out where this opportunity falls.

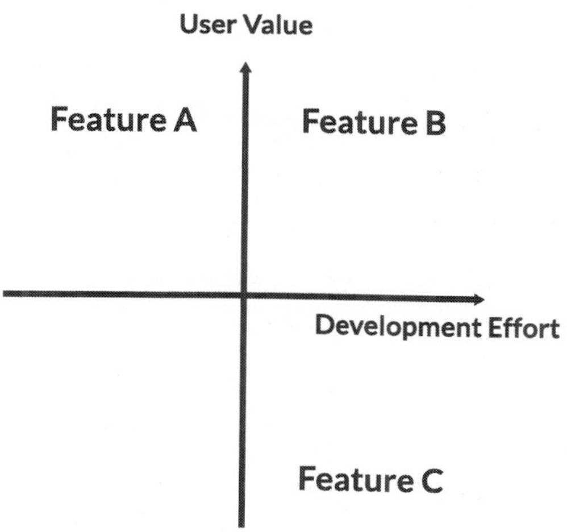

Figure 4-1. Creating a grid to compare development effort to user value is an easy way to visualize and compare different opportunities. Ideally, you will do low-effort/high-user-value tasks first (Feature A) and avoid high-effort/low-user-values tasks (Feature C) as much as possible.

Unfortunately, this isn't a litmus test for opportunities because sometimes we have to do high-effort things that users won't value, like rebuilding a back end, but this grid will help you put things in context. Low-effort, highly valued features or products are nearly always worth pursuing.

For some opportunity hypotheses, like "fixing a bug will help us achieve our goal," this level of validation might be all you need. If it's clear from data that the bug significantly affects a lot of users, it prevents users from winning, you have the resources to fix it, and the cost vs. value doesn't outweigh something else you want to do, then great—you've validated that it's worth fixing the bug! Other hypotheses require more effort in order to validate them.

This internal validation can also help with a soft skill: Respect. You'll often have people throughout the company giving you product ideas—in fact, you'll have more ideas than you can implement. This means you'll spend most of your time saying "no" to good ideas because you want to focus on the best ideas. But if you simply say "no" without a reason, people will feel that you don't listen to them, affecting how well you work together, and they will stop coming to you with ideas, which could prevent you from finding a great one. Doing an internal validation will let you easily and explicitly provide a reason for why you're pursuing one idea over another, making people feel like you listened to them and aren't just making arbitrary product decisions.

CHAPTER FOUR TIP

This chapter's tip comes to us from Nik Laufer-Edel. Nik teaches at Product School and helped design the curriculum. Beyond Product School, Nik leads the core passenger-experience team at Lyft. Previously, leveraging his background in design and research, he led the initiative to reimagine the online learning experience at Udemy, a 13-million-student marketplace worldwide. He loves discussing the product-discovery process, learning science, communication design, and the future of work, and you can find him in coffee shops across San Francisco or on Twitter @nikdotca.

YOU NEED CONTEXT TO MAKE GOOD PRODUCT DECISIONS

At the end of the day we know what's most important is focusing on helping our users win. To do that we know we first have to understand our users. We know we should validate our riskiest assumptions. We know we should gain confidence that our problem makes sense to work on and that our solutions actually solve the problem. But there's more we need to know to make good product decisions.

Over the years, I've designed a simple customer-journey model to remind myself of the context needed to define problems and evaluate solutions. The base of the model came about during two years I spent doing customer-development research at an early-stage start-up. It's evolved since to incorporate some of the research around motivation theory as well as concepts discussed in the realm of the Jobs to Be Done framework.

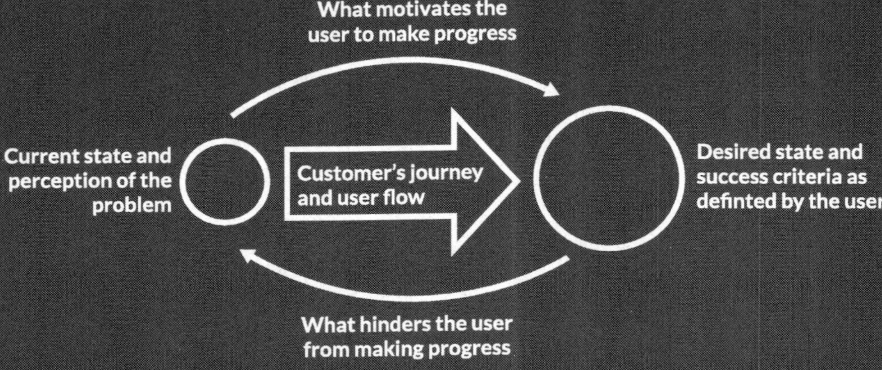

Assuming you're not trying to create an entirely new behavior, the model acts as a reminder that your users already have a perspective on the problem you're solving, a way in which they measure success, and a means by which they work towards that desired state. These are the basic building blocks of understanding users and today this information is often captured in personas, metrics, and user flows. What can be missing from these artifacts is what motivates users to make progress towards a desired state and what holds them back.

You can use this model of the customer journey as your North Star when articulating or reflecting on any product initiative.

CURRENT STATE

- What's the users' current perspective of the problem? How do they think and feel about it?
- Journey
- What are the current steps they take? This is often the flow of your application but might also include taking steps outside of your app or using competitors.

MOTIVATION

- What about the current solution are they not happy with?
- What about the new solution is uniquely appealing?
- Do they believe that following the journey will get them to the desired state?
- Do they believe they have the ability to do what will be asked of them at each step?
- Do they believe they will be supported if they run into problems?

HINDERANCES

- What about the current solution do they like?
- What about switching to the new solution worries them?
- Desired State
- How do they measure success? What is winning?
- How does getting to this state move them closer to other, larger goals?

I start all initiatives by drawing out the model to align the team and develop research questions. For mature products and iterations on existing features you may already be able to speak to all parts of the model. For new products or features you'll discover gaps in the team's knowledge or risky assumptions to tackle through internal or external validation. Ultimately, understanding what winning is for your customer, their current situation, and the factors that will help them or hinder them from making progress will equip you and your team to make better product decisions. Good luck!

EXTERNAL VALIDATION

External validation simply means getting feedback from real customers to see if your idea makes sense. Even though you might think you know what they'll say, you don't know for sure until you check.

There are many ways to get feedback. The simplest one is to be a data detective. What external data about real customers can you find from existing research sources to validate your idea? Are there relevant research reports, whether it's Mary Meeker's Internet Trends report (available for free), NPD Group's reports on what people are buying and their behavior (these reports are expensive but the data's very valuable and spans numerous industries), census data, or even Google Trends to see what people are searching for?

Sometimes it might not be obvious where to look, and you'll need to see if there's a similar or analogous vertical whose data will inform your decisions. Your primary goal is to focus on the need people are trying to meet, and to find research relevant to that need. This data isn't always easy to find, and it might be spread out across multiple research reports. Financial-analyst reports are often great additional sources of overall industry trends.

As an example, when on-demand food-delivery services like Postmates were getting started, they could have looked to food-industry reports about how often people order carryout/delivery, how much they spend per order, what demographics tend to order carryout the most and where they live, which segments of the food industry are growing vs. shrinking, and more. Secondarily, Postmates could have researched a specific interaction mechanism, push-button ordering with mobile apps, by looking at on-demand apps like Uber. If Postmates' hypothesis was that people would like push-button food delivery, it would've meshed these data points, using the food-industry reports to validate demand for food delivery along with the mechanism data to validate that people would be willing to order from an app.

Make sure to watch out for confirmation bias. This is when we look for only evidence that confirms our hypothesis and ignore evidence that contradicts it. Again, our hypothesis might be wrong, and that's OK.

Reading market data can be very useful, but it doesn't always give you great insight to what your customers are feeling, and their needs not captured by data. Empathy can be a powerful validation tool: Is there some way for you to *be* your customer so that you can accurately understand his needs? Sometimes this is easy; for example, if you're a PM at Slack, you use Slack internally to communicate. You'll know how people use the product because you use it daily, and you can validate your idea by analyzing how useful it'd be to your life and if there's a tradeoff or cost that'd reduce the value. Be careful here, as you'll need to make sure the way you use Slack is similar to how your customers use it.

Other times, being your customer is doable but takes effort. Ford Motor Company built a special suit, the Third Age Suit, which effectively simulates what it feels like to be an elderly driver, with reduced joint mobility, a simulated feeling of arthritis, simulated impaired vision conditions, and more. This suit lets Ford employees "be" an elderly customer to test features in their cars without having to bring in a pool of elderly test drivers to observe and talk with.

The trick to being your customer is to make sure you're representative of an actual customer. Even though we all like to think we're an average customer, we're not—you're a PM, you're above average! And especially if your product has multiple personas, you'll likely represent only one of them.

Unfortunately, sometimes it's not realistic to be your customer, especially for enterprise and niche products. In these cases, you just have to find another approach to understanding your customers.

Customer Development

Finally, sometimes it's necessary to go outside the building to talk with customers, both current and potential. Keep in mind that the goal right now is to figure out whether to build a given thing, not to conduct user testing/research to see if we've built a particular thing well. The former happens at the beginning of the product process, and the later will happen once we've started building something.

So what is customer development? It's a way to validate if the people you think are your customers truly are the right customers and confirming you're on the right path. This includes finding out what problems customers are seeking to solve, what they're doing right now that either creates those problems and tries to solve them, what they're able to do (technically, financially, socially, etc.), and how they find out about and decide if a new product/feature is worth it. Fundamentally, it's a conversation and an exchange of information.

It's also useful to know what customer development is not. It's not a way for people to give you a wish list. It's not a focus group to only see how people respond to ideas. It's not a place to observe how customers use your prototype. It's also not a replacement for product vision. Customers will give you a huge wish list, but they'll often ask for more than they actually need, end up not using features, and —in really bad cases—might get confused by all the extra features. This is a big part of why we recommend having some opportunity hypotheses in mind first.

Interviews

We've found that, of the various steps in the product-development life cycle, people new to product management have the least experience with customer interviews. But interviewing is an incredibly valuable skill because it's an effective and low-cost way to validate your opportunity hypothesis. And since a product manager's ultimate goal is to help the customer be awesome, spending time with customers is critical to your role.

There are entire books, such as Cindy Alvarez's excellent *Lean Customer Development*, that cover in detail how to prepare, do, and learn from customer interviews. We'll do our best to give you a detailed overview, but we'd recommend doing further research and practicing your own interviews before actually talking with customers.

Preparing for Interviews

Just like how you don't walk into a job interview without preparing, or a meeting without anticipating a desired outcome, customer interviews take preparation. These steps are largely based on *Lean Customer Development* because we believe in them!

To get started, write down a list of what you know factually and what you're assuming about our customers, including their needs and how your product satisfies them. The Business Model Canvas can help you identify key assumptions. Of course, customers can help you validate only parts of the canvas that apply to them: segments, value propositions, channels, relationships, and maybe revenue streams. But given how fundamental these are to your business/product, they're quite important to turn from guesses into facts.

Use the Value Proposition Canvas to identify what you know for sure and what you're assuming are your customers' existing pains and desired gains. Also try to identify what tradeoffs they're willing to accept for these gains. For example, does a smartwatch provide enough functional and fashion gain that they're willing to trade off the sentimental value of their existing watch? Or does your augmented-reality headwear provide enough value that your customers are willing to make the social sacrifice to wear it? Google Glass learned customers' feelings about that tradeoff in a very public and expensive way.

It can be helpful to explicitly write your opportunity hypothesis in terms of these canvases: "I believe that <personas/segments> experience <this pain> when doing <task> because of <limitation>, and alleviating that pain would let the customer <achieve this gain>, although she'd have to <accept these limitations>."

Don't forget about what you think your key metrics are and who you believe your competitors are. Your customers might not see the same people as competitors, or they might know of existing solutions that you don't.

Also, it's useful to know your company and product roadmap: How'd you get to where you are, where are you thinking about going, what are the open questions, and what information from customers might help you make better decisions?

It's useful to look at any other persona trait relevant to your opportunity hypothesis to think about who to talk with, and if there are enough potential customers to pursue this opportunity. For example, if your product provides a convenience service for a fee, you'll want to focus on customers who will pay for convenience rather than people who have *coupons.com* as their homepage—still talk to a couple of people who value cash over convenience to get a sense of where their tipping point might be, however. Other traits to look at include where potential customers fall on the risk vs. reward, low-tech vs. tech-savvy, bored vs. busy, and frequent vs. infrequent purchase spectrum.

A—hopefully obvious—technique to help make sure you're finding the right customers is to create screener questions you ask potential interviewees. Try to hide the "right" answer so that people don't answer with what they think you want to hear. If you want people who use streaming music services, ask what product they use to listen to music. Also ask questions to exclude people, like, "How often did you listen to music last week?" Braden Kowitz at Google Ventures created a useful template to help you screen for participants, available at *https://goo.gl/uPBXD6.*

Once you've figured out who you want to talk with (more on finding these people shortly), let's figure out what to ask them. The most important thing to know is that, whether they realize it or not, people are going to try to please you. The most valuable thing you can do is to get the customer to tell you about how they currently deal with whatever problem you're thinking about solving. Even if you think you have a new service (imagine someone considering a food-delivery service like Postmates for the first time), your customer might already do something in this space (ordering from restaurants that aren't their favorite specifically because they deliver, getting carry-out, etc.) that you'll want to ask about.

There's a phenomenon called "ideal self" where if you ask someone about what they might do, they never give a good answer. Would you like to lose weight? Would you like to save time? Would you like to have delivery from your favorite restaurants that don't currently deliver? Of course the answer is yes to all of these!

Instead, if you ask questions about what people currently do, you'll see what actually happens in their lives, which is a much better predictor of what they'll do in the future. How often do you go to the gym? What diets have you used in the past six months? Do you pay a handyman or fix things around the house yourself? When did you last order delivery? Did you make a restaurant choice based on who delivered?

Similarly, asking what someone will pay is useless because no one will give you an honest and meaningful answer. But it's useful to ask what they've *already* paid to try to answer this question. If they haven't spent anything in the area you're asking about, it's likely not an issue for them.

Rather than asking customers if they'd like your feature/product—because they'll say yes—it's better to find out about how they deal with the fundamental problem you're trying to solve. The simplest way to ask a question like this is, "Tell me about how you do <topic> today."

Unfortunately, it'll take some prompting to get useful information. For example, someone might have a situation or limitation that he doesn't see as relevant to your discussion but that could play a huge role. Maybe your product needs a fast cellular connection to work well, but the person you're interviewing barely has 3G where he lives. It's very helpful to get context. Here are some sample questions:

- *How often have you dealt with this topic?*
- *What were you doing right before this topic came up?*
- *Once you finished, what'd you do?*
- *How long did it take to deal with the topic?*
- *What made you buy the product relevant to this topic?*
- *How often do you buy the product?*
- *Where do you go to buy the product?*

It's also really valuable when you ask questions that get customers to tell you stories rather than giving simple yes/no answers. They'll automatically provide you some background context, or you can politely interrupt and ask them to clarify any needed context. Stories help you go up to a slightly abstract level because you'll often find out why someone was using the product, what their goals were, and what they prioritized. You'll also find that people say things implicitly in stories so that you don't have to prompt for more—e.g. they might mention using Siri, which means they are iPhone users.

Sometimes you'll have customers who think they know exactly what they want and will tell you specifically. For niche products with advanced users, these people likely *do* know exactly what they want, and they know enough about how the product works to know what's possible. But that's a very small group. Most customers don't know what's possible or impossible, and you'll likely want to ignore specific feature requests. Instead, it's your job to figure out people's underlying pains and see if your idea will address them. Think about the Henry Ford's "faster horse" example here: The feature request is a faster horse. The underlying desire is the desire to get to a destination faster.

Restating someone's feature request to make sure you understand it and asking what she thinks it'd let her do or how she envisions using that feature is an easy way to start to get to the underlying desire. You could also use the "magic wand" question: *If you could wave a magic wand and be able to do anything you can't do today, what would it be? Anything you can imagine is possible. What would you like?* This might seem like an ideal-self question, but it's not, because we're not asking if a customer *would* do something. We're actually asking, "What's your biggest pain point around this topic?" in a more fun way. Hopefully our hypothesis addresses it!

It's also useful to ask about tradeoffs. "If <new feature/product> were to happen but it meant that <tradeoff>, how would you feel?" This does start to hit on the ideal-self question, but it can give you a sense of what a customer values.

Sometimes customers are used to seeing the world one way, and might not realize that they have a real pain point. Did you realize how annoying the taxi experience was before you tried Uber or Lyft? You might need to think of questions to tease out if there is an unrealized pain point, like asking how often someone walks to a hotel to find a taxi rather than trying to hail one on the street.

If you have an existing product and a fairly detailed opportunity hypothesis, you can also use a hypothetical situation. Have part of the interview where you say something like, "I want to tell you a story about how we imagine someone like you using the next version of our product based on what we've heard from other customers. Please interrupt me if you have questions, if you disagree with anything I'm saying, or if I'm just plain wrong!" This approach can help you find out about any limitations customers have, if your product has unused features, and if your customers are using your product how you imagine they're using it.

Generally, avoid showing any existing products or prototypes, as that focuses the conversation on what you have rather than on what the customer needs. However, it can be useful for customers to show you any existing solutions they have in place, and you might notice aspects of the solutions that the customers don't explicitly realize.

You'll also want to avoid loaded and leading questions—that is, questions that imply an answer or encourage the customer to answer in a specific way. "Mr. Smith, do you still beat your wife?" is a loaded question because it implies guilt even if Mr. Smith wouldn't harm a fly and never ever beat his wife. "Do you have problems with your PC?" is leading because it implies the customer uses a PC and that his PC has problems. "Tell me about your primary computer" is better because it doesn't imply any judgment and lets customers respond with what they care about.

Put together your first list of questions, but don't worry about making it perfect. As you start to do real interviews, you'll refine your questions based on if you're getting the information you want—this doesn't mean you'll get the answers you're hoping to hear. Your list will never be perfect, but keeping this advice in mind will help you get a great start.

We recommend taking a step back once you have a list together, and really thinking about if these questions will deliver the information you're hoping to learn from the interviews. One way to do this would be to imagine what the most useful results would look like—which you could derive by thinking about how you intend to use the results from the interviews—and working backwards to see if your questions will deliver.

There is one question you should always ask at the end of an interview: "Is there anything else about <this topic> that I should've asked about?" Here's when you account for the known unknowns—that is, the category of things the customer cares about, and that you know exists, but you have no idea what else might be in there beyond what you asked. For example, maybe you were focused on how quickly a customer can access Google Now or Siri on his phone, but it turns out the customer hates voice recognition because it doesn't work with his accent.

Once you have your question list together, start preparing the logistics. Here are some key issues to consider:

- **What's the last date where interviews can give you useful information?** Customer development takes time, and often there are internal milestones beyond which new information isn't helpful. Knowing these milestones in advance helps you craft an effective interview schedule.

- **What level of quality and confidence in the results do you need?** Do you have a bit of time to really do a thorough job, or do you have to work as fast as possible even if the results are imperfect?

- **What's the right medium for the interviews: in person or on the phone?** In person is always best, but that might not be feasible if your customers aren't all in the same city. Phone chats are often easier to schedule and more convenient, but you'll miss any non-verbal cues, like facial expressions. Video chat solves that problem, but it can be rather frustrating if it's not working or if the interviewee isn't tech-savvy—you don't want to spend your interview time debugging a connection.

- **How much time will each interview take?** Interviews tend to run long—people run late, you find interesting things to ask about, etc.—so if you plan on conducting a 20-minute interview rather than a 30-minute one, you'll likely hit your time goals. Make sure to communicate your time expectations clearly to your interviewees.

- **Should you pay your interviewees?** In general, yes. Somewhere between \$50 and \$100 per hour is common, and it's often as a gift card rather than cash. You're asking people to work for you and provide their expertise, and you'll use that input to make money. The one exception would be if you're talking with someone who reached out to you, such as a current customer who emailed the support team. The best way to pay those people is to make the product even better for them! You can also make them feel special by including them in early-access programs.

Finding People to Talk With

We've got our hypothesis, we've got our interview goals, we've got our questions, and we know the type of interviewees we want to talk with. Now all we need are interviewees! This might seem scary, but it's easier than you expect. People like to help others, especially if they can sound like experts. Approach people humbly, saying you'd love their help and want input from their experience, and you'll find willing interviewees.

Look at your connections first. Do you know anyone directly who fits your target persona, or do you know people who might know people? Don't hesitate to ask your connections directly. Make your request explicit: tell them why you're asking, make it clear what the interview would involve (time, format—like on site vs. phone call), and mention how helpful it would be. If you're asking a connection to reach into her network, create an easily forwarded email so that it's simple for your friend to press "Forward" and send the email to anyone she knows without adding a long note.

Social networks can be great resources, too. Reach out on LinkedIn, Quora, subject-relevant forums, or even Twitter to see if you can find people willing to help. If there's a particular physical place your customers hang out, try going there in person and talking with people, or at least posting a notice asking people to contact you if they'd be willing to provide input.

Craigslist and other online classifieds will be very hit-or-miss, and more miss than hit. You really don't know who will stumble upon your post given Craigslist has such a wide audience, and it might take more time to filter for the right interviewees than it's worth.

If you're really stumped, ask yourself this: Once you've built the product, how are you planning to find customers to sell to? Or, if you already have a product, how do you reach your existing customers? Use similar techniques to reach your audience, but rather than asking them to open their wallets, ask for their wisdom.

For existing products, you should have already had customers reach out to you to offer opinions. People who speak up might not represent the silent majority who won't complain or comment, though, so you'll still want to find what the quieter people want. Your sales and support teams can point you to good customers to talk with. When reaching out to these people, make it clear you're exploring opportunities and not changing the product, and give them permission to complain. They'll let you know about their pain.

There are also many market-research firms you can hire to help you find the right customers to talk with, and they will also often help conduct interviews. These firms can be a bit pricey and take a while to produce results, but they make your life a lot easier.

No matter how you find your interview subjects, remember to use your screening questions to make sure these potential subjects fit your criteria.

After you've found the right subjects, schedule the interviews. Provide very clear instructions for everything your interview subjects need to know, such as parking availability for onsite visits and your direct contact information. Once scheduled, confirm the interview, and consider a reminder call or email the day of, too. Multiple tools that help you schedule interviews, such as PowWow, will send the reminders for you.

Conducting the Interviews

Now comes the fun part—talking with real people. Before you begin, take a breath and smile—you're a friendly researcher right now, no matter what else is going on during the day.

As soon as you greet your interviewees, make them feel comfortable. You want them to open up and have a conversation with you, not feel like they're being interrogated or rushed. Watch the time, but be courteous about it. Talk with them as a human, and call them by their names—don't call them "customer." Make it clear that there are no right or wrong answers—you want their expertise and you appreciate their time.

It's helpful to get interviewees talking right away by starting with simple questions that the customers won't have to think too hard about, like asking them how they deal with the topic you're looking at now. Imagine an arc: start with small talk, go to easy questions, move to meatier questions, recap key points, and then thank them for their time.

Your job is to be quiet and listen—don't jump in and start talking when the other person takes a breath. You'll even want to wait a few beats after someone finishes a thought before saying more, in case she's thinking and planning on elaborating on her answer. If someone criticizes your product, don't get defensive; remain neutral and encouraging, getting the person to talk. Even smile and sympathize!

To make sure you understand what your interviewees said, ask for anything you want clarified, and even restate what they said into your own words. You'll also want to clarify vague expressions. If someone says, "I hate waiting for this," find out where his tipping point is—is he OK waiting one minute but five feels like a waste?

In terms of taking notes, you'll generally want to record what your subject says verbatim rather than summarizing. This will help you avoid confirmation bias, and it'll make it easier to analyze the conversation later on. It's very useful to have a notetaker so that you can focus on the person rather than writing. Failing that, use a smart pen like Livescribe, which records your conversation and lets you tap on any notes you take to immediately jump to that part of the conversation.

Make sure to note any non-verbals, and star any emotional utterances ("I hate/love this"). One exception to the verbatim-recording goal is if they say "maybe"; write it down as "no."

At the end of an interview, thank the subject for his time, and ask if you can follow up later.

If you've never done an interview before or you're not sure about your questions, do a practice interview or three with someone you know. It usually takes 5 to 10 interviews to fully get into the zone, and unless you're changing your questions, 15 to 20 interviews is usually when you stop hearing new things.

Drawing Conclusions from Interviews

Take some time immediately after each interview to pull out 5 to 10 of the most interesting points. Focus on things the subject said that validated or invalidated your hypothesis, carried emotion, or surprised to you.

Each interview should help you figure out if your hypothesis addresses a valid pain point the customer has: whether the customer has tried to solve that pain point before, whether the customer cares enough about this pain point to want it fixed, and if there's nothing that'd stop the customer from using your solution. You should have a good sense of how your product would fit into the person's life day to day, if it'd replace anything, and, if she wouldn't buy your product, the specific reasons why.

Make sure to pay attention to actionable vs. wishy-washy words your customers use. If they say, "I keep meaning to," then they don't actually care about the topic at hand. If they say, "Here's what I've tried and what I do," then they care. "<This> would help me achieve <this goal>" is meaningful, whereas, "<This> would be interesting to have" and "I think I could figure out how to use it" mean this person won't use the product. If they say, "I wouldn't use it, but others would," no one will use it. Similarly, "Maybe it's just me" means lots of people feel that way.

Pull the data from all your interviews together into an overall summary that you update as you go. Categorize what the customers say as appropriate, including pain points, emotions, existing solutions, and so on. Even try sorting their words into "validates hypothesis" and "invalidates hypothesis" buckets. Try to see if you can identify trends with multiple customers having similar comments.

If you haven't found anyone excited about your idea in five or so interviews, either you're talking to the wrong people or your problem isn't a real problem for customers. Try changing who your target subjects are, and if the trend continues, you just invalidated your hypothesis. Also, if your questions aren't giving you the insights you want, change them!

If only a few people see your opportunity as a pain point they care about, the potential market for your product might not be large enough to matter. You'll want to do more (like a survey, which we'll cover next) to try to gauge the market size, but this should be a warning sign.

Sometimes you'll notice customers discussing the same pain point again and again, even if it's different from your opportunity. Absolutely note this pain point, and analyze if it's a better opportunity (has a bigger value, lower cost, etc.) than the one you're looking at now.

After 15 to 20 interviews, you should have a good idea about how valid your opportunity hypothesis is.

Surveys

"The plural of 'anecdote' is not 'data.'" (This sentence is attributed to Frank Kotsonis and Roger Brinner.) Interviews are great because they help you figure out customers' underlying pain points and motivations, but they're just a small sample of your user base (or potential user base). They don't help you quantify issues or measure overall attitudes. Analytics don't provide that type of information either. Analytics are great at exposing what customers actually do, but they don't tell you anything about what's going on in a customer's mind.

Surveys occupy this murky area, where we can get a view inside a lot of customers' heads. In general, the data surveys provide isn't as high quality as that from customer interviews, but it's a low-cost way to see if our conclusions from customer interviews scale to a large number of people.

There are multiple ways to use surveys—one example is how we used them in Chapter 3 to gauge your overall NPS as a potential starting point for finding an opportunity. We'll focus now on using them to validate a hypothesis.

In the validation step of the product-development cycle, never start with a survey—you'll find out better questions to ask and get more real data about people's needs with interviews, but once you think the interviews have validated your hypothesis, surveys will help you see if the bulk of your customers agree.

Creating Surveys

Good survey design is also a bit of an art. Because you're not there to ask clarifying questions or to pay attention to non-verbal cues, you need to be careful of how you design them. You'll also want to test any survey before sending it to a broad group.

Like you would with an interview, start by explicitly focusing on your goal. It should be "to further validate my hypothesis by seeing how many people have this pain, have invested significant resources trying to solve it, are unhappy with the solution, and could implement my solution."

In general, keep surveys short! They should take only a few minutes to fill out. Survey fatigue is a real thing, and the quality of the answers in the middle of a survey drops compared to the beginning and end, especially on longer surveys. To help account for that fatigue, wherever possible, randomize your questions (or more commonly, randomize the ordering for the groups of questions you present).

You'll also want to randomize how the answers are presented to account for a bias anyone has toward just picking a specific answer number—remember when you guessed "C" on every question you didn't know in school?

It's critical to keep your questions and answer choices very clear—you might know what industry jargon means, but your customers might not. Even phrases that seem obvious, like "Q4," can be ambiguous—do you mean a fiscal or calendar Q4? Just specify the months instead.

When picking questions, you'll also want an arc for the survey. Start with broad questions, move into specifics, and close with a place for the customer to add any extra thoughts. Group related categories together, too, to help the customer with context.

Like with interviews, always aim for actual instead of ideal-self questions—i.e., ask what customers have done, not what they might do. Also avoid leading and loaded questions. For example, rather than asking if the customer has recently used online billing tools, ask how a customer pays bills, with an option for online billing.

Comparison questions, whether between what the customer uses now and something else or between two hypothetical products, are implicitly leading because analyzing a hypothetical is very hard. It's better to present the two options separately and to have people rate their experience with or thoughts about each specific option. Later, you can compare the results.

Comparison questions also often ask two questions in one because you're evaluating each product's value. It's always better to ask separate, simple questions rather than one question that really includes multiple questions.

Tables that explicitly ask a user to rank her thoughts about specific items are useful to figure out how many customers value this potential pain point and how much, and to analyze how trends change over time. For example, "Are you completely dissatisfied, slightly dissatisfied, neutral, satisfied, completely satisfied, or n/a with your ISP's download speed?" is a useful question, and you can ask it again and again as the speed and what customers do online changes. Ranking like this is also great because it lets you build an importance/satisfaction graph with real data. Simple agree/disagree questions are frequently biased because people want to please you and are more likely to select "agree." Use a scale instead to get more accurate answers.

Ask for specifics when a bucket has a lot of variability. Age is a great example because surveys often have questions asking which age range you fall into. But between 18 and 40, there's a lot of potential variability in your life, especially depending on where you live. People in cities might still be single, living with roommates, and have lots of disposable income at 30, whereas a person in a rural area might be married with three kids. Instead, ask the person's age specifically, and ask specifics for any other data you need to correctly segment the customer. And, of course, remember what we've mentioned again and again about segmentation around pain/needs/jobs being more effective than around demographics.

At the same time, allow for flexibility when needed. Fifty years ago, people were much more likely to join a company, stay there their entire career, and then retire. Today, you could be employed and looking for a job, or self-employed but in between contracts (essentially unemployed).

It's totally reasonable to have empty text fields where people can type stories, rather than radio buttons where they're constrained to fixed answers. Asking how someone's last flight experience on an American carrier was will yield more interesting results than, "How satisfied were you with your flight?" Make sure that if you ask for a detailed answer, you don't set a low character limit on your survey's answer box.

Asking "why" questions can be dangerous because people are not very self-aware. As with interview questions, aiming to understand a customer's goals helps dive at motivation more explicitly. "What's the top thing you hope to learn from this book?" is a better question than "Why did you buy this book?" (Please email the authors if we're not meeting your needs!)

When conducting a survey about an existing product, it's also good to ask a Net Promoter Score question (see Chapter 2), as this will implicitly help you measure the score over time as you conduct more surveys.

Executing Surveys

There are many tools to create surveys: Google Forms, SurveyMonkey, Typeform, etc. The best tools will let you add conditional sections so that you can ask follow-up questions based on how your customers answer questions. If they're unsatisfied with something, you might want to dig into more specifics about why to help you validate your hypothesis, but if they're completely satisfied, you don't need to ask more questions.

Finding people to take your survey is similar to but arguably easier than an interview because a survey is much less of a demand on someone's time than an interview. If you have an existing app, add a pop-up in-app or email existing customers that meet your filter requirements to ask if they have five minutes to take a survey to help improve the product. Note how that sample text has the survey's goal, "help improve the product," which explains why it's valuable for customers to take it. This makes it more likely a customer will complete the survey.

Posting on various forms and social networks where your target market resides is useful, too. If you're doing minimal manual filtering when sending the survey link, though, you'll want more filter questions at the start of your survey to make sure only the people you want to hear from are actually progressing through the survey and answering the main questions.

There are also services like Ask Your Target Market that have a large mailing list, and you can pay to send your survey link to exactly the right people. Paying for targeted ads on Google, LinkedIn, Twitter, Facebook, and more is another way to find potential respondents.

Generally surveys are unpaid, but companies often offer a lottery-like reward at the end to add an incentive for people to participate ("Provide your email address to be entered in a raffle to win a $100 gift card").

Analyzing Data

Run your survey until you feel you have statistically significant results or until you stop getting new/useful/different results.

When you're ready to start looking at results, the very first thing to do is validate the data. What do you do with incomplete surveys? Do you want to ignore them or manually look at them to see where—and maybe why—people stopped answering? If you use the data, you'll have a different sample size for each question.

Next, do you want to do any partitioning based on background questions? People who listen to streaming music daily may have different answers than people who listen once a week. What about cohort analysis? People who came from a professional forum might be different than people who started replying only once you added a raffle.

You'll likely want to do a basic data analysis with any numerical questions—i.e., convert scales to numbers, look at the mean, median, variance, etc. You'll also want to look at the distribution to see if it's standard/normal—that is, most people are around a mean—that says the data trends to a point. However, if it's bimodal, answers fall into two discrete categories, that tells you something else, and a mean isn't useful for that question.

In general, like with interviews, you're still looking for anything that validates or invalidates your opportunity hypothesis. But the other aspect you want to look for with a survey is how many people feel this is a pain point, and how significant of a pain point is it.

If everyone agrees it's a pain point but no one has spent any time or money trying to solve it, your opportunity is likely not worth building unless a solution is very cheap to build or you have reason to believe your solution will make customers realize the pain point is bigger than they thought. You could imagine what a survey about voicemail would've looked like before visual voicemail on the iPhone—finding, listening to, and saving a specific voicemail message was a pain, but no handset manufacturer spent money to solve it because it required service carrier cooperation.

If you used satisfaction questions to build up an importance/satisfaction graph—both in terms of how customers perceive importance and how you internally rank importance—you can see if your opportunity is the right one to pursue next or if there's something more important.

Because it's very easy to fall victim to confirmation bias, try focusing only on data that invalidates your hypothesis before looking for data that validates it. At this point, you should have a very good sense of whether your hypothesis is valid and if it's a valuable enough opportunity to pursue.

Experiments

An additional way to validate a hypothesis is to run an experiment where you build something to test your hypothesis. This isn't always possible, but if you can run one, it'll yield incredibly informative results.

Experiments are complementary to customer development, not a replacement, as they'll help you see what people do when you make a change, but they won't help you understand *why* people do it or what their fundamental needs are.

A/B Tests

One of the most common experiments to try with an existing product is called an A/B test. The idea's simple: if you make a change to your existing product and address the opportunity you're focused on, what impact does it have on your key metric? You'll implement the change, randomly give some users the current "A" version and some users the new "B" version, and then see if the metric changes in a significant way.

The hardest part of an A/B test for people to understand is that you're not fully building out the B version in a well-designed and engineered way. The goal is to hack together something quickly and cheaply that will let you determine if this opportunity is worth pursuing in a more thorough way.

A/B tests are a great way to validate if your hypothesis achieves your goals with iterative/refinement opportunities. For example, Google had a hypothesis that the shade of blue used in advertising links affected click-through rates, and A/B (and C/D/E, etc.)-testing different shades let Google find a shade that generated an extra $200 million in revenue, according to Dan Cobley, managing director of Google UK.

It's most common to A/B-test navigation, user flows, layout, and messaging/content. If your opportunity doesn't fall into these buckets but you think you can A/B-test it anyway, go for it! In fact, sometimes companies beta-testing a completely redesigned, blue-sky-opportunity version of their website will randomly direct part of their traffic to the new site and see how the users' overall behavior differs from behavior on the main site.

Optimizely is a very common tool for implementing A/B tests, and its expanding feature set includes support for web, mobile, and desktop apps, custom segmenting/test targeting, analytics, and more.

Simple MVPs

We like to talk about two types of minimum viable products, similar to Lean Startup (discussed in Chapter 3). The one people most commonly talk about is the version you'll actually build and release (covered in

Chapter 5). The other type is a very simple MVP that you can create to help validate your hypothesis—a scaled-back version of your full product vision. These super-simple MVPs will be inexpensive to put together and not actually implemented how the real product will be implemented. But they should provide enough to a potential end customer that you can gauge if your opportunity's worth pursuing.

The simplest MVP is a *preorder MVP*. This helps you evaluate if people are interested enough in your idea to open their wallets for it. Create a fake marketing website for your product, describing it as if it already existed with the features you feel are important, and put a "Buy" button at the bottom of the site. Then, market this product like it actually exists, take out different display ads, and see how many people click "Buy".

To avoid being completely deceptive, we recommend adding a note when someone clicks "Buy" that says you haven't finished building this product, are currently working on it, and they can enter their email address to be updated when you have new information. This is also a nice way to capture a list of customer email addresses you can market to when your product is available.

For an existing product, you could create a "New Feature" section on your website, see how many people watch an explainer video showing how you intend for the feature to work, and use a "Learn More" button instead of a "Buy" button to reveal the truth and again capture email addresses.

Another type of MVP is a *concierge MVP* (these names are from Eric Ries in *The Lean Startup*). In it, you'll manually work with your customer just like a real concierge would to perform a task, where the task is the overall focus for your opportunity hypothesis. If you have a hypothesis that people want a restaurant-recommendation app, you'd act like a concierge to help them select a restaurant. During this process, you'll want to explicitly focus on the steps you go through to figure out an answer—which questions matter and which don't, and what's involved in completing each step—so that you can eventually automate them.

Looking at this restaurant-app idea, if no one asks for your concierge's help, that's a big initial sign that something is wrong. Either you're not appealing to the right customers or you're not making your value proposition clear. Then, when someone expresses interest, you'll manually discuss with that person what type of food he likes and dislikes, what type of restaurant ambience/price point/etc. he's looking for, and you'll run a Yelp search for him. You could even offer to arrange transportation.

As you go through this process, you'll find out if customers are interested in the overall idea, which steps are the most useful and what goes into them, which steps are unexpected but delightful (like arranging transportation), and which steps customers don't care about. This helps you refine your hypothesis and create a better cost/value estimation. For example, maybe you find your customers really want a feature that lets them push a button and simply have a Lyft show up to take them to a nearby open restaurant that they'll probably like: they care about instant fulfillment over making a reservation and planning.

Many service start-ups initially began with a concierge MVP, helping them gauge interest and better understand the overall problem space and customer needs. Wealthfront, an automated investment service, even started with a concierge MVP by having financial advisors manually working with clients.

A *Wizard of Oz MVP* is another simple type, sometimes the next step after the concierge MVP. Here, you'll create a product that looks like it's fully built to an end customer, but humans are doing the work behind the scenes. The Zappos founder didn't start by making an e-commerce site or stocking tons of inventory: he took photos of shoes at different shops (with permission), put them online, and when an order came in, he'd manually buy and ship the shoes. But to a customer, it looked like Zappos had a full inventory and was a store by itself.

This style of MVP also doesn't scale, but it's another way to validate the demand for your opportunity. If you can manually keep up with the demand, this idea probably isn't worth pursuing. But if people love it and you're overwhelmed, that's a good hint it's time to automate it.

The last type is a *fake door MVP*. If you're thinking about building a new feature into your product, add the UX elements you'd use to trigger the interaction, but rather than actually delivering the feature, provide a notification that the feature's coming soon. See how many people use your "fake door." For example, if your hypothesis is that people would find a live group chat feature useful on your online education site, add a "Chat" button and see how many people click it. If only a tiny percentage do, reconsider if it's worth pursuing this opportunity, depending on the value of those customers vs. the cost of implementing the feature.

The key to remember with every experiment is that you want to keep it simple and cheap. You don't want to spend so much time designing the perfect A/B test or preorder MVP that you're burned out before you've even run the experiment. You're going to throw away every experiment, regardless of the result. If the result's positive, you'll have to build the product or feature for real.

MOVING FORWARD

At this point, even if it took a lot of changes and retries because your initial hypothesis was wrong, you should have an opportunity hypothesis that you've validated as worth pursuing. Woo! It's time to get going on your roadmap!

There's one more step to think about, and that's your opportunity's priority on the roadmap. Even though you've found a great opportunity, you have limited resources, and another PM might have found a different priority that's more important to the company's goals. Every feature has an opportunity cost: working on one thing means you're not working on something else. As a PM, you want to think strategically to make sure you're always working on the things that matter most. You might have a great idea that you've validated, but is it what the company should work on next?

A helpful litmus test is whether this product or feature will help the company achieve its current goals. If not, you should likely table it and work on it when the company is focused on the appropriate goal.

The Kano model (Chapter 3) provides a useful way to gauge how critical your product or feature is. Is it a basic feature? If so, it's probably a high priority to do next because your users expect it and you're not doing it—or at least not well enough. If it's a satisfier or delighter, you can prioritize it based on its value (how much you think it will provide towards your goal) vs. cost.

A simple way to compare priorities is to come up with a value vs. cost number. Work with an engineering lead to put difficulty values on different opportunities. From your customer-development work and other internal analysis, create business-value numbers for each opportunity. Use higher numbers to indicate more expensive cost, or more valuable. Because it's tough to estimate value and difficulty precisely, use an exponential series rather than a linear one—i.e., use 1, 2, 4, 8, and 16 rather than 1 through 5. This way, it's very clear when one opportunity is harder or more valuable than another. Next, for each opportunity, figure out a score using *score = value÷cost*. Focus on the highest-scoring opportunities first, as they provide the most value for the lowest cost. You might choose to change priorities based on other factors, but this will give you a good starting point.

We'll conclude this section with a warning: you might have a run of good luck where you create hypotheses that customers vehemently validate. Keep validating your ideas, though; just because you were right before doesn't mean you'll always be right. Taking time to validate your idea is a lot more effective than skipping this step, building the product/feature, and finding out you were wrong.

MOOVER'S OPPORTUNITY-VALIDATION STRATEGY

In Chapter 3 we came up with a hypothesis for Moover that if we integrate into the app everything that happened in the follow-up call for planning a move, our customers will be happier. We came up with this from data—NPS survey results—plus internal discussion. During the internal discussion, we essentially did the internal validation, and we agreed it made sense to work on.

But Moover has a lot of possible things to work on next, and we want to make sure in-app messaging is the right one. This means we want to do customer development, interviewing real customers. We want to learn if messaging really is an annoyance, if our in-app messaging feature would solve that pain, and if there's something else we've missed that we should work on instead.

Here's the first version of our interview template:

- Have you moved before, without Moover? If so, what was it like?
- How did you hear about Moover?
- What was your experience like using Moover?

- Which moving company did you pick, and what made you pick them?
- How did you communicate with the moving company outside of Moover?
- (If they say "phone"): How many times did you attempt to contact each other before you actually talked? (That is, you call them and get voicemail and you miss their return call.)
- How do you feel about talking with someone on the phone?
- Could you tell me what your first and second preferred forms of communication are (e.g., phone calls, email, SMS, something else)?
- What additional information did the moving company need to give you a final estimate?
- How long did it take to go from starting to communicate with the company to providing your information to getting a final bid? Did that delay affect your planning?
- Did you have any special items, like a piano? If so, what was it like to arrange moving that?
- (If the move has happened already): How did things go the day of the move? Was there any preparation with the movers that didn't happen that would've made the actual move smoother? Post-move, how did things go with the moving company?

- (If they've moved previously): What parts of Moover saved you time compared to when you moved before?

- If I could wave a magic wand and change any part of the moving experience (aside from packing and unpacking—say this with a laugh), what would you want me to change?

- On a scale of 1 to 10, with 10 being "definitely" and 1 being "not at all," how likely are you to recommend Moover to a friend? (If you don't think you've gotten answers that reflect this number, probe more and ask about the single biggest factor that led to their picking that number.)

- Is there anything I didn't ask you about communicating with the moving company that I should know?

We'll refine this as we do interviews, but this is a good starting point that will give us a sense of what customers think about the whole experience, if there's another pain point that comes up commonly, and if communicating with moving companies to figure out details really was a pain point.

We'll also want to reach out to customers who leaked from the funnel at the phone-call step to see what was painful about that step. Those interview questions will be similar, but we'll ask questions about what they did to book the move instead of using Moover and what about the phone-call step specifically caused them to choose that alternative.

After doing these customer interviews, if in-app messaging still looks like the biggest pain point, we'll look at the development effort needed to build it. If it's fairly low, we'll just build it. If it's high, we'll implement a Wizard of Oz MVP next. The customer will send a message, we'll contact the moving company on the customer's behalf, and we'll reply to the customer on the company's behalf. We'll run this experiment for a while and see how the NPS numbers change and if any customer explicitly comments on the in-app messaging. Then we'll use that data to decide if we should build this feature for real.

CHAPTER FIVE

FROM IDEA TO ACTION

Finding and validating the right opportunity to work on next has gotten you to the starting line of the product-development life cycle. Now we need to run the race and actually build the product. In this chapter we'll look at how to transition from an opportunity to something actionable, and in Chapters 6 through 8 we'll dive into the entire "get it built and launched" process.

Fundamentally, this chapter is about an important PM soft skill—communication—and how to effectively communicate, discuss, and finalize the opportunity you've found with key stakeholders.

WHY NEW IDEAS STRUGGLE

A product manager's job includes anticipating what might cause the product to flop and addressing that risk up front. The biggest reason new products struggle isn't a technical reason—it's because customers don't want or need the product you end up building. In other words, it happens because you don't achieve product/market fit. Fortunately, there are things you can do to give your product the best possible chance of success.

Taking steps to validate your idea, like we went over in Chapter 4, will help get your product started the right way, as you'll have made sure there will be some need for your product or feature—from this point we'll say "product" for simplicity. But numerous issues that might crop up and prevent your finished product from achieving product/market fit, as you go from "idea that we believe customers want" to released product. It's your job to anticipate and prevent these issues before they cause harm to your product.

Here's an example. What if there's a hidden barrier you never learned about or addressed that prevents customers from using your product? Remember the Kano model from Chapter 3? There are often basic expectations that a customer won't explicitly mention, but if your product is missing those features, the customer will be unhappy and might not even use it. Imagine if you booked a hotel room and there was no bed. Or toilet paper. Or sink. Would you stay or would you immediately go to another hotel? Early test phases with key customers as you build your product can help make sure you don't miss a hidden barrier.

But hidden barriers are just one thing that might prevent you from achieving product/market fit. Other obstacles include the following:

- It takes you so long to build and release your product that your customers' needs have changed or they found a better solution.
- Your product has so many features, new customers can't figure out how to use it, quickly getting frustrated and abandoning it. Or if you're adding a new feature to an existing product, perhaps it ends up being hidden where no one finds it.

- The product's value wasn't even clear in the first place, and customers didn't purchase it because they didn't realize it would address their needs.

To be fair, you won't be able to anticipate every possible obstacle, nor does anyone expect you to—that's what iteration is about. However, as you start to build your product, there are steps you can take that will give your product the best chance of success possible. These steps start with writing a few key documents that will help you clearly establish your goals and desired outcomes, create empathy for your customers, and allow for clear communication with stakeholders. Those traits combine to help you and your team make smart decisions as you build your product, giving it the best chance of success.

WORKING BACKWARDS BY IMAGINING THE FUTURE

Building something new involves imagining the future and making it happen. We frequently find it useful to start development on a new product by describing what the world will be like when the product's done. Imagine you're writing a science fiction story about a near-future world with your product.

There are two great "imagine the future" documents to try writing before anyone's written a line of code. These documents are a press release and a product review. Amazon often has its product managers write a press release when starting development. But press releases are internally focused, and they cover how you imagine talking about the product when it's done. Writing the product review you want to receive before starting development forces you to think about how you want the product to be *perceived externally* when it's done.

Both of these documents are useful to write, as they help answer key questions up front and help communicate with key stakeholders. When you start to build a new product, writing these documents forces you to take your product ideas out of your head and get them down on paper, making it much easier to share your ideas with other stakeholders. Furthermore, writing down your ideas will help ensure you have initial answers for important product questions like, "What are the key features customers will care about that we'll want to promote?"

Over time, as you build out the product, come back to the review and the press release, and update them whenever you're at a critical decision point. How do these documents change if you choose not to build a specific feature, for example? If you're unhappy with how your review is changing, what can you do to get it back on a good track?

Writing an Internal Future Press Release

While not the most fun prose-wise to write, writing a press release before you start product development forces you to explicitly write down your target market, the problem you're addressing, how you're solving it, and the key features of the solution—succinctly, in less than a page.

Sharing the press release with stakeholders, including the engineering and design leads, will also help you start to uncover any internal barriers and figure out what questions you need to answer before the team can start fully building this product. Perhaps this product relies on building a new piece of technology, and you need the engineering team's help to build a prototype to see if it's even technically feasible. You'll need to find time on their schedule, and that prototype will be a milestone towards the overall project, affecting the release date even before you've started planning the project.

Writing a press release will also help you start to determine how you communicate the product's value to customers, along with how customers will find and get started using the product. You'll likely change both of those as you actually build the product, but thinking about them up front helps address two major reasons products flop.

Furthermore, it's one final validation step to make sure this is really what you want to do next. If you're not excited to write this press release, and no one is excited to read it, are you working on the right opportunity? Is there something else you would be excited to write, and excited for customers to read?

Similarly, ask yourself if the product described in the press release really will help you hit your goals. You could try writing a press release as if you achieved your goal. For example, if your goal is to grow your engaged customer base to a certain target number, write a press release about how you've hit that milestone and the role this product played in hitting it. If the press release feels contrived or very hard to write, then perhaps this product isn't the right thing to build to help you achieve your goals.

A basic product press release usually includes these elements:

Headline: If you were to tell your friend about this product in a sentence, what would you say? Included in that is the key target market, how it helps them win, and a tentative product name that the target market can understand. Sometimes you will need two sentences, in which case you should write a headline and a subheading.

Summary paragraph: The first full paragraph in your press release should call out the most important aspects of the product and how it solves the customer's problem. Imagine you're reading this press release on Flipboard or Apple News—most people will read only this first paragraph, so it needs to be concise but complete.

Problem and solution: The next section should elaborate on the problem and your solution in more detail.

Spokesperson quote: Include a quote from you, the product manager, about how this product is great for your customers. It's fine to include this in the solution text.

Customer quote: Include a quote from a fictional customer about how the product fits into his life.

Conclusion/how to get started: Explain how new customers can find/sign up/buy/use this product, and pull everything together with a call to action.

If you find you need to write more to help make your thoughts about the product clear, especially around issues that relate internally to your company and how you'll get the product built rather than around issues related to the customer, then also write a product FAQ document.

Writing a Review

The other "imagine the future" document you might write at the start of the project, especially for a major new version of a product or a brand-new product, is the review you want your product to receive. Imagine if Recode, or whomever is appropriate, were reviewing the released version of your product—what would they say?

In a press release you think about how you want to talk about your product, but a review forces you to think about what customers will hear and how they'll experience the product. Therefore, this is where you need to be honest about what tradeoffs you're willing to make with the product. Maybe your product will be amazing but also pricier than the competitors. The reviewers will call this out—Are you OK with that? If not, and you start taking steps to reduce its price, what tradeoffs will occur? Will you need more customers to make up for lost revenue? Is that achievable? Will you need to reduce the feature set? What impact would that have on the review?

Similarly, what parts of your product do you think a reviewer will focus on, and which will they ignore? The parts you discuss the most are the parts where you'll later spend most of your design and engineering effort.

Mostly importantly, the review should have a conclusion about why a customer should buy your product, especially over a competitor's or whatever the customer is doing now. This conclusion should reflect the unique, differentiating value your product offers. If it's something minor, such as identical features at a slightly lower cost, then your product might struggle to stand out—if a competitor has a sale, there's suddenly no difference in your products, and you'll be seen as a copycat.

Writing that conclusion will force you to connect the concepts in the previous three chapters: What are your company's core competencies? How do those connect to this opportunity? For example, especially at first, Google Docs was much more limited than Microsoft Word. But it was cloud-based, collaborative, and platform-agnostic—in addition to being free. Those three factors are how Google used its strengths to build a differentiated word processor. If it had been a free app you downloaded and installed on your Mac or PC, a review would've concluded that it was a very limited free word processor, and that's it—that product wouldn't have taken advantage of Google's strengths.

Just like your press release, your review should be concise. Most product reviews don't exhaustively look at every feature. They give customers enough information to help them know what problem the product solves, if it solves the problem well, what tradeoffs the product has, and if they should buy the product.

Defining a Minimum Viable Product

Clearly defining the MVP you want to ship and working backwards to determine how to achieve it is another way to help set your product up for success. In Chapter 4 we talked about using one type of MVP—simple ones hacked together and not built like the actual product—to validate your opportunity hypothesis. Now let's look at MVPs from a "what will we actually build?" perspective.

As you wrote your press release and product review, you were forced to pick out the most important parts of your product to talk about. The single most important aspect of your product, the one that delivers the real value for your customers, is the starting point to define the MVP. You'll prioritize building that part first, and at some companies that will also be the initial product you release.

Before we go further, let's clear up a big misconception about MVPs. *Minimum* doesn't mean *bad*. Your product is still going to be designed and engineered well, tested thoroughly, and, most importantly, it will deliver value to the user. It should be a product that people are willing to buy and use. Even if it's not fully featured, it should work well enough that it becomes your customers' go-to solution.

Imagine a product that has only one button. It's easy for customers to use this product, because their only option is to press a button. Now imagine you add a second button. Suddenly the product is a lot harder to use because customers have to choose which button to push. Every button or feature you add increases the friction for customers—it makes them have to think more about what they're doing.

Minimum simply means the fewest buttons or features you need to build to deliver the most important value. This prevents you from building features that no one ends up using, or, worse, making the product so complex a customer doesn't use it at all. In an ideal world with lean methodology, you'll release your MVP to real customers and then determine what to do next based on what they're actually doing with the product and what limitations they encounter. In other words, you're always just building MVPs and iterating.

Unfortunately, we often end up in non-ideal situations where we iterate less frequently, like building a major new version of our product, and we'll be expected to ship more than just the pure MVP. In these cases, defining the MVP will help you prioritize the pieces you absolutely have to build to deliver on the product. For the beyond-MVP features, rather than arbitrarily picking features to build, test your MVP with key customers before release. Then, use their feedback to figure out what extra features to prioritize. Even though the end release will be more than an MVP, this approach helps you use an MVP internally, effectively.

So how do you come up with your MVP? Using your press release and product reviews as a guide, let's make a list about your product.

1. Write down the overall thing you're doing and why you're doing it. That is, what value will it deliver for your customers and what goal will it help you achieve? Explicitly put this statement at the top.

2. List the features you think you need to achieve that top-level goal, along with why that feature's important. Rather than just writing "cloud data store," write "cloud data store so that customers can

access their data from any device."

Now here's the kicker: as you work on this step, you're not allowed to add any new feature category not listed in the press release and product review. You'll define each feature in more detail (e.g., you might need a way to log in, so that people can access your service, and a way to reset passwords), but you can't add something major. For example, if you wrote a fictional press release about the iPhone 5S and never mentioned Touch ID, you can't suddenly list Touch ID as part of the MVP. Whether you realized it or not, writing the press release and review helped you prioritize the most important parts of your product, which in turn helps define the MVP.

3. Go through your feature list and cross out whatever items customers don't actually require to address their core need. This step is the really hard part—MVPs should be uncomfortable. You as the product manager should feel like the MVP is not feature-rich enough, but there should be enough functionality that customers can accomplish their goals. For example, even though two-factor authentication is more secure, is it really critical to your customer or can it have a lower priority?

   Eliminating features might even eliminate certain personas from using your product. That's OK, as long as it doesn't prevent your key target market from using the product. If your product is very risky, such as relying on technology engineering hasn't built yet, you might even define a "single use case MVP," which can be used by only one persona for one situation—a risky one. If the MVP works for the key market, then over time you can build the needed features to support more personas.

By the time you're done, you should have what you believe is a clearly defined MVP, along with explanations about why each feature is part of the MVP.

MVPs, Plussing, and the Kano Model

We love MVPs because they let you focus on delivering a product your customers want and will use. But remember, minimum doesn't mean bad. You need to be continuously seeking ways to make sure what you're doing is great. In Chapter 3 we talked about the Kano model, and we introduced the idea of delighter features, features that customers don't ask for but that deliver a huge return in customer satisfaction.

As you're defining your MVP, it's easy to inadvertently dismiss delighter features as non-essential work, after all, customers aren't explicitly asking for them. But it's your job as a PM to advocate and to keep these features part of the MVP when possible, as they're critical to building innovative, differentiated products that your customers love.

To help you think about these features, we want to share an idea from Walt Disney. He came up with the idea of "plussing," which is simply finding ways to make a good idea great and to deliver beyond what people expect. Sound familiar?

Disney historian Les Perkins tells a story from the early days of Disneyland. Walt was holding a Christmas parade, which cost $350,000. His accountants begged him not to spend that money, because people would already be in the park. Walt's reply was, "That's just the point. We should do the parade precisely because no one's expecting it. Our goal at Disneyland is to always give the people more than they expect. As long as we keep surprising them, they'll keep coming back. But if they ever stop coming, it'll cost us ten times that much to get them to come back."

To this day, The Walt Disney Company's culture has integrated plussing in everything they do. At a park, a cast member might go out of his way to unexpectedly help your family skip a long line, and this unexpected delight makes your day even more awesome. The sunken ship and sharks explosion sequence in *Finding Nemo* was a lot of fun, and the final shot with two birds sitting on the water completely plusses it (we're not going to spoil the surprise in case you haven't seen it). The results of continuously delivering more than people expect, in both revenue and customer satisfaction, speak for themselves

When you're defining your MVP, an extra filter as you're cutting potential features is to ask, "Does this plus the core idea?" If it really does, spend some extra time considering if you should cut it or not. Conversely, if you're struggling to find ways to define delighter ideas, ask yourself, "How could I plus this?"

While plussing is arguably not fully in line with lean thinking, you'll likely discover that plussing your initial MVP is key to building products that customer's don't just use, but also love.

Next, let's look at how to effectively discuss the MVP and the project as a whole with other stakeholders.

COMMUNICATING VIA A PRODUCT REQUIREMENTS DOCUMENT

One of the most importantly tools to help you communicate is a well-written *product requirements document* (PRD). A PRD is an explanation of the specific product you're building. It clearly explains why you're building this product, both for your internal goals and for your customers, along with the exact scope—the features and functionality—of the product. Similarly, it should convey what you're *not* building.

For better or worse, PRDs have become a controversial topic in the product-management world. In very waterfall-oriented companies, a PM will spend a long time writing a very detailed PRD. These huge documents, often 20 pages or more, specify every aspect of a product up front, they are difficult to read, and they are essentially immutable once finished—this is what the team is going to implement no matter what. Advocates of lean methodology use the PRD as an example of everything wrong with waterfall development. Specifically, they believe in quick iteration and using new knowledge to plan what to do next, and long and detailed specifications for what you'll do are contrary to that approach.

We believe that a PRD, if done well, is a fantastic communication tool, and we're going to help you create effective ones that others will read. Furthermore, we view a PRD as a living document. You'll update it as the project progresses, documenting changes in scope along with key decisions and fleshing it out with relevant information like user design tests. Unlike when product management first emerged and people created detailed PRDs before a project began, we believe that the PRD is finished only when the product's released.

The PRD is a tool for everyone involved in the product. At first you'll use it to get all the key stakeholders on the same page and help the team understand the project. Having an initial PRD can be reassuring and inspire confidence in your project, as it's clear to others in the company that you have an idea for where to take the project. We believe that, throughout the project, the PRD should be the project's home page—or at least the very first link on the project's homepage. As you near release, your support and sales teams will use it to find out everything they need to know about the product. And when you're done, it's a historical reference for why you made certain decisions.

We should mention that you won't need a PRD—or an imaginary press release/product review—for every opportunity you pursue. A bug fix, for example, won't need a PRD. There's no exact division as to when you do and don't need to write a PRD. Our recommendation is to write one for any opportunity that is more of a project, involving communication between various teams and potential confusion rather than a clear, small change.

Let's look at what goes into a PRD and how to use it as a communications tool.

Breaking Down a PRD

These are the key sections in a PRD:

Title: Give this project a distinct name.

Change history: Provide a description of each important change to the PRD, including who changed it, when, and in what specific way.

Overview: Briefly, what is this project about? Why are you doing it?

Objectives: What will this let the customer do? What are our high-level internal goals for doing this project?

Success metrics: What are the success metrics that indicate you're achieving your internal goals for the project?

Messaging: What's the product messaging marketing will use to describe this product to customers, both new and existing?

Timeline/release planning: What's the overall schedule you're working towards?

Personas: Who are the target personas for this product, and which is the key persona?

User scenarios: These are full stories about how various personas will use the product in context.

Requirements/features in: These are the distinct, prioritized features along with a short explanation as to why the features are important.

Features out: What have you explicitly decided not to do and why?

Designs: Include any needed early sketches, and link to the actual designs once they're available.

Open issues: What factors do you still need to figure out?

Q&A: What are common questions about the product, and answers to those questions?. This is a good place to note key decisions.

Other considerations: This is a catch-all for anything else, such as if you make a key decision to remove or add to the project's scope.

The exact format of a PRD varies company to company, but the overall content is similar. Let's dig into each section in more detail.

Title and Change History

The PRD's header contains the title, which is a unique, identifying name for the project. This might be a code name or it might be something simple, like "Moover Web App" for the first version.

The change history is just a way to quickly tell if there's new information so that readers don't have to reread the entire document only to find out nothing's changed. Some wiki tools have automatic change-tracking widgets, so if you're writing your PRD online, this section is automatically written for you.

Overview and Objectives

Next, you write an overview paragraph that will be very similar to the first paragraph of the press release you wrote. It will describe what this project is and why you're doing it now. You'll also create a short bulleted list explicitly listing what you want the customer to get out of this project and what internal goals you're trying to achieve—your objectives.

Success Metrics

You'll also explicitly list the most important success metrics, the key performance indicators that you will need to be able to measure to figure out if you've achieved our goals.

As you start to write the PRD, you might find you have a general sense of your goals (increase the number of users), but not necessarily a detailed goal (increase our user base by 10%). Write whatever you can and add some placeholder indicator, like "???" if you're not certain or need to more clearly define something. You will also call out this uncertainty in the "Open Issues" section.

New PMs often make the mistake of listing every possible metric they could measure. Instead, focus on the key success metrics you want to watch for, and later in the PRD as part of the features section or within the Q&A, list the specific metrics you want to measure that will affect the success metrics.

Messaging

Messaging is how you'll explain the product to a current or new customer in a short sentence, and we'll cover it more in Chapter 8. It's quite likely that your product messaging won't be clearly defined at the start of the project. Take a stab at writing something, indicate it is tentative/uncertain, if it is, and add figuring out the exact messaging to the "Open Issues" section.

Timeline/Release Planning

Even though you're most likely not acting as a project manager and owning the project schedule, you'll want to include some rough timing information here and eventually provide a link to the full schedule. Maybe your marketing and sales team want to release the product for a holiday push—this means it needs to be for sale by mid-November. Knowing that date might significantly impact your development planning and how much you're able to build and test in time.

Personas

Call out the key personas this product is intended for. If you have personas defined elsewhere, link to the full personas and remind the reader of the key traits in the PRD. If they're not fully defined elsewhere, define them here so a reader understands what the eventual customers will be like, and their goals.

User Scenarios and Storytelling

Now we come to the secret sauce of our PRD format: user scenarios. We believe user scenarios will help you write PRDs a cut above everyone else's, making people want to read them. In a user scenario, you'll combine personas, customer development, and empathy to write full-paragraph stories about how your customers will use your product in different scenarios.

Stories are the oldest form of entertainment we have, and scientists have argued that narrative experiences are the basis for far more of our lives than systematic logic. Think about the last bad presentation you saw. Chances are the presenter had slides chock-full of bullet points and just read each one. After three minutes, you were checking your email, daydreaming about being anywhere but in that seat. And when you looked at the bottom of his slides and saw "3/101," you started praying for a fire to get out of the room. Poorly presented content can make even the most fascinating of subjects boring.

Conversely, think about a TED Talk. These presenters easily hold your attention for 15–20 minutes and make you want to hear more. Each starts with the presenter sharing a personal detail about her life, and the slides, if there are any, are images with no text. Instead of reading bullets, we listen to the world the presenter crafts for us and imagine ourselves in it. TED Talks are formatted as stories, and these stories engage our brains.

There's scientific evidence that our brains are wired to think in stories, not lists of bullets. Scientists have found that just reading a list of bullet points activates the language-processing parts of the brain (Broca's area and Wernicke's area), but when we read a story, areas in the brain that we'd use when *experiencing* the events are activated, too. If we read about a person walking down the street, the same parts of the brain that activate when we walk down the street will activate. Stories let us imagine another's experience.

One of the big reasons a product manager needs to communicate effectively is to make everyone on the team empathetic with the customer so that they can clearly understand the customer's needs and how the product fits into his life. Writing stories to talk about the customer and the product you're building is the most effective way to help your team empathize with the customer because it makes your teams' brains behave as if they're the customer, implicitly communicating the results of your customer-development work.

Storytelling also provides a way to take vague opportunities and raw data and make sense of it. When we're young, we're taught that there's one right answer to a problem. 2 + 2 = 4. Even in English class, we're taught to write to one right answer: write an intro, hypothesis, supporting data, and conclusion. The way most schools work are a relic of preparing students to work on assembly lines where there is only one way to do each task.

Product management isn't like that. We have a lot of seemingly disconnected data that we have to weave together to create a product narrative. And there's not always one perfectly clear, right answer for every problem. Instead, we want to focus on the customer's underlying needs and motivations to make sure whatever answers Design and Engineering come up with will solve the problem. Stories are an effective way to give meaning to data and to express that need in an understandable way. They let us imagine a world that doesn't exist and think about the steps we'll take to get there—which is also useful when crafting a product roadmap.

Writing user scenarios is a great way to turn a list of customer needs and product requirements into a format that others will understand and want to read. Storytelling will help you not only craft great PRDs but also give effective presentations, explain your product clearly, and more.

Crafting Great Stories

Fortunately, good stories aren't hard to write! By reading books, watching movies, and just being human, you already implicitly know how to tell a great story. Let's make that knowledge explicit. All stories have a similar structure. They first give you context: they set up the world. For a user scenario, who's the persona? Remind us quickly about the customers that persona represents. What situation is he in? What are the key details we need to know—Is he in his car? Holding a baby?

The transition from the setup to the next part of the story, action, is the "inciting incident." The inciting incident is when conflict shows up. What problem causes the persona to need your product, or to need a specific feature in your product if he was already using it in the setup? Why does he think to use your product? If he's a new customer, how will he find/buy your product?

Now is the action section. This is where "stuff" happens. When the persona is using the product, what's he doing? What happens as he tries to use it? What roadblocks or conflicts does he encounter while trying to use the product, and what product features help him eliminate those roadblocks? In a user scenario, this is where you'll justify why various other features are important.

Finally, what's the result? Now that he's addressed his need, how does his world change? It's fine if it's a small change, not every product is saving the world. "Having scratched his itch with the Acme backscratcher, Jeff puts his backscratcher down within easy reach, knowing it's the perfect tool to scratch his back." Hopefully you see how even that simple result implies that we'll achieve a customer satisfaction/engagement goal in the end.

Setup. Action. Result. That's it. The challenge is in the execution! As you write the story, include the relevant details to help a reader imagine the situation you're describing, but just like when writing personas, you don't need to include every possible detail. If you're not sure what to include, start by writing a detailed story and then begin eliminating details. If the overall meaning doesn't change and the customer need/how the product addresses it is still clear, then you likely don't need those details.

Write your stories so that if a customer in your target persona were to read it, she'd go, "I've been in that situation before, and this product sounds fantastic!" Also, your customers likely don't know your jargon, so avoid using it as much as possible. This will also help other stakeholders to understand the story clearly—there'll be no ambiguity because you used jargon they don't recognize.

Last, as we've mentioned before, be authentic. You want your stories to be real and believable, as that will help you figure out your potential weaknesses, both in terms of execution and where your customer might encounter friction. Once you know your weaknesses, you can take steps to address them!

Like product management, crafting great stories is easy to learn but can take a lifetime to master. Keep using stories for your PRDs, presentations, and more, and you'll become a better and better storyteller.

Writing User Scenarios

In a PRD, you'll likely write multiple user scenarios covering different personas and their use cases. Your MVP definition will help you figure out the most important stories to write and what features to focus on in those stories—each use case or major aspect of a use case will be one user scenario. If you find yourself not mentioning features that are on your MVP list, adjust your list accordingly. Everything in your MVP list should be in the user scenarios, but not every feature called out in the user scenarios will be part of the MVP. If you narrate how each feature will help the user win—that is, how will customers will use it to address their problems—you'll make the feature's value clear to your readers. For new products or features, don't forget about the onboarding part of the user scenario: How will a customer first encounter this product and learn to use it?

There are three key tips to keep in mind when writing user scenarios. First, remember that your goal is to make readers feel like they're sitting next to each persona, using the product in each scenario. Provide the relevant detail so that readers know what's going on in the customer's life when they use the product, but don't drown the reader in unnecessary detail.

Second, you want these stories to be as truthful as you can imagine, as being authentic will help you get the best possible understanding of your customer so that you can make smart product decisions—we're reiterating this because it's that important. If one of your product requirements is a 100-page user manual, is that reasonable? When was the last time you read a product manual? Why should we believe the characters in your user scenario will read a long manual?

We once read a PRD where each user scenario ended with "and then the customer tells all her friends about the product and everyone buys one." While it's nice to have a happy ending, that wasn't authentic about what people actually did! Instead, try to be realistic about what impact each persona's product use will have related to your goal. A realistic statement is, "Because this is an ongoing problem and the customer was so happy with our trial product, she signed up for the monthly plan."

Being authentic can also help you eliminate unnecessary product features. If you find yourself trying to force what you thought was a key feature into the story, that's a great hint that the feature isn't essential.

Last, do not define in too much detail or be too prescriptive about what the solution entails. As we'll discuss more later, we want to leave the PRD focused on goals and requirements rather than specific solutions to a problem. Design and Engineering will figure out the right solution to help the customer achieve her goals and to meet your requirements. For example, rather than describing how a customer turns a doorknob on a restroom door to leave, describe how the customer exits the restroom with clean hands. Maybe Design will conclude that using her foot to open the door is a much better solution than a doorknob in this case. Being prescriptive to Design or Engineering is an easy way to get those teams annoyed with you—you need to trust them to do their jobs.

Requirements/Features In and Features Out

Next up in the PRD structure is a feature list, which is sometimes also called a list of requirements or, more confusingly, user stories (these are not actually stories). This section is a list of what features you're going to build into the product, ideally with some rough prioritizing around *essential*, *really want*, and *nice to have.*

You already have the basis for this: your MVP definition list. Each of the items on your MVP list should be prioritized as essential. Your user scenarios will provide the rest of the list—go back through them and explicitly break down the prose into tasks. Note that the prioritization labels aren't set in stone. As you develop the product and share early versions with customers for feedback, your feature prioritization will likely change.

It's OK if you don't have the full knowledge for how to break down the top-level tasks into specific subtasks. When you share the PRD with the design and engineering leads, you can work with them to break down each item into more specific user stories.

Just like the user scenarios, you'll want to avoid being prescriptive and instead focus on goals and requirements. An easy way to do that is to write each item in this format: "As a <persona>, I want <specific feature goal> so that <reason>." Some PMs prefer to use the *Given-When-Then* format: "Given <some context>, when <some action is done>, then <a set of observable behaviors happens>." While

Given-When-Then makes it easier than other ways of writing requirements to tell when the user story is implemented completely, be careful, as the When and Then blocks can easily become prescriptive.

Regardless of what format you choose for your user stories, it should be clear what the feature will do and how to measure success/proper implementation of the feature.

We've found it also useful to explicitly list "features out"—that is, what you're not doing and why. For one, multiple readers might ask about adding a feature/supporting a use case, and this preempts the question. Second, if you choose to reduce the scope of the product and cut out a feature, you will note the feature, that decision, and the date on this list. This list can also be a source of inspiration for the next product iteration. It's also a great place to write down suggestions others give you that don't fit in the current scope so that the people who made the suggestions feel like you listened to their feedback.

Designs

Having defined the product's requirements, in the design section you start to look at the solutions. Even though you don't want to be prescriptive, sometimes it's effective to create a low-quality, high-level "napkin sketch" of a possible design to help everyone understand what you're talking about. A picture can be worth a thousand words! The design section is the place to include those sketches.

We'll cover working with the design team in the next chapter, but we recommend making these sketches very rough so the designers don't think you're trying to do their job! And even if you were a designer before becoming a product manager, you'll want to make your sketches rough. You need to trust that the design team will do a better job designing a solution than you will. You'll add links to the actual designs as they become available.

Open Issues, Q&A, and Other Considerations

The last few sections in the PRD are a catch-all. Especially on your first draft, there are likely some parts of the project you're unsure of, from what your specific success-metric goals are to if you should include a use case or not. Note these questions under Open Issues.

As you discuss your PRD with others, you'll find some common questions come up again and again. Include a Q&A to provide the answers. If you created a product Q&A to go with the press release, you might already have a good start to this section! The Q&A is also a great place to address edge cases—how will you handle them?

The last part of the PRD is a general Other section in case something comes up that doesn't fit anywhere else. As you write the PRD, we recommend including all of these headers even if the only content is "nothing yet" so that they're there when you need them.

Using a PRD

Now that you have a PRD, here's how to use it to get stakeholder buy-in and as a tool for communication with your team/company.

We recommend you write the first draft of your PRD in a private format, such as a Word doc or a non-public Google Doc. It will change the most in the first few drafts, and you don't want someone stumbling upon it and panicking! You'll define the core of the product in these early drafts, and you want to make sure everything on the page is coming from the work you've done to identify, validate, and scope the opportunity.

After you've written it, you'll start sharing it with others for feedback. Even though you'll want to listen and address their feedback collaboratively, remember that product isn't design by committee. You're the person responsible for the product, and you should approach these discussions from a perspective of "This is what I believe is right. Did I miss anything?" as opposed to "What do you think we should build?"

However, this does *not* mean you should approach this sharing process as just telling people, "This is what we're building. Now, go do it." You'll want to solicit and address feedback, both to make the product better and to keep your relationship with various stakeholders productive and respectful.

The first people to share your PRD with are leads and fellow product managers. People who have been at the company longer, have experience with the product, or have more experience in general might have valuable insight to make the product—or the path to getting it built—better.

Once your team is on board, engage the other key stakeholders, such as the design and engineering leads. Again, view this as a conversation—you're seeking their feedback, and you'll incorporate their thoughts into the PRD. Perhaps the engineering manager will note a technical issue you need to figure out, and you'll add that to the Open Issues section. Or maybe the design lead will have an idea for a solution that changes the technical scope. Maybe the marketing lead will really want you to have something for a certain release date. They might also ask you to break down one of your user stories into more detail to make the project's scope explicitly clear.

Sometimes you hear people say that a PM owns the problem, Design owns the solution, and Engineering implements it. We've found a much better approach is to define the problem and generate solutions together. You, the PM, might take the first stab at the problem's definition, but that doesn't mean what you write is perfect and that

Design doesn't have valid input. Similarly, if you used to be an engineer, perhaps you'll have a valuable insight as to how Engineering could implement a solution. When conflicts arise, remember your core role and focus on the product's requirements, not how to build it. A lot of conflict comes about when someone tries to do someone else's job, such as a PM trying to design the solution or a designer wanting to change the product's scope.

After discussing the PRD with this group, you should all be in agreement about what you're trying to build and why, along with what your key success metrics are. You should have a basic idea about if the project is feasible with the defined scope and on the desired timeline. You'll also likely come up with various questions and answers for the Q&A section, and the other leads might have ideas that impact the user scenarios and feature list.

Now is the time to start sharing the PRD more broadly. If you have an internal wiki, move the PRD to a wiki page and make that the product's homepage, or, at the very least, link to it from the product's homepage. Start sharing the PRD with the teams who will be working on it. Be sure to incorporate their feedback, as people in the weeds day to day often have valuable practical insights.

Last, it's quite possible that you'll be asked to share the PRD with a broader group, be it at a company all-hands meeting or even at a board meeting. In this situation, don't read the PRD or your user scenarios to the audience verbatim. Instead, distill the PRD down to the essence of what you're doing and why, and present that information to the group. The press release you wrote can be a great guide. It's OK to call out specific things to make the project's scope clear, but try to leave plenty of time for questions.

And while you're sharing the PRD with broader audiences, the design and engineering teams are starting to actually work on the product! In the next couple of chapters we'll look at how you'll work with them to shepherd the product.

CHAPTER FIVE TIP

This tip is from Mike Belsito. Mike is the cofounder of Product Collective, the company behind INDUSTRY: The Product Conference. Mike has spent more than a decade in executive and product management roles at various early-stage technology companies. Mike is also author of Startup Seed Funding for the Rest of Us, is a contributor at Rocketship.fm, and serves as an adjunct professor of design and innovation at Case Western Reserve University in Cleveland, Ohio.

USING EXPERIENTIAL IMMERSION TO PREPARE YOUR TEAM

Communication within your internal product organization is perhaps one of the most overlooked, yet important, factors that determines the success of your product. As product managers, it's easy to focus on the customer-facing side of defining the initial problem—and then, later, actually overseeing the buildout of the solution. But the portion of work and preparation in between can be the difference between a product properly launching to address the actual problem, and going off track before the build-out even begins.

Clearly defining the problem and requirements through well-organized documentation as described in this chapter is one way to properly prepare your team. Consider supplementing your documentation with an experiential immersion with your entire team.

An experiential immersion is simply finding a real-world experience that your entire team can go through together that will allow you all to really live through the problem you're solving for. Even if your team members are generally not your target market and aren't who you're designing your solution for, you should all become method actors and live as if you were.

In the case of Moover, your team could actually become a moving company for a day. Set up a simulated office for your moving company. Assign roles to different people—including those who play the customer. Spend a couple of hours doing the type of back-office work that you might envision at a Moover client moving company. If the Moover team were to go through this experiential immersion, they might start to get an even keener understanding of why the problem they're solving for needs to be addressed. Or even better, it might bring up serious questions about whether any of your core assumptions about the problem you're solving for should be reconsidered.

How to do this?

1. As a team, pick the core problem that you feel you're ultimately solving for.
2. Identify a customer persona that experiences this problem often.
3. Create a scenario where your team can "act" and simulate actually being the customer experiencing the problem.
4. Allow your team to live through this problem together for a while—at least a couple of hours.
5. Discuss as a team what it felt like to live the problem and whether any of your core assumptions have been even further validated, or need to be readdressed.

MOOVER.IO'S DOCUMENTS

After validating the idea we came up with in Chapter 3, that Moover should add in-app messaging so that customers don't have to play phone tag with moving companies, we're going to clearly define our ideas. We'll do so by writing an imaginary press release, working on an MVP list, and then writing the PRD.

Sample Press Release

Move on Your Schedule With Moover's Latest Update

The leading app-based moving service now provides easy in-app communication with moving companies.

Moover, the iPhone app bringing moving into the smartphone age, is proud to release its latest update. This update removes the need to exchange phone calls and emails with moving companies, completely digitizing the moving experience. Rather than having to schedule a phone call and email photos back in forth, with Moover you can now message with each moving company in-app, dealing with questions and contracts at your convenience to finish planning your move.

Since its release six months ago, Moover has transformed urban moving. Instead of having to search out moving companies, call them, and deal with an annoying game of phone tag just to get an accurate bid, Moover brings moving companies to you. Enter a few details about your home and when you want to move, and moving companies will compete for your business, with bids appearing in-app. The latest update simplifies the process by providing in-app messaging with each moving company so that you can share photos and address your home's unique traits. This new feature ensures accountability and lets Moover guarantee that the bid you receive is the price you pay.

Product manager Jane Doe believes, "in-app messaging is the biggest win for customers since we released Moover. It means you can provide answers to the moving company's questions when you're home at night, thinking about the move, instead of having to stress during the day to call the moving company at work between meetings."

Recent customer John Smith tried a prerelease version of messaging and "started planning the move at 11pm, sent photos of the apartment two days later at 2am, and moved the next weekend." He went on to share, "This is the third time I've moved, and even though I have more furniture now than ever before, this was the first hassle-free move I've had."

Download Moover from the App Store today to get started planning your first hassle-free move.

Sample MVP List

Goal: Add in-app messaging so that customers cay stay in-app and don't have to exchange phone calls/emails with a moving company to get a bid or complete a move.

MVP Requirements

- Initiate a conversation with the other party so that I can address questions to provide a more accurate bid or finalize the moving details.
- See when there are new messages so that I know I have information to deal with.
- Respond to messages to keep a thread going.

Features We Removed from Moover's MVP

- Send documents like photos, videos, and PDFs as attachments to further help avoid email while communicating beyond words.

- See a history of all communication/attachments with each company for accountability and reference.

Sample PRD

Here's what the first version of a PRD for our Moover messaging feature looks like. Notice how we call out an MVP with our prioritized-feature list in the PRD, and it's definitely an uncomfortable MVP. However, the PRD doesn't just talk about the MVP features. It talks about a range of features to give a complete view of the product and how the product manager expects customers to use all of the features together. Non-MVP features just have a lower priority in the requirements list.

As a product manager, you really hope Engineering will be able to do some of the lower-priority features to make the overall messaging feature more functionally complete. But, as long as you get the highest-priority features done, all the personas will be able to achieve their goals, even if it takes a little more work than if every feature were implemented. This also gives you flexibility to release just the MVP version, get feedback, and then adjust what you're working on next rather than building the entire PRD feature list before considering the product release-ready.

Title

In-App Messaging

Change History

First version

Overview

Our mission is to be the Uber of moving companies, making it convenient to book a move on your smartphone. We've done a great job bringing the first part of moving to your fingertips—finding vendors and getting initial rough bids—but we've found that there's a second part. Despite using Moover, our customers still have to talk on the phone to figure out details, get exact bids, and finalize their moves. That means move prep still has to take place from 9 to 5. We're going to bring the second part of the moving process into the smartphone era by adding in-app messaging. This will make it convenient for our moving companies and customers to interact to plan details, allowing the moving company to message from 9 to 5 and the customer to reply when convenient.

Objectives

- Improve customer satisfaction by continuing to reduce the hassle of moving
- Increase revenue by having more completed moves

Success Metrics

- Improve the number of completed moves by a significant margin. [??? What's our precise goal? 10%?]

Messaging

- Moving on your schedule [???]

Timeline/Release Planning

Summer is a popular time to move, so we want to have at least the MVP done by May. That gives us about eight weeks. Ideally we will release the MVP by April so that we have an iteration or two of the feature by the time the moving season really starts.

Personas

Our primary target is Ant Moving, our mid-sized moving company. They're the ones who will have to ask for more information, so we need to make this easier for them than using the phone. Really Busy Rob is our second target, our persona who doesn't mind paying a premium to use app services over traditional services. We'll need to provide an intuitive messaging/notification system so that he doesn't have to look up a help page about how to talk with the moving company.

User Scenarios

Ant Answers a Bid

Linda is the office manager at Ant Moving. Ant Moving signed up for Moover when it first became available, and it's given the company a nice bump in its business: Moover is now promoting Ant to potential clients, without Ant having had to do anything more. Linda is happy with Moover and is willing to be a first adopter on new features to help the business keep growing.

Currently, Linda gets an email from Moover when there's a new bid request. The email has the basic information for the bid and a link to the Moover web dashboard. When Linda clicks the link, she's taken to a website that lets her reply to the bid, see its status: unanswered, bid sent, or customer accepted/rejected. She can then link back to a master list of all bid requests received and the status.

If the customer accepts the bid, Linda then receives the customer's contact info, and she can call him to finalize details and give a more accurate bid. Although Linda's bids are pretty good, sometimes unexpected things happen. Moover has the standard field for how many stairs are in each location, but it doesn't account for tight staircases you can't fit furniture down, for example.

Now, with Moover's latest version, when Linda gets a bid request she still looks over the basic information and clicks a link to open the dashboard. However, there's a new group on the customer page with messaging information. Since she noticed the customer said he has stairs inside the current unit, Linda uses the messaging tool to ask the customer if he could take a photo of the stairwell and the rooms upstairs, with the furniture inside of them, so that Linda can look for any potential problems.

Rob is the customer booking the move. He receives a notification that there's a new question waiting for him in Moover. He checks it and makes a reminder to take photos when he's home that evening. At home, Rob takes and sends the requested photos to Ant.

The next day, Linda gets an email from Rob, via Moover, with the requested information. The stairwell looks quite large, with no sharp turns, and there's no obnoxious furniture upstairs that could cause a problem. Linda determines her bid, provides it to Rob via the dashboard, and moves on to the next potential customer. Being an office manager at a moving company keeps Linda busy! She appreciates that the new Moover messaging feature lets her not play phone tag with customers, too!

Moover archives the conversation so that later, should Rob accept the bid and need to reference his photos, he can look them up on his customer page on the web dashboard. Furthermore, Linda can continue the conversation with Rob since he accepted the bid, finalizing any details. If he'd rejected Ant's bid, Linda could see the previous conversation but not initiate a new conversation. While that means she can't reach out later and offer him a coupon, it also provides her incentive to give Rob the best price up front.

Rob Answers Ant's Questions and Asks for Insurance Information

Living in downtown Metropolis, Rob loves app services. He uses Lyft to get around, Rinse for his laundry, and more. He's about to move apartments downtown, and he's trying Moover for the first time.

After downloading Moover and answering a few questions about his old and new places, he sits back and waits to receive bids. The next day, he gets a notification from Ant Moving asking to see photos of his staircase and upstairs rooms. No worries—he takes the photos that night and sends them in-app to Ant. Ant gives him a bid, and it looks good.

However, that afternoon he gets an email from his landlord, reminding him that moving companies have to meet a certain minimum insurance requirement to comply with the homeowner association (HOA) rules, and he has to provide a copy of the company's insurance certificate unless it's an HOA-approved mover. Ugh! Ant isn't on the approved list, but its bid is half the amount of the HOA-approved movers.

Rob goes to the Open Bids section on his app, and creates a new message to Ant. He provides them with the requirements, asks if they meet them, and asks if they'd be willing to provide a copy of their insurance information for the HOA if so.

Linda at Ant gets the new message notification and is prepared. She's had this request from other clients. She double-checks the numbers, Ant meets them, and she replies with that confirmation. Since she already has a copy of Ant's insurance as a PDF, she attaches it for Rob, too.

Rob gets a notification about this reply, and when he checks it he sees that everything looks good. He even can open and save the PDF attachment. He accepts the bid and sends the insurance PDF to his landlord and the building HOA to get the move process started on their end.

Linda promptly sends him the contract PDF. He saves it and signs it using a PDF app on his phone, and he sends the completed contract back to Linda via Moover's message attachment feature. Rob's excited that this move just got real, and it was easy to organize at a great price thanks to Moover.

User Stories/Features/Requirements

- P0: The minimum viable product.
- P1: Medium priority.
- P2: Low priority.

P0

Web Dashboard

- As Ant Moving Company, I want to initiate a conversation with a potential customer so that I can ask any questions to provide a more accurate bid or finalize the moving details.
- As Ant Moving Company, I want to see that there's a pending message so that I know I need to reply to a potential customer.
- As Ant Moving Company, I want to read messages so that I know what a customer's asked/sent.
- As Ant Moving Company, I want to respond to a question so that I can ask follow-up questions and send answers.

Mobile App

- As Really Busy Rob, I want to receive a notification of a new message/reply so that I know there is a pending message.
- As Really Busy Rob, I want to be able to read a new message so that I know what the question or answer is.
- As Really Busy Rob, I want to create a new message so that I can send messages and replies to each moving company.

P1

Web Dashboard

- As Ant Moving Company, I want to see my conversation history with each customer separately so that I can easily remember what I talked about with this customer.
- As Ant Moving Company, I want email notifications of pending messages so that I don't have to log in to the dashboard to know a customer just emailed me.

Mobile App

- As Really Busy Rob, I want to view my conversation history with each company so that I can remember what specifics I discussed with each and to retrieve my contract to sign when it's convenient.

P2

Web Dashboard

- As Ant Moving Company, I want to see and save attachments so that I can see any photos a customer has taken of his space or view a signed contract.
- As Ant Moving Company, I want to respond to a question with my own attachments so that I can send annotated images to request measurements or send contracts.
- As Ant Moving Company, I want to see attachments in my conversation history so that I don't have to manually save and organize every attachment a customer sends.

Mobile App

- As Really Busy Rob, I want to send attachments so that I can quickly send a photo of my space and stuff rather than trying to describe it, along with returning signed contracts.

- As Really Busy Rob, I want to receive attachments (JPEG, PDF) so that I can provide more specific answers and handle the moving contract in-app.

Features Out

- **Cloud storage support for attachments:** While it might be nice to save a contract to the cloud, open/sign it on another machine, and then send the completed contract via Moover, there are a lot of possible cloud storage systems we'd need to support to cover our customers (Dropbox, iCloud, Google Drive, One Drive, etc.). Plus if customers want this for only contracts, we should explore providing a standard moving contract that can be created in the dashboard and signed in-app, no attachments required.

Designs

None yet!

Open Issues

- Need to figure out exact success-metric goal
- Need to figure out exact product messaging, especially for any existing customers who could benefit from messaging now

Q&A

None yet!

Other Considerations

None yet!

CHAPTER SIX
WORKING WITH DESIGN

So far, you've been responsible for each step in the product-design life cycle. You've found and validated an opportunity, communicated it to your stakeholders, and gotten everyone onboard. Now we'll shift into the execution phase, which starts by figuring out the product's user experience with the design team. A lot of thought goes into this phase to ensure we craft a great product! Put another way, now that we've figured out we're building a house, we need to draw up blueprints and sketches, to figure out everything from where the toilets go, to how thick a wall needs to be to support the roof, to how we want to decorate.

WHAT IS USER EXPERIENCE DESIGN?

Put simply, *user experience* (UX) design is about how we interact and engage with the product. Because building products is fundamentally about making a new experience or making an existing experience better, a good user experience is fundamental to a great product. This includes everything from the box—if there is one—for the product, to how a customer achieves her goals within the product, to what the product looks and feels like.

There are two primary approaches to design. The first is that the customer should adapt to the product, and the second is the product should work in a way the user expects/understands. For a long time, UX took a backseat to engineering. Because the engineers who built the product were also responsible for the design, the UX directly represented how the product worked internally. In those cases, if there was a design team it was relegated to making nice icons for the interface the engineering team created. This is why many people think design is just about making something look pretty.

People are adaptable, and this approach worked—and continues to work—just fine for many products, but the result is a product that most people don't want to use. Figure 6-1 shows an application where the UX matches the engineering. Each field and option in the UX maps directly to the software's internals, and the result is a confusing mess. With some time and effort (and cheat sheets), we all could figure out how to use this product, but very few of us would want to.

Over the past few years, the second type of design, called *user-centered design*, has become far more popular, and it's what we'll focus on. In this type of design, the product's UX is a well-thought-out solution to help the end user effectively achieve her goal using the product. Compare the design of the original iPhone to the Blackberry and other smartphones of the time, for example.

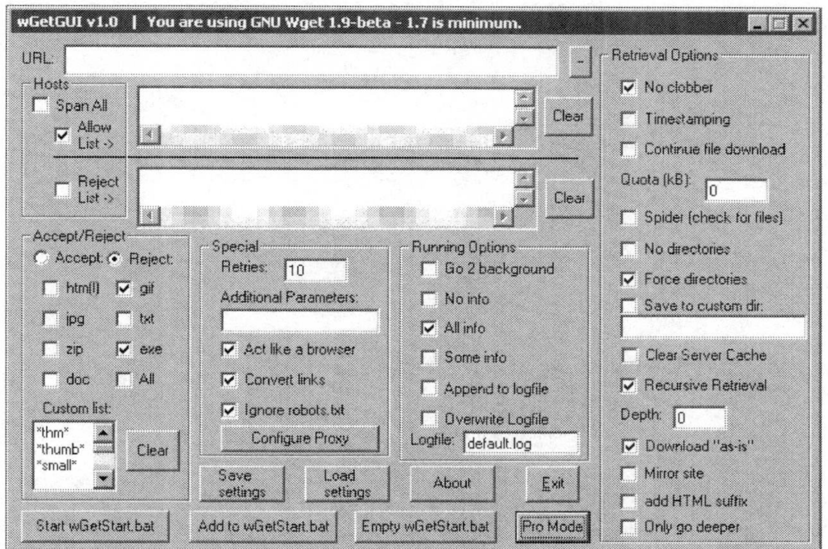

Figure 6-1. This app's UX is a visual representation of its internals, and the results aren't pretty!

In many ways, Apple's iPod and iPhone are responsible for the design priority change. Mac OS put design front and center for years, always trying to create a great experience, thereby building a loyal customer base. But its market share was so small most people never had a chance to appreciate what a difference a good UX made—software design on Windows tended to reflect how things worked internally. When the iPod came out, its functionality was the same as that of many other MP3 players, but its overall experience, from putting music on to it to finding and playing the song you want, was so great it crushed the competition. (Figure 6-2 shows the original iPod's competition.) The iPhone kicked this into high gear with an incredibly intuitive touch experience. Even toddlers can use iOS. Apple's earnings reports show the result of this focus on user-centered design.

Figure 6-2. The Creative Nomad Jukebox had a 6GB hard drive compared to the iPod's 5GB, but can you guess how you'd select a song? User experience matters!

As people used the iPod, the iPhone, and other products with a great user-centered design, they came to appreciate how much easier the products were to use, letting them achieve their goals—from listening to music to checking their voicemail—faster. People began to want great experiences in *all* of their products, whether it was HR software or a thermostat. When faced with two products that solve a problem, they often picked the better-designed one. Slack, for example, has seen exponential growth by taking a product that's been around for years—group chat—and building a much better UX around it. This trend has led to far larger design teams and making design a full part of the product-development life cycle rather than an afterthought.

Back in Chapter 2 when we discussed enterprise vs. consumer software, we mentioned that for a long time UX design mattered very little, in enterprise products especially. As long as the product solved a problem, customers would adapt and learn how to use it. But as people started to experience well-designed UX in the consumer products they used at home, they wanted better experiences at work. This had led to significant disruption in enterprise software lately, with new, well-designed tools like Basecamp replacing big, traditional tools like Microsoft SharePoint.

So what goes into making a great, user-centered experience? At a high level, UX designers need to understand the customers, come up with ideas for how to address their needs, help define requirements for the solution, and create a specification that they work with Engineering to build. This should sound similar to a product manager's role, and it absolutely is. In fact, this is why some start-ups won't hire a PM—they feel a UX designer can do it all—or conversely a start-up will want a PM to handle design tasks. However, the difference is in the details, and while the roles are complementary, they really do need different skills!

Product Managers vs. Designers

To use an analogy, a PM is like the typical president of the United States and the lead designer is like the typical secretary of state. This fits nicely with Guy Kawasaki's claim that a product manager has "all of the responsibility and none of the power." The president will set policy goals and provide reasons he picked those goals, but it's up to the secretary of state to work out the details of achieving the goals. The secretary of state will also make recommendations to the president to help him make good decisions and craft useful goals. Essentially, the president focuses on strategy and not tactics, and the secretary of state is tactical. The president works with people beyond the secretary of state, too, be it the secretary of education or Congress—he has to keep a broad view every day! And while the secretary of state isn't responsible for education, she should still have some knowledge of the president's goals for the secretary of education—she can't just work in a vacuum.

The product manager owns and writes the product requirements and goals. She will lead the product requirements document (PRD), roadmap, cross-team communication, and sometimes even the budget to help get the product built. The lead designer will own the user-experience strategy: What UX do we want to create, both short-term and long-term, to help deliver the best overall product experience? However, the lead designer will also likely do user research and come up with requirements. Her research can help the PM figure out what the final product requirements are, and design will also be tactical and determine how to meet those requirements. Like the typical president, the PM will work frequently with every team, not just the lead designer, to shepherd the product, so the PM will have to balance everyone's needs. And a good lead designer will have a basic understanding of the product's business context so that she's not working in a vacuum and can help the product manager understand tradeoffs for different design decisions.

THE DESIGN PROCESS AND KEY DESIGN SKILLS

The design process generally breaks down into six primary phases:

1. User research
2. Information architecture
3. Interaction design
4. Prototyping
5. Visual design
6. Content strategy

Each phase requires a different dominant skill. While some of these skills are complementary, you rarely find one person who's great at every part of the design process. That means you usually have a design team with different people specialized in each tactical element, or some combination of elements.

During each phase, you'll give feedback on the work the design team creates, answer questions about the project's requirements and customer/business needs for the design team, facilitate any needed communication with the engineering lead and other stakeholders, and shepherd the process along. One way to help keep things moving is by having a reoccurring Design/Engineering/Product meeting each week for the project, but make it clear you're always available to answer questions the design team has beyond those meetings.

Let's look more at the typical design process and the types of designers you'll encounter. The design process starts before you've written the PRD, as you work with the lead designer and a user researcher, if that's not the same person, to figure out the right strategy and scope of your opportunity. Just like a product manager, a user researcher is focused on understanding the customer, what his needs and goals are, what he's using now to address those needs, and what we might do to make his life better. The lead designer and a user researcher will often accompany you to customer interviews, and you'll work together to figure out the user value you want to deliver, business goals to focus on, and the features/functionality you need to meet those goals and deliver the value. They will likely have valuable input to your PRD, and as we mentioned in Chapter 5, take that input constructively.

User researchers also help with user testing. That is, later in the design process, once you've built a prototype, user testing will help you learn how well the customer accomplishes key tasks using your prototype.

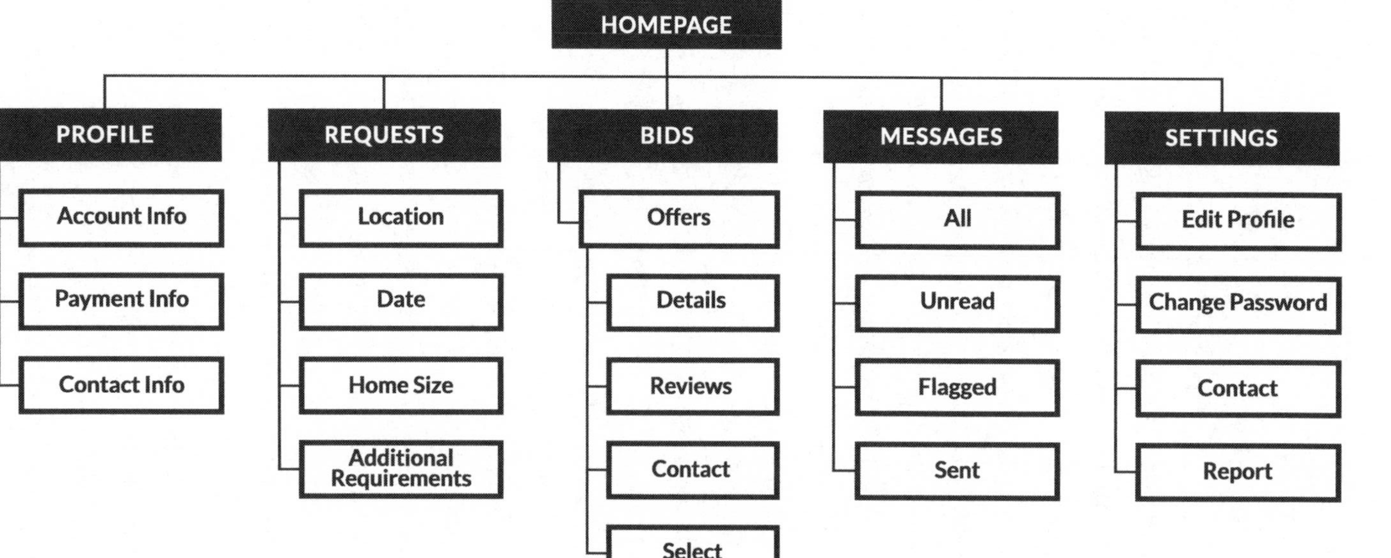

Figure 6-3. This is whvat an IA diagram for messaging in Moover might be like.

Once you've figured out what to build with a user researcher's help, an *information architecture* (IA) designer will figure out how to model and organize the data we're working with. IA is very much a structure step, asking what information a user should see first, second, and so on. IA might create a data model, explaining how the underlying product will conceptually be presented to the customer, along with block diagrams expressing in what order to present the information. Figure 6-3 shows a sample IA diagram for Moover's messaging feature.

Interaction designers then take the information architecture and figure out how to present it in the product. They're the ones who focus on how a customer navigates through the product, what UI controls you use (e.g., should you use a slider or a text field?), how many steps it takes to achieve common tasks, and more. As the skill implies, they're the ones really focused on how you use the product. It's quite common to find designers who specialize in IA and interaction design. This is also the step where the engineering lead will start to get involved, providing the design team with feedback about the technical feasibility of its designs.

The most common delivery from this phase is a set of wireframes. These are rough, block diagrams showing how a user will interact with your product, like we see in Figure 6-4 for Moover—we're showing only one wireframe, but typically you'll have a series representing various views and key interactions. Wireframes help you visualize where your customers will find various pieces of information, how they will navigate through your product, and more. Wireframes are not interactive, and they might even be sketches on paper rather than digital assets.

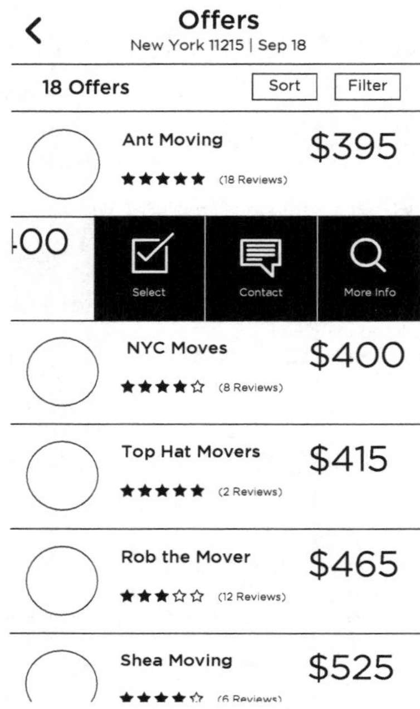

Figure 6-4. Sample wireframe for Moover's messaging feature, showing one of the steps of the workflow after swiping to reveal the available options for a company.

Design teams will often have prototyping experts who turn these static wireframes into interactive prototypes using anything from HTML to specialized tools like Balsamiq and InVision. Prototypes are incredibly helpful for three reasons. First, they help everyone working on the product internally to understand what you're building, be it people on the direct team, your boss, or beyond. Having something visual is more easily understandable than a written PRD, and having something interactive is even better. Second, the prototype helps Engineering provide more accurate estimates for how hard parts of the product will be to build. Using a standard UI control might take minutes to implement whereas a custom control the design team created might take days, for example, and all the teams will have to discuss if the custom control

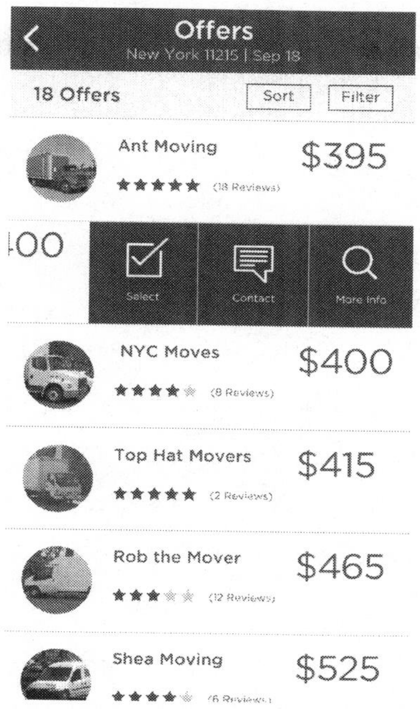

Figure 6-5. Sample mock-up for Moover's messaging feature, indicating how one view should look when finished

is worth the time tradeoff. That decision will then affect the prototype. Third, prototypes help with usability testing.

After prototyping, you will have a great idea of how the product will work/flow, but you won't know what it will look like. Visual design is the focus on how the product will look. Your team's visual designers will often work in parallel with the people creating wireframes, establishing the overall look and feel of your product. They will create mock-ups, like Figure 6-5, usually based on the wireframes, that look pixel-perfect but aren't functional. These mock-ups are designed to help the product's overall team gauge how everything will come together, and the end product will visually look similar to the mock-up.

Visual design is more than just making the app look pretty, though.

Visual designers need to consider usability (e.g., is the font large enough to read and are the buttons large enough to tap accurately on a phone?), emotions (conveyed through colors and icons), and consistent brand messaging. Visual designers will often work with marketing to create a company style guide that influences everything from customer announcement emails to the marketing website to the actual product.

Sometimes visual designers and prototypers will create a higher-fidelity prototype using the mock-up and wireframes, giving the prototype a more finished feel to help you judge the product more effectively.

After you've created your wireframes and mock-ups for Engineering to implement, a content strategist will help make sure your product is using the right media and text, such as how to word an alert. Like visual design, content strategy applies to marketing, too, and you want to use consistent words and have a consistent tone. It detracts from the overall experience and can confuse your customers because of misaligned expectations if your app is very formal and your website is very whimsical. Some companies will have one copy manager who is responsible for all text, be it in-product or in an ad.

The main design process is done when your prototypes and mock-ups are validated as a solution and Engineering has agreed to their viability. As you hand the designs over to Engineering, you will likely discover questions about how part of the product should behave, unanticipated edge cases that need to be designed, new alerts you need the proper wording for, and parts of the design that are problematic to implement.

Your primary role throughout this process will be facilitator, but you'll also want to make sure early test customers are happy with the designs and able to achieve the product goal satisfactorily. You'll likely want to keep running a meeting with the design and engineering teams throughout the project to make sure everyone is on the same page and to address early user feedback and additional engineering needs. For example, if you have a ship-date deadline, you might need to cut a feature and change part of the product's design so that the feature doesn't appear to be missing. The entire design process isn't truly done until the product ships.

Usability Testing with Prototypes

As your design team builds a design, it's useful to test various aspects of it with customers when possible to see if the design is easy and pleasant to use and ensure that your customer can complete tasks the tester gives them with the design.

User researchers and prototypers will work together to perform this testing. Tools like UserTesting (which lets you get videos of random people that meet specified criteria performing tasks with your website, mobile apps, or prototype), and UsabilityHub (which provides data, including heat maps, about how people perform tasks with your static mock-ups across different categories) help simplify the task.

Usability testing is critical to making a successful user-centered design, but it isn't perfect. It doesn't test for questions like "Is this product valuable to a customer?" The hypothesis validation you did in Chapter 4 should have answered that type of question. If you're testing a new feature in isolation from the main product with a prototype, usability testing won't test whether existing customers are able to find and use this new feature. It also can't account for things like taste. A test might reveal that customers are most successful when you use an orange-and-green color scheme for the feature, but unless you're building a pumpkin-themed product, you might choose to trade some usability value for a better aesthetic.

Once in a while, even a user-centered design team has to make choices that seem more like they force the customer to adapt to the product rather than being user-centered. Sometimes this is due to an internal limitation, such as engineering or design resources. Other times it's because this choice is in line with the company's vision and general attitude, such as Apple's not providing removable storage on the iPhone. A great design team will also think about the future and the roadmap, and this might lead to making choices in the current product that seem weird but are better for the future, like removing the floppy drive and serial ports from the original iMac. While testing is important, design is often more of an art than a science.

However, this doesn't mean you should ship an unusable design because it's in line with your company vision! If a customer can't use your product to solve his problem, or if it's very hard to use your product, he'll look for a different solution. Your product must be usable in addition to providing utility!

Just like how you created an opportunity hypothesis and then worked to validate it, design will create various UX possibilities and then work to converge on the main design. Just like your opportunity hypothesis, bigger ideas will need more work to validate. Some small projects might not require any design iteration. If you're responsible for the schedule, make sure to incorporate the appropriate time for design to iterate.

WORKING WITH DESIGN

While product and design will often have a fantastic relationship, all too often they have a frustrating relationship. Let's dig into why that happens and look at some tips to help you work well with your design team.

Judging and Giving Feedback About Design

As a PM, you will be expected to give feedback about designs and to have informed opinions. While we highly recommend you take the time to learn about design, reading books like Donald Norman's seminal *The Design of Everyday Things*, it is possible to have an educated opinion about design without being an expert. We can form that opinion by using a framework with specific criteria and then looking at how the design meets those elements.

The most important criteria we're going to set is "Does this design let the customer achieve his goal with the least friction possible?" As you look at a wireframe and imagine using the product step by step or as you actually try a prototype, are you able to accomplish the key tasks the product promises? Does the design ask for irrelevant information or require complex actions that prevent you from achieving your goals?

Ask yourself this question for every use case, and you'll be amazed what you find. On some cameras, for example, it's easy to put the battery in backwards because the battery's a rectangle with no special grooves. The only indication that you've put it in wrong is when the camera doesn't turn on. A design change might have spared users the hassle of putting their batteries in wrong!

With software, is the information users need easily at hand, or are they constantly having to bounce between parts of the app to get the needed data? What about the sign-up process—do you have a simple one that lets users immediately engage with the app, or do you ask a lot of irrelevant questions before they can start using it?

To go a step further in our criteria, we're going to recommend using Dieter Rams's 10 principles of "good design." Rams is a well-known designer, primarily having worked at Braun throughout his career. His designs are highly regarded, he's influenced numerous designers, including Jony Ive, and his 10 principles are easy to understand.

Good design is innovative. Technological innovation is constantly creating opportunities for new and innovative designs. This doesn't mean that you need to reinvent the wheel with every design. Often, there are standard design elements that will make sense for your product, like a button. But especially when you're building an innovative product, it's worth asking if you're being innovative with your design or applying old design ideas to something new.

Good design makes a product useful. We want our products to be used and loved, which means they need to be useful. The design has to make the product functional but also psychologically pleasing. Dental headgear is a great example of a functional product that's not psychologically pleasing, which means a customer won't want to use it.

Good design is aesthetic. Quoting Rams, "The aesthetic quality of a product is integral to its usefulness because products are used every day and have an effect on people and their well-being. Only well-executed objects can be beautiful."

Good design makes a product understandable. Design can help make a product's intended function clear, and great design makes the product usable without any training. When it fails to make the product understandable, the customer often gets frustrated trying to use the product or remembering how to use it.

Good design is unobtrusive. Products exist to help a customer be awesome and achieve a goal, not to be revered by themselves. If a design is neutral and restrained, it lets the focus be on the customer rather than calling attention to itself.

Good design is honest. A well-designed product doesn't make the customer believe it does something that it doesn't actually do or that it is something more valuable than it actually is. Painting the product gold won't make it actually be as valuable as if it were made out of gold.

Good design is long-lasting. While it can be tempting to make something trendy and fashionable, good design will last so that even as styles change, your product won't go the way of the mullet.

Good design is thorough down to the last detail. You want to think out every aspect so you make sure that no matter how customers interact with your product, they're encountering a great experience.

Good design is environmentally friendly. Design can help us preserve our planet for future generations by minimizing the resources it needs, whether we're talking about compute cycles that require power or physical design that needs raw materials.

Good design is as little design as possible. As Rams puts it, "less, but better." As you evaluate a design, ask yourself if you can eliminate elements. Focus on reducing the design to its essentials, as that purity and simplicity will help make your products aesthetic, understandable, unobtrusive, and honest.

Not every principle will apply to every design with equal weight. When you're building an app, you likely don't care as much about its long-lasting or environmentally friendly nature. But when a designer gives you a wireframe, prototype, or mock-up and asks what you think, these criteria give you a way to provide thoughtful and precise feedback.

Design Relationship Skills

The biggest source of conflict is that both product and design feel like they represent the customer. Both groups do represent the customer, just in different ways. Like we said earlier, PMs have to think about the big picture and about different teams' needs, whereas the design lead will be more tactical and focused primarily on a great design. A handy way to think about the difference is that product managers focus on the ideal customer, whereas lead designers often focus on the ideal user.

Let's look at an example to understand the difference. If you were designing a keyboard, your goal would be to help users type quickly and accurately. The design team would come up with a fantastic keyboard layout, and it almost certainly wouldn't be the most common keyboard layout, QWERTY. QWERTY has been proven to not be the ideal design for fast or accurate typing.

But QWERTY keyboards have been around for a long time. They're everywhere, from your computer to your smartphone to some TV remotes! Customers know how to type on them relatively quickly and accurately. A non-QWERTY keyboard will have a potentially steep learning curve, meaning customers won't type quickly or accurately while they learn the new layout.

While our design team could come up with a new keyboard layout for the ideal user whose goal is to type quickly and accurately, the ideal customer most likely wouldn't buy it because of the short-term tradeoff.

To understand customers comprehensively, it's useful to focus on their personas. In addition to their goals, what other factors are at play that will affect the customers' behavior? In our keyboard example, while their goal was to type quickly and accurately, their prior familiarity with QWERTY is a big factor that affects our product choices.

Sometimes, especially with consumer products, it's easy for PMs to believe they represent the target persona accurately, even when they don't. These PMs often ignore the details of the persona, using their own taste, not persona details, to make product decisions. This can be frustrating to designers, as this can make the PM's decisions feel arbitrary.

Micromanaging every decision design can cause friction between the design team and the PM, too. PMs are ultimately responsible for the success or failure of the product, and that responsibility can cause them to try to tell the design team how to design the product. We mentioned earlier that wireframes, mock-ups, and prototypes are great because they're so much more immediately comprehensible than the PRD. The flip side is that because design is so visible, it's easy to have an uninformed opinion. Trust your design team to make smart decisions, and use criteria like Rams's design principles to assess if they're good decisions and to give informed opinions.

So how do you build a constructive relationship with the design team? A simple but important step is to get to know the team. Building individual relationships with the people you work with will help you respect each other as people and deal with conflict more productively.

Beyond that, in no particular order, there's a variety of things you can do to have a great relationship with your design team. We recommend that you learn a bit about design, if you don't know about it already. You don't need to be an expert, but you should be able to talk about why you think a product is well-designed or not. For software, learn common design patterns and accepted layouts for functions like search, settings, and more, especially for different platforms. This will help you learn not to force an Android app to look just like an iOS app or vice versa, for example.

As you learn about design, focus on developing an appreciation for what goes into design so that when you see a wireframe, you can ask good questions about why the designers made certain choices and understand the implication of those choices rather than arbitrarily telling them to do certain things. Words like "white space" and "hierarchy" should eventually be part of your vocabulary.

Similarly, don't overstep your bounds. In the PRD, do not specify the design. Your job is to give requirements and constraints along with how you'll consider the problem solved, and let Design and Engineering find the solution. For example, rather than incorporating mock-ups of a new onboarding process, specify what data is required and what's optional for a user to enter, then let design create a wireframe showing how to enter that data. Even if you used to be an amazing designer, your primary job as a PM is to focus on giving clear personas, requirements, and goals.

Your design team will love you if you're clear on those three elements. This clarity will be part of a well-written PRD and true at the highest level—the overall project objective—and with individual user stories. Rather than just saying, "We need to improve the onboarding process," explicitly say who the target customers are, what you need the onboarding process to achieve, and how you measure its success.

Furthermore, never, ever vaguely say a product is for "everyone." There is no such persona, and no product is perfect for every single person. Instead, make sure your target market is a clear part of the requirements in the PRD and that a persona is defined so that design can make the right choices to address that persona's needs.

Once in a while, you'll find that you really, really want to sketch out a UX, as it'll be the fastest way to share your thoughts, be it in early conversations about the product or even in a PRD. When you first join a new team, you'll need to work with other stakeholders and earn their respect. We recommend putting together a whiteboarding session with the design lead (and maybe the engineering lead) to discuss initial, rough ideas. Together, you can draw on a whiteboard and then take photos of the board to incorporate into your PRD or share with others.

After you've worked with a team, you'll usually find it's OK to sketch out a UX concept on your own rather than only including photos of whiteboards, but you need to recognize and make clear to others that this sketch is just to convey what you mean, not to imply design answers. The best way to do this is via a *napkin sketch*. A napkin sketch is a drawing that's low quality and created quickly, as if you drew on the back of a napkin with a pen. We recommend using a tool like FiftyThree's Paper for the iPad instead of a prototyping tool like InVision or Balsamiq for any UX sketches you create. This will make sure your sketch is clearly hand-drawn and force you to create something unpolished but give you a digital drawing with a nice stroke quality.

As the design team starts to ideate using your PRD, work with them and other stakeholders to discuss the pros and cons of each idea beyond just if it's a good design or not, especially thinking about the ideal user vs. customer. Furthermore, ask if the team's thought through all the implications of the design. If you're designing a social network and the design team has a flag button in the design to mark inappropriate content, what happens when a customer presses that button? Does that button mean someone on the support team will manually have to look at the content and possibly remove it? Does that team have resources to do so?

All of this advice rolls up into one key point: your job is to provide clear communication between all stakeholders while keeping the end goal—making the customer awesome—in everyone's mind. You are not here to do the stakeholder's work—you left Design/Engineering/Support/etc. behind to move into product management. You need to keep everyone moving towards your goal.

There's a great story about when President Kennedy visited NASA in 1962. The president asked a janitor what he was doing, and the janitor replied, "Well, Mr. President, I'm helping put a man on the moon." NASA did a great job making sure everyone knew what they were working towards, and that helped every individual think about how his actions affected that goal. You might feel like a broken record sometimes, but if you focus on keeping your product's goal front and center in everyone's mind, you'll be amazed at how the whole team rises to deliver on that goal.

CHAPTER SIX TIP

Conrad Albrecht-Buehler, an amazing designer who's also worked as a product manager, provides us with this chapter's tip. Conrad has designed an award-winning in-car interface for BMW, designed some of the first mobile applications for VMware, and worked on several products at Apple. In addition to being a designer, he has worked as a software engineer, a product manager, and a user researcher. He lives in Munich and the Bay Area with his wife, two kids, and a Shiba Inu.

BEING OPEN AND FLEXIBLE

Aaron Sorkin, who's written some of my favorite television and films, recently said that for many episodes of *The West Wing*, he would start with just an idea for a moment, and then let the story build as he wrote it. To paraphrase: he didn't always know exactly what he was writing until he wrote it. In interviews, many of my favorite authors and, yes, even designers, have said the same thing. It's not because they lacked discipline or were not methodical in their work, but stories and products are complex, and, until you get deep into creating either one, much of that complexity isn't revealed. Because of that, as a PM working with a designer—be it a user-experience designer, user researcher, or industrial or visual designer—my advice is this: be open and be flexible.

As a designer works to accommodate requirements from product and from engineering (and myriad other sources described in previous chapters), compromises must be made on one aspect or another. Be flexible, rather than authoritarian. Don't try to push a singular agenda an call it a "vision." Be open to compromise as the deeper complexities of the product reveal themselves. The best designers learn how to make the best compromises. But not without your help and the help of all stakeholders and contributors. However, as the PM, you may have to referee the debate around these compromises, and that's always tough because you will never be a neutral observer in those debates.

The various sides of the debate will be framed in terms of cost vs. benefit. Most stakeholders will see the costs in terms of financial costs or time costs—things that impact the company and employees. The designers will see the costs in terms of impact to the user. That is where things go off the rails most frequently. Another stakeholder will claim, "I'm a user, and I'd be fine with this." Maybe the customer will be, as well, but it is the responsibility of the designer to know how people who are not just like the designer will perceive and interpret the product. Even if all the debate participants claim that they, as users, would also be fine with a compromise, don't treat that as a majority of a sample size and imagine that the designer arguing for something else is obviously mistaken. Be open to their experience, and value the time they've spent trying to get into the heads of people different from themselves to help you predict how a customer will see, use, and value your product. It may help you make the best, if not always the most expedient, compromise as you address the complexities of a product.

GOOGLE DESIGN SPRINTS

Google Ventures came up with a great way to use design thinking to solve critical business questions. It has used this process with its portfolio companies to solve problems ranging from "Is our new business viable?" to "How do we develop this new feature for existing products with millions of users?"

We like design sprints because they're collaborative (involving key stakeholders from each department), focused, effective, and user-centered ways to solve big problems. Furthermore, as we've just spent a long time explaining, PMs often have to be hands-off with the actual design work, but in a design sprint you get to be hands-on. This can be fun, letting you use your creativity, and it will help you gain an appreciation for what your design team does day to day.

These sprints typically last a week. You start the week with a specific challenge to solve, and you end the week with a design the team's agreed upon and that you've validated with real customers. Of course, once in a while you end up invalidating the design and/or raising new questions, but then you can run another sprint using what you learned. Let's dive into how to run a design sprint!

Sprint Preparation

Start by picking a sprint master. This person will set the context for the design sprint and facilitate each stage of the sprint. This will usually be someone who is familiar with UX research and interaction design, but this person should also be able to lead a meeting productively and get every participant contributing. The sprint master will do a fair bit of planning around content and logistics before the sprint to make sure it runs smoothly. Google recommends about one day of preparation for each day of the sprint.

For content planning, the sprint master will write a design brief that clearly defines the challenge (the PRD can be a great reference here), the deliverable, and the timeline to launch. She might also do a design audit beforehand, pulling together the current designs, user research, and more, to provide context to the sprint team. This is especially critical if the team has already done work on this problem, as there will be existing learning you can build from.

For the sprint logistics, she'll start by determining the right team to have on the sprint. The best teams are five to eight people and include the PM, designers, engineers, and other experts or stakeholders. Sometimes, especially in start-ups, the CEO will be part of the sprint team. It's also possible to have multiple teams working in parallel on the same challenge. The sprint master will even schedule the room and make sure she has all the needed supplies, including paper, tape, sticky notes, voting stickers, a timer, and pens.

Understand

The first part of the sprint is devoted to understanding the problem you're trying to solve, why you're trying to solve it, who the customers are, those customers' needs and capabilities, and more. As we discussed in Chapter 2, understanding the overall context for your customers and company/product is always the first step towards creating new solutions.

The sprint master might arrange short talks, user interviews, field visits to customers, competitive overviews, or beyond to facilitate this step. If you've done previous research or work with this sprint challenge, this step is when you'll present that previous work.

You as the product manager will likely play a key role here in helping the rest of the team understand your goals and strategy.

During the first day of the sprint, you'll also schedule your customer-testing interviews for the last day. This will put pressure on your team, forcing you to create something to show customers, given real people are coming to see your work. After all, the best creativity happens when you have constraints!

Define

After the team understands the problem space, come up with a clear problem definition. This is when you narrow the problem and come up with the key principles and goals to help you measure your solution. You might define your design objectives, such as building a "fun to use" product, or you might think about the messaging and tag line for your solution, like "a thousand songs in your pocket."

Diverge

After you clearly know the problem and what you want your solution to achieve, you and the sprint team will brainstorm as many ideas as possible for how to solve the sprint challenge. You might have everyone work individually to generate ideas using "Crazy Eights," where you fold a piece of paper in half three times, to create a page with eight segments, and take five minutes to draw eight ideas, one per segment.

Or perhaps you'll work together to brainstorm ideas. Make sure not to reject anyone's ideas during this phase—your goal is to generate as many ideas as possible, even bad ones. In fact, sometimes working together to come up with the worst possible solution can help you think of new ideas for the best solution.

You don't need to be able to draw well to participate in the Diverge phase. But you should make sure anything you draw or create is understandable on its own, without an explanation from the creator. It's OK to put some text on your drawings or to use multiple drawings to show a flow. Give the concepts titles to help you refer to them. However, don't put the creator's name on each. You don't want any company politics to influence which ideas you pick.

Get crazy, get creative, and don't filter yourself. Ideate, ideate, ideate.

Decide

Once you've come up with a lot of ideas, you'll pick the best ones, so far, by voting.

For the first round of voting, everyone gets an unlimited number of voting stickers, and you vote on what ideas, or pieces of ideas, you like the best. You can use lots of stickers if you love something.

Even though each idea should be self-explanatory, spend some time discussing each one. For example, take three minutes to look at each idea, and discuss what you like about it, what you don't like, what could go wrong, and more. Don't let the creator explain the idea first, as it should stand on its own, but if the others miss an aspect of the idea, the creator can point it out.

Don't worry about achieving consensus during this first round—talk about what you like with the various ideas.

After you've discussed each idea, you'll super-vote. This is the decision-making vote. Each team member will get a limited number of voting stickers, and the CEO and PM will get extra voting stickers. Again put these stickers next to what you believe is the best idea, or part of an idea. This voting process will help you uncover the best ideas, regardless of who created them.

Prototype

After picking a key idea or two, create a prototype. Building this prototype will take the most time of all the steps, but you will emerge with a mock-up, demo, physical prototype, or other way of demonstrating the idea that you can show to real people.

You might end up having multiple prototypes to test the overall utility of the solution separate from the usability or to test the usability of different ideas. The key in this step is to make some artifact that will help you validate your solution. After all, you'll be showing it to customers shortly!

User Testing

The final step in the sprint is showing your prototype to real customers and getting feedback. Try to find out what they like and dislike, if the solution will meet their needs, and if there are hidden factors that could stop them from using this solution.

You can also ask for feedback to measure how well you achieved the goals you set forth in the Define step. For example, ask each user to rate how much fun they had using your product and what made it less fun.

Make sure to validate this solution with the key stakeholders, including the engineering team, too, to confirm that this is the solution everyone is onboard with pursuing and believes can be implemented.

When user testing is finished and the sprint is over, take some time to review the process and analyze how it went. Did these customers like the solution, or did the design not work? Do you need to do another sprint? Ideally, you'll have a basic design that you know has promise, which you can take, flesh out, and turn into a real product.

If you like this approach and want to run your own sprints, we highly recommend reading Google Ventures's book *Sprint: How to Solve Big Problems and Test New Ideas in Just Five Days*. This book contains lots of tips from Google Ventures's experience running sprints, to help you run the best sprint possible.

At this point, you should have an appreciation for what design involves and see that it's more than just making things look pretty. You should also have an idea about how to work collaboratively with the design team. Remember, we say that design is done when our prototypes and mock-ups are validated as a solution to the problem we're trying to solve and Engineering has agreed to the designs' viability. Now that we've drawn up the blueprints for our product, let's turn our attention to how we'll work with Engineering to get our product built.

CHAPTER SEVEN

WORKING WITH ENGINEERING

Now that you've figured out your product's requirements and come up with—and hopefully tested—a design, it's time to actually build your product! In practice, this phase of the product-development life cycle is where you will spend the bulk of your time as a product manager. You'll work closely with Engineering day to day to help oversee the product that's being built, making sure it meets the product requirements, making scope changes if key features are taking longer than expect to develop, prioritizing the backlog, and eliminating whatever obstacles you can for the engineering team.

You'll want to do your best to establish a strong relationship with the engineering team because although a great relationship doesn't guarantee success, a bad relationship guarantees failure.

While this phase can be a lot of fun as the product comes to life, it can be very hard for product managers for two reasons. The first is that if you started your career as an engineer, you might unintentionally frustrate the engineering team or imply you know better than they do. Alternatively, if you don't have an engineering background, you might not understand how engineers work—or how to work with them—causing them to not respect you. Fortunately, these problems are avoidable! Let's start by looking at soft skills, interpersonal relationship skills that will help you work with engineering. Then we'll look at common ways engineering teams work and see how you as the PM fit into those workflows.

PRODUCT/ENGINEERING RELATIONSHIPS

Just as design is more than just creating pixels, engineering is more than just typing code. Programming is very much like an art form: you're building something from nothing, and all of the pieces must function pretty much perfectly or the whole product won't work. This artistic complexity leads to some common traits in engineers worth knowing about, as understanding these traits will help your interpersonal communication and relationship with engineers.

In general, engineers are highly intelligent people motivated by working on hard problems and leaning something new. They're often very independent and care more about crafting an elegant solution to a complex problem than about specific business needs. Engineering is hard, and every product needs engineers. Given that, their skills are incredibly in demand and talented engineers are worth their weight in gold!

However, because their skills are in demand, if engineers feel like they're not being respected or mentally challenged, or if they don't believe in the overall product and direction, they'll likely look for a new opportunity. Replacing an engineer is very costly, both in terms of actual cost and productivity costs. PMs can help engineers, and the whole company, by making sure engineers feel respected and recognized and have confidence in the product.

So how do you keep a great relationship with Engineering? You're starting off the right way by recognizing that it takes work! The biggest thing you should keep in mind is that coding is hard and you should trust that your engineers know their craft—contrary to what some designers and PMs think, engineers are not just code monkeys typing on keyboards. Especially if you have an engineering background, one of the worst things to say to an engineer is "can't you just...." Those three words imply that whatever the engineer is doing is easy and that you know better.

We recommend that you view working with Engineering as an educational experience, both for you and for them. For example, ask them to help estimate how hard a task might be. And if the estimate is higher than expected, ask if they could explain what goes into that estimate and where the tricky parts are. This will help you understand the full scope of the task, and if the engineer is making assumptions because you hadn't accounted for something, perhaps you can decide to limit the scope of the task and make the engineer's life easier. As a simple example, if you're building a streaming-video player, it takes a lot more work to make a 4K video stream efficiently than a normal HD one. If it makes sense, you could make a product choice to not support streaming 4K content, thereby reducing Engineering's workload.

Another big mistake that PMs make with Engineering is that they don't take time to get to know the engineers and how to best work with each person. Some engineers work best when they have a to-do list, and they don't care about the broader picture or why you're making certain choices. But other engineers get frustrated when you don't clearly explain why you made certain choices. To those engineers, this makes you come across as dictating, not collaborating. A well-written product requirements document (PRD) like we described in Chapter 5 can help both of these situations, as it makes the information available for the engineers should they choose to read it.

As you continue throughout the development cycle and have to make hard decisions, cut features, etc., make sure to work with the engineering lead and perhaps individual engineers to understand the technical side of these decisions. They're the only people who can tell you how technically feasible something is and provide an estimate for how difficult it will be to build. This doesn't always mean Engineering just has bad news for PMs. Sometimes they'll even tell you that something you thought impossible is actually feasible! Do make sure to write down key decisions, such as in the PRD or in key user stories—or in epic requirements if you're using scrum—so that there's no confusion about what the state of that decision is.

Furthermore, change and tradeoffs happen in every product. Projects often get behind schedule because many small things pile up, such as someone being out sick for a while, family emergencies, jury duty, and more. If you work closely with Engineering to watch the balance between time (When are we aiming to have this done/shipped?), quality (Can we take on some technical debt now?), and money (Would more people or overtime help us get this project done?), you'll keep the process collaborative and deliver the highest-possible-quality product on the best-possible schedule.

Working on projects that have a lot of technical debt can also be very frustrating for engineers, as accumulated debt can make even polish and bug fixes painful. We've talked before about how it's important to the project's overall momentum to periodically pay off any technical debt. It's also important to your engineers' sanity and your relationship with them to periodically do so.

A lot going on in an office inherently conspires against engineers. Specifically, solving hard problems requires deep concentration. Interruptions, whether for meetings or to reply to high-priority messages via email, Slack, HipChat, etc., can be very frustrating and tough to recover from mentally. Open office plans make things even worse, as there are so many distractions and so much noise that developers often wear large, noise-cancelling headphones so that they can focus on their work.

While some of this is beyond your control, like floor plans, there are some things you can control, especially around communication. Do what you can to give the engineering team time to focus on getting its work done, even if it means you have to wait for an answer to a question. Not every question you have is urgent, and interrupting someone's coding flow for a non-critical question is never appreciated.

As Engineering completes each task, make sure to provide feedback, whether it's that they did a great job and exceeded your expectations or that you found a bug or something isn't quite right. And when the project's over, make sure the engineers—and everyone else involved—get their share of the credit for getting the project done. Don't hog the credit—be humble!

To be clear, the engineering team is not the PM's boss—you don't need the engineers' approval on everything, and they're not the most important people in the company. But they're the ones building the product and the ones you'll spend a lot of your time with. If you put in the extra effort to do your best for them and to help them feel like part of the overall project team and not just code monkeys, they'll feel happier and more respected, and the work they do will be higher quality.

Finally, no two engineering teams are the same. While you should keep our advice in mind on the whole, sometimes with junior teams you need to step in a little more and make sure they're following best practices. For example, you might need to explicitly encourage them to add more automated test coverage and to take time to do thorough code reviews.

SOFTWARE-DEVELOPMENT METHODOLOGIES

A development methodology is simply the framework you use to structure the work to build the product. These methodologies are really more about project management, not just how developers write code. We've touched on two of these methodologies—waterfall and lean/agile— previously, but they have such a profound impact on how your engineering team works, we'll cover them in detail here. We're going to focus on various software-development methodologies, but many of the same principles apply to hardware development.

At one end of the spectrum, you have workflows where you, the PM, create a detailed spec and the engineering team disappears for months—likely more than you anticipated—reemerging with the product built exactly as specified. At the other end, the engineering team divides the project into the smallest tasks possible, programmers work in pairs on the same computer to complete one task, and then they come back to see what task they should do next. The next-up tasks might change while the programmers are working on their current task, and it doesn't matter to the programmers. Let's compare the two most common approaches along this spectrum, waterfall and agile.

Waterfall Development

The *waterfall* method is the oldest style of software development. Early software engineers simply adopted stages from the hardware world (manufacturing), and over time this approach became more refined. In 1985, the US Department of Defense formalized the waterfall process in its DOD-STD-2167A document, which specified that its contractors would use this approach to write software along with detailed descriptions of how they'd use it and the deliverables they'd create.

As you might guess, the waterfall method is very structured, with explicit, formal stages. It's even called "waterfall" because you can't move to the next stage until the current stage is done—everything goes from one stage to the next in a big dump, like water over a waterfall. Waterfall development starts with the requirements phase, where the PM has the most to do, finding the right opportunity and writing a very detailed PRD. Unlike the PRDs we discussed in Chapter 5, waterfall PRDs need to be detailed and complete, specifying as much of the project up front as possible. They are not living documents, but rather large and detailed bibles for the product.

After the requirements phase, Engineering and Design take over, beginning with a design phase, a coding phase, and a testing and integration phase. Products often ship with known bugs, as they'd never release if you fixed every bug. PMs are often involved in prioritizing bugs to make sure the ones that will affect customers the most are fixed before release.

Waterfall has a few benefits. For one, everyone will have a great idea of what the final product will look like early on since you create a detailed spec. Furthermore, since you do a lot of work up front creating the requirements, you might find and fix an issue in that phase. It's significantly cheaper to fix a problem early on. Because the scope is fixed early on, Engineering can make close-to-optimal design decisions for the project rather than designing for potential unknowns. Third-party development firms often like working with waterfall with clients because they can budget a project based upon the work they've agreed to do. Clients (and PMs) often like it because they don't need to be involved day to day in managing the project. Management also often likes the clear and easily understandable milestones in a project, and you can measure progress by what percentage of the spec is implemented.

But there are also significant drawbacks to waterfall that have caused many software teams to move away from it. These problems include the following:

Customers might not know their exact requirements up front. Because waterfall focuses on specifying and building something complete rather than on fast iterations, what you build initially might not meet the customers' needs. And by the time you have a new version addressing their needs, you might find that the customers have long since stopped using your product and sought out another answer.

There's no good way to handle changes. After the requirements stage, you might find new data that affects the product, and waterfall doesn't let you go back upstream to change decisions in earlier stages.

There is no time-boxing on each step, and the release often slips. One of the most common problems is that there were technological unknowns and coding the solution took much longer than intended, so a three-month project estimate actually took six months to complete. You had to invest those extra three months because otherwise you wouldn't have a product.

It can take so long to move through stages that a good decision you made initially might be the wrong decision when you release the product. For example, maybe you thought customers wanted a certain product, but after building it you discovered the market conditions changed and they no longer wanted it.

If you're working on a product where the requirements and technology are well known, waterfall is a reasonable approach. If your company is using a waterfall system, the best thing you can do as a PM is validate the PRD as much as possible initially to prevent changes later, and try to learn quickly if the market likes your idea.

In most cases, waterfall's shortcomings outweigh its benefits. Many software teams—including that of the Department of Defense—have switched to more iterative development approaches. There are numerous ones with various names, and some are still very waterfall-ish, but eventually you will encounter the second main development methodology, *agile* development.

Agile Development

Agile development is fundamentally about being flexible, iterating quickly, and embracing changes. Unfortunately, "agile" has become a somewhat generic and vague term much like "big data." Many companies claim to follow agile practices or use words from agile methodologies to describe their process, when in fact their workflows aren't at all agile. Let's look at what agile really means and then at specific implementations.

The Manifesto for Agile Software Development defines key principles of agile, including these:

- *Individuals and interactions* over processes and tools
- *Working software* over comprehensive documentation
- *Customer collaboration* over contract negotiation
- *Responding to change* over following a plan

Instead of a fully fleshed out, staged approach, agile follows an incremental approach. With agile you plan out a relatively small unit of work, build what you need to, and evaluate what you built. Then you use that knowledge to plan the next work to do. These small units of work can be organized either around time, in which case they're called a *sprint*, or around the number of tasks a team can work on at once, called a *cycle*.

There are multiple agile development methodology implementations you can use as starting point for your team's agile workflow, and you can adapt an approach for your team's dynamic. What matters is that you're open to change, iterating quickly, and building working software, not focused on how you get there.

For agile to be truly effective, you need to embrace the lean principles we've advocated throughout this book, like building a minimum viable product (MVP) rather than the fully featured product. In other words, build something small as quickly as possible, learn from it, and then iterate in the next sprint/cycle.

Short sprints—one or two weeks—or continuous deployment are ideal with agile, as they let you move quickly and get feedback. If you were to try to execute an agile process with a six-month sprint, you'd encounter many of the disadvantages we listed for waterfall, like how the customer's needs might change while you're building the product and you have no mechanism to get feedback or make changes during a sprint.

Agile and lean also lead to a breadth-first approach where each sprint or cycle will—ideally—produce a usable piece of software that you can use to get feedback from customers or clients. In waterfall you're much more likely to schedule milestones so that part of the product is deemed feature-complete before moving on to another part, scheduling for depth. With agile, sprints/cycles are usually focused on getting to a very minimal but functional app initially and then adding features to each section as needed, scheduling for breadth.

Furthermore, the team will do incremental testing on the code during each sprint/cycle, which leads to a higher-quality product with fewer bugs. Studies have shown it's up to 20 times cheaper to find and fix bugs as you build a product rather than doing separate development and testing stages like in waterfall.

Unfortunately, there are some downsides to agile, especially for PMs. Agile workflows frequently put a lot more demands on you, sometimes even having you handle quality assurance/bug testing in addition to everything else you're doing.

Having more milestones more often also puts additional demands on you to keep validating builds with customers, but you'll need to work to find the right balance of wanting feedback and deciding which builds to validate. Making sure a customer wants something before spending tons of time building it really is a big net win. After all, if you find you're building the wrong thing, you can pivot before spending more time on it. But it would take all of your time and not always yield useful information if you tried to validate every build.

Similarly, in an agency model clients sometimes dislike agile because they have to be more involved in the project, consistently scheduling and prioritizing.

One of the biggest criticisms of agile, however, comes from developers. If you're building something new/trying to solve a hard problem, agile's heavy focus on delivering something usable within a sprint (and the various associated practices) is counter to thinking deeply and solving a problem. Often, developers discover that the best way to find a creative solution to a hard problem is to isolate oneself, focus deeply, experiment, and reemerge when they have a solution. There are ways to avoid this shortcoming, such as leveraging scrum spikes—a user story to investigate something—or having explicit R&D sprints where a developer's only task is to try to solve one problem. Just being aware that this is a frustration for developers will help you make planning decisions that take it into account.

Agile can also be tricky to scale to large teams. See the "Further Reading" section for information about Agile Release Trains to help scale. There's also a ramp-up curve before you hit full productivity when implementing an agile workflow.

Agile critics say that it leads to reactionary development, as you're responding to what customers want now, rather than planning out a roadmap and maintaining a product vision. We feel it's quite possible to have an overall thematic roadmap with projects defined and communicated by PRDs, built using agile/lean methodologies, where the exact details change as you find out how customers use your product.

Despite the various criticisms, the Standish Group, an IT advisory center, tracked 50,000 projects from 2011 through 2015 and found that the success rate (shipping a working product) of agile products was 39% vs. 11% with waterfall. That's a huge difference, but note that even with agile 61% of projects don't have a working product by the end.

Let's look at two of the most popular ways agile methodology is implemented: scrum and Kanban.

Scrum

Scrum development is based on an idea from rugby, specifically that a team's functioning as a team, and not as a group of individuals, is key to success, and the best teams are given direction but can devise their own tactics for how to achieve their goals. Scrum came about in the early '90s whereas agile was formalized in the early '00s, but scrum's architects were part of the group that created the Agile Alliance.

At a high level, with software development, using scrum means that the team comes together to prioritize what to do next and set short-term goals for what work to finish. You as the PM will have very strong input into that part of the process. Then the team goes off and figures out how to best do that work. You'll check in with the team members at the start of each day as they work, addressing any questions, and you'll validate the work when they say it's ready. But you don't micro-manage them or change their goals before they're done with the current set.

Scrum is one of the most common approaches to agile because it has a very clearly defined project structure with clear team roles. This makes it easy for a company transitioning from waterfall to agile to adopt scrum. And even if companies don't fully implement scrum, they often borrow ideas from it, such as daily stand-up/check-in meetings.

Scrum uses time-boxed sprints, most commonly one or two weeks. Each week, you meet with the engineering team to perform *backlog grooming*. A product's backlog is the collection of all the bugs and suggestions, generally written as user stories, for the product.

Grooming simply means you make sure the bugs and sugs are organized and have enough clarity to act on. For example, we've all seen—and maybe sent—poorly written software bugs that just say "it crashed." That's not helpful. In grooming, you'd do what you could to add steps to reproduce the crash and attach a crash log to the issue so that the team could eventually fix the bug. In addition to adding clarity, during grooming you will make sure each new item for the backlog has acceptance criteria: How do you know the item is done properly?. Furthermore, we like writing backlog tasks as user stories because that format helps explain why something is an issue so that Design and Engineering can determine the best approach to address the issue.

Also during the grooming meeting, the engineering team will assess the complexity of the new or updated stories, breaking them down into sub-tasks if necessary. It's tough to know exactly how hard a task is or how many hours it will take, so you'll often see complexity measured using relatively weighted story points. Teams might assign one point to an easy task, two points to a medium task, four points to a hard task, and eight points to a very hard task. The idea is that you don't know exactly how hard something is, but you can say that one thing should be twice as hard as another.

After assessing the complexity, your role as the product owner will be to provide rough prioritization for any new items along with existing backlog items based on customer need, business value, and longer-term goals/needs. Your goal with this prioritization is to have the most important thing to work on next at the top of the backlog.

Backlogs often grow quite large, and there's usually a big chunk of stuff on it that you're just not going to be able to get to, along with things that are cool but not relevant in the immediate future. Teams often create a second list, called an *icebox*, for these less-immediately-relevant-but-things-you-don't-want-to-forget stories. Stories in the icebox can be "unfrozen" and moved to the backlog, but you won't actively work on icebox items. As we discussed in previous chapters, there will be a lot of potential features and ideas to make the product better. You will be saying "no" a lot to make sure the project doesn't get out of hand! Putting something in the icebox instead of explicitly saying "no" is a nice way to make people feel their input is valued while avoiding feature creep.

Later, you'll have another planning meeting where you determine the *sprint backlog*. The sprint backlog is simply the list of user stories the team intends to complete during the sprint. You'll pick the key things you want to work on based on priority/business value, and the engineering team will agree on whether they can commit to it during the sprint.

A common question is, how do you know how many backlog items to pick for a sprint? Over time, you'll find that the team tends to complete *n* story points per sprint. That number is called the *sprint velocity*.

During this planning meeting, if you add up the story points on the tasks everyone agrees to do, it should come out to that velocity.

If you're struggling with how to prioritize what to do, try calculating a priority score by adding a Business Value field to each story, like we suggested in Moving Forward section at the end of Chapter 4. Factors that go into the business value can include how much you believe this will help you achieve a goal, how many customers are asking for this, if there's an important technical reason you need to do this, and so on. Then, calculate a priority score by dividing the business value by the complexity. High-value, low-complexity stories will have a high score. High-value, high-complexity stories will have a mid-range score. Low-value, high-complexity stories will have a low score. This approach is especially useful if your team is responsible for multiple products and you have to balance each product's needs during sprint planning.

Note that you won't change the sprint backlog during the sprint, as that disrupts the team and can throw off the sprint velocity, which affects planning. This lack of change encourages you to have shorter sprints, especially when priorities are shifting, so that you can balance reacting to change with letting the team function effectively.

You'll also find that scrum requires more attention to the balance between building the right thing (what PMs want), building the thing right (what engineers want), and building it fast (what scrum masters want so they can get feedback quickly). It's quite likely that you will accumulate technical debt—that is, the code will have some funkiness in it that Engineering had to build to deliver something in time.

It's OK to have a little technical debt to get short-term customer value, but lots of technical debt can reduce your team's velocity. During sprints, you'll periodically need to accept work that pays off that technical debt even though there's no visible customer value. For example, if we rewrote

Moover from Objective-C to Swift, there wouldn't be any immediate customer value, but it could make it easier to add new features going forward, improving the team's velocity.

During the sprint, you'll have short, 15-minute meetings called *stand-ups* at the start of each workday, where each team member states what she did during the past day, what she aims to accomplish today, and if she has any blocking issues.

At the end of the sprint, you'll have a demo meeting with key stakeholders/the customer/the client to show what you've built and gauge their feedback, and an internal sprint retrospective to assess how the sprint went.

When done well, while combining scrum and lean methodologies, scrum tends to provide a very nice balance of planning ahead and tolerating change, which we've found valuable. Since each sprint ideally produces something usable, you can break down a bigger plan specified in a PRD into smaller milestones and validate what you're building at key points with customers and stakeholders to make sure you're on the right path. If you're not, pivot before building more.

When you start a new project, scrum is especially helpful. Early on in a project, there's a lot of risk (business, technical, and more). By focusing on sprints and tasks that de-risk the project, you might have low initial customer value but enable rapid progress later.

For example, when planning Moover's new customer messaging feature, we might focus on making messaging back and forth between customers and movers work initially, not paying any attention to a good user experience. This will let us test and make sure that this core piece works. If the development team finds out that its initial approach has some big limitation (e.g., maybe it's constantly blocked by a firewall), the team can come up with a better solution. And if it turns out that the core piece isn't do-able, you can reassess what you're building without the team's wasting time on non-core pieces.

Scrum also makes project management easier, as you can use story points and the total story points for outstanding items in the product backlog to create trend lines. These trend lines let you estimate when the project will be done with a feature set, along with how much work will be done on a certain date.

If you have to make a schedule tradeoff, we'd recommend reducing the project's scope rather than extending the schedule. That way you make sure you have something done by the deadline, and if you finish early you can increase the scope.

Unfortunately, scrum has some problems. Some of these problems have even led to cries that "agile is dead." The heart of that argument is that the agile movement was supposed to be about individuals and interactions and responding to change. Scrum has become synonymous with agile, yet implementing scrum is often more about process over individuals, and change has been limited to enable better planning. In other words, "agile" has been bastardized to be just as rigid as waterfall.

Stand-up meetings are a great example of that rigidity. The goal is to keep the team apprised of what's going on and to help unblock any issues at the start of each day. But if your team starts its day at different times or works in different time zones, stand-up meetings aren't effective because they'll be at the start of the day for one person but hours into the day for another. Plus, these check-ins all too often become an easy way for managers to micro-manage while claiming it's part of scrum. Despite these shortcomings, the teams still hold their stand-ups because that's what scrum says to do. A better approach would be to create new ways to communicate, like agile encourages, such as posting a status update to Slack at the end of the day rather than holding a stand-up.

Scrum can also create headaches for you. It's often up to the product manager to do acceptance testing, making sure each user story is completed correctly and without bugs. This can be very demanding of your time, and when you combine it with everything else you have to do, it's easy to get sloppy and miss bugs that a dedicated QA team would have caught.

A final downside to scrum is that while you're seeing progress more frequently than with waterfall, in the best-case scenario you still have to wait a whole sprint to see the latest and greatest. While that might be fine for a new feature, it can be very frustrating for bug fixes! Given how easy it is to release software in today's world, such as with web apps, there are alternate agile approaches worth looking at, such as Kanban.

Kanban

Kanban development comes from Toyota, which came up with this methodology by looking at how supermarkets stock shelves. Specifically, supermarkets aim to be "just in time" so that the shelves are neither empty nor overstocked with wasted, expired food. While Toyota used this technique to build cars efficiently, it is often applied to software, too.

Kanban's goal is to match the team's capacity to do work with how much work is actually happening. Additionally, there should be a few tasks ready to go so that if a team finished *n* story points of work, they can immediately start working on a task requiring another *n* points to complete. This is nice because your future priorities can change with very little impact on the team's current work.

In Kanban, you will typically create a task board showing what's up next (to-do), in progress, ready to be tested/verified, and done. Tasks will move from one column to the next, and you'll know how much work the team can handle at once along with how many things it can verify at once.

While many agile methodologies are time-based, Kanban isn't. Instead, the PM will work with the dev team to reprioritize the backlog and make sure that the most important items are always next up and their difficulty estimates are accurate. This leads Kanban teams to focus on *cycle time*: how long it takes from the moment you start a unit of work until it ships.

Many little things can hurt cycle time, such as one person having specialized and required knowledge for the task, along with multitasking. Therefore, Kanban encourages teams to learn skills outside their domains—so that everyone could test, for example, if there's work piling up in the "ready to be verified" queue and holding up the next phase—and to stay focused by keeping the amount of work in progress small.

One of the biggest benefits to Kanban is that it enables continuous deployment. Once a change moves through the cycle, it's ready to be released. Especially for web apps, this is quite nice and enables immediate customer feedback.

Kanban is also nice because it can be implemented on top of other methodologies. It's really just a focus on incremental, continuous improvement to the product. In general, if your team is already using a workflow and executing well, Kanban might help the team move to the next level. But if your team needs help becoming more efficient in general, shaking things up by focusing on implementing another agile process, Kanban might not be the right place to start. That's because Kanban is a much less formalized method than scrum, and it can be harder to understand how to implement it initially.

Sometimes you'll see Kanban combined with scrum—called "scrumban")—which was originally intended as a way to transition from scrum to Kanban but has become a methodology of its own. Here, the team will have a planning meeting, execute a very short sprint, and then have another planning meeting when the work in progress falls below a certain number of story points. There are no predefined roles or fixed schedules, and the iterations are focused on points delivered rather than time.

However, while Kanban is great for development teams, it can be very hard on PMs. PMs are frequently quite busy, working with customers, shepherding products, working with marketing, and more. Kanban requires us to also be available continuously to verify each task is completed (acceptance testing) and to make sure the next set of tasks is prioritized and ready to go (backlog grooming). If you don't continuously do these tasks, you might become the bottleneck for the whole team!

Overall, remember that with agile, individuals and interactions are the most important element—more important than processes and tools. This means that you shouldn't worry about following a word-for-word implementation of a specific methodology. Start somewhere and figure out what works best for your team. And don't be afraid to try a new approach.

CHAPTER 7 TIP

Mohammad Musa, a Product School instructor, provides this chapter's tip. Mohammad is cofounder of a stealth start-up focused on virtual reality for enterprises. He used to work at Google on companywide efforts to enable teams to build products more effectively. He worked specifically on infrastructure products for tracking user-centered metrics, bug management, and user-feedback loops. Prior to that, he was the head of Launch & Readiness at Google Apps for Work, where he led a cross-functional team managing product launches, product roadmap, trusted tester, and launch communications. Before joining Google, Mohammad worked in software engineering and technical sales positions in the video games and semiconductor industries, mostly in small start-ups.

WORKING WITH JUNIOR DEVELOPMENT TEAMS

If you are a software PM, you will need to work hand-in-hand with the software engineering manager (often called tech lead manager or TLM in companies like Google, Facebook, and Twitter). The TLM manages a number of software engineers with variable seniority levels. The more senior engineers are often referred to as tech leads (TLs). The TLs may or may not have management responsibility over the other team members.

The TL reports to the TLM and handles most of the day-to-day work assignment and helps the team unblock technical challenges for a particular project.

If you are lucky, you will be working with an experienced TLM and/or TL who has mentored and managed many engineers in the past. The TLM or TL will take care of training and advising the junior developers on the team without requiring extra cycles from you as the PM.

However, in reality you don't always get an experienced TL or TLM. Or sometimes you may get a great but busy TLM that has 15-plus engineers reporting to him/her. In these cases, your role as the PM will need to expand to best help the team succeed. In my experience, I found that working with junior developers requires the PM to do more work around scrum management, quality, and product or feature definition.

First off, with regards to scrum, the junior developers are not used to user story estimation. Their estimates are usually off and they often think that a story is complete while there is still a lot of work left to be done. These premature stories can cause embarrassment in front of stakeholders if not enough QA has been completed. Second, and closely related to the first point, you really need to do a lot more QA around the work that junior developers have completed. You may not have a QA team at all and even if you do, the scripted tests may not catch all the errors that have been introduced by someone who does not know the system very well. This is exacerbated in complex software systems that are already suffering from coverage and quality problems.

Finally, around requirements and definition: As the PM, you need to assume that the junior team members are like new users who have only casually used your product. You can't count on quick hallway or chat conversations to agree on minor details and just move on. You really have to document and make sure that junior team members have internalized what you are asking them to do. This will include more detailed user story descriptions, detailed mocks and user journeys/scenarios, and detailed acceptance criteria.

Within six to eight sprints, the junior members will better understand the product complexities and requirements. To speed up understanding and shorten the learning curve, it would be ideal for your team to develop more user empathy. Encourage your engineering team to monitor user research sessions or conduct informal customer-discovery conversations with users directly (if possible). More knowledge of the user persona and their pain points helps the entire team become more experienced and helps junior developers take more ownership and pride in their work.

WORKING WITH REMOTE TEAMS

A common challenge PMs face is how to work with development teams that aren't in the same physical space or even the same time zone. While there's no one right answer, clear communication is the key. This doesn't mean an expectation of non-stop communication and constant availability, but rather having regular check-ins and using tools like Google Hangouts to see each other and remember that you're working with a person.

You can play a big part in helping remote teams be successful by over-communicating requirements, goals, decisions, and the definition of "done" for the project so that everyone feels like they're on the same team and has a clear understanding of what they're working towards, regardless of where their desks sit. Sometimes important decisions or clarifications happen in a hallway conversation, and unless you pay attention, a remote developer might not hear about that decision, or might feel left out of the decision-making process.

Creating a culture where people don't think twice about having a quick video chat can help replicate the face-to-face interaction that happens naturally in a single location. Too often, we still think of a video conference as a formal, scheduled time—it doesn't have to be that way.

Furthermore, be aware of when people are starting or ending their days. Is there something that team A can do at the end of its day that you need for the start of your day? Or is there something you can get done by the end of your day so that when team B starts, it's not blocked? It can even be helpful to establish "golden hour" handoff meetings so that these needs get communicated clearly at the start and end of each team's workday.

Agile helps a lot with remote teams because it forces you to think about the adaptable nature of agile to figure out workflows that work well for you. For example, scrum works well with remote teams because you can plan what to do, let people work independently, and still conduct daily stand-ups. Depending on what time zones people are in, you might have to conduct daily stand-ups asynchronously via email or instant message throughout the day rather than having everyone together at the same time. Additionally, at the review meeting, rather than trying to accommodate everyone's schedule and possibly making the meeting inconvenient for the stakeholders, try having the product owner, rather than individual developers, present the overall team's work to the stakeholders.

The biggest thing that remote teams miss out on is the natural team-building that happens when people spend their days together. It's important to get your team together in the same place periodically, even if it's just for team-building exercises. Product managers should have empathy for their teams, not just for their customers. Spending time together is a good way to develop solid relationships.

WORKING WITH THIRD-PARTY DEVELOPMENT TEAMS

If you're a software PM, there's a good chance that at some point you will work on a project with a third-party development team. This means that the project's developers aren't company employees, but rather employees of a development agency you've hired. Companies usually engage a third-party development team when they're resource-constrained—a start-up may not have had time or funds to build a full-time development team, or in an larger company may want to take on a project its internal team doesn't have time to do. Sometimes you'll also hire a third-party team because they have a particular skill that you have a short-term need of, such as expertise in a specific API.

As a product manager, you'll handle a lot of the interaction between your company and this team, and you can do a few things to ensure success. The biggest is to make sure you're communicating the requirements, goals, and deadlines to the third-party team clearly. Take the time to address any potentially confusing elements as they arise. Writing everything down on a shared project-management resource such as Basecamp will help ensure everyone has access to the same information and key decisions. Coordinate the timelines and progress with any stakeholders internally to make sure everything looks good. It's often better to over-communicate, especially at first.

It's also very helpful if you establish frequent milestones with the external team. If that team is internally using an agile process, this should be easy. The benefit is that you can see what they're building, and if something isn't heading in the right direction—whether because of a miscommunication or because you made a mistake in what you needed to build—you can address it early. Just like with an internal development team, if you give a third-party team a large spec and then only check in three months later, what they've built might, unintentionally, not be what you wanted or what you need.

Having a solid short-term plan is also very helpful, as it lets agencies schedule their developers efficiently on your project. In fact, some agencies prefer to let work queue up until they have a sprint's worth on your project before prioritizing it. Frequently changing what you're asking for is frustrating for development agencies, as it makes it hard for the agency to to plan the project longer term and to gauge when it'll finish your project and when it can take on new work.

Above all, just like you would with an internal team, look at an external development agency as a partner. Be respectful of the agency's skills, time, and needs, and it'll likely do great work for you.

However, while there are many great external development firms, there are some sketchy ones, so you should know a few warning signs. Like when you're buying a used car, if your contact keeps telling you what a great value you're getting, he's likely overcharging you. If your contact never asks questions to clarify each user story or make an effort to clarify and deliver the acceptance criteria, you should be wary. If your contact ignores questions you ask except on your check-in calls, you should also be alert.

Be watchful of how agile agencies assign story points to user stories for which they use a pre-built in-house framework. Specifically, many agencies have built up libraries of common functions, such as server code for account management. A good agency that's using its library to complete user stories will estimate these user stories as "easy." This is honest and lets you calculate sprint velocity effectively. A sketchy agency will list a hard estimate for the user stories, claiming all the original work it took to develop the library as part of your story, even though it's trivial for the agency to implement. Then the agency will tell you how much it kicked butt for the sprint because its team accomplished hundreds of story points, even though it really only did 10 story points' worth of work. That claim messes up the sprint velocity and planning calculations, and it's a sure sign you should find a new agency.

No matter where your team members are located, whether they're in-house or external, and whether they use Kanban or waterfall, we say that the development phase of the product life cycle is done when working, tested software that meets your product requirements is ready for release. Your role during the development phase comes down to providing clear requirements for the engineering team members, working with them to prioritize and reprioritize as needed, and trusting them to build great code. Now that we've built our product, let's look at how we launch and market it.

CHAPTER EIGHT

BRINGING YOUR PRODUCT TO MARKET

At this point you've found an opportunity, validated it, gotten your team on board, and built a product. You've done a lot! In fact, if you come from an engineering or design background, you might feel like the hard work's over and you can take a vacation. But for a product manager, there's still more work to do to get your product into the market successfully. As the team at Pragmatic Marketing, a product-marketing-focused agency, puts it, "Launch isn't the end of development but rather the beginning of selling."

As much as we'd like to believe that if we built the perfect product it will sell itself, the harsh truth is that it won't. If none of your target customers know about, find, or buy your product, it will flop. If the wrong people buy your product, they won't be happy and your product will flop. Unless you have a solid plan to bring your product to market, it will most likely flop. Fortunately, marketing and sales teams exist to make sure the right customers learn about, find, and buy your product!

To ensure a successful launch, you will work closely with the marketing team. Some companies even have a second role within marketing related to product management, the product marketing manager (PMM). Put simply, the PMM is focused externally and is an expert on the customer—and the buyer, if that's not the same person, such as in enterprise software—whereas the PM will focus internally on getting the product built. Companies that have a PM and a PMM call the PM "inbound" and a PMM "outbound" to reflect this differing focus.

Workflow-wise, the PMM will often handle customer development and outreach, the PM will take that feedback and research and get the right product built, and the PMM will step back in for launch. During launch, a PMM is responsible for figuring out how to explain the product to the customers, crafting the right go-to-market (GTM) plan to bring the product to market successfully, and helping the sales team. We'll go through this chapter as if the PM and the PMM are the same person to give you the best understanding of how product and marketing come together during launch.

By representing the customer, the marketing and sales team will often ask for the PM's input when forming strategies. For example, if your product is aimed at teens, the PM will know that teens currently use Snapchat and Instagram more than Facebook. The marketing team will use that input as a starting point to determine where to buy display ads. While you won't be responsible for the details of buying display ads, your input will affect where those ads are and what they say.

Throughout this chapter, we'll look at launch preparation, at the launch itself, and a bit at post-launch activities. Launch preparation starts way before the product launches with understanding your customers and product messaging. Even though we're covering this material after the product's been built, you will implement this advice while you're building this product.

Whether you're releasing a new version of an existing product with minor fixes or releasing a completely new big product, the advice in this chapter will help you. You'll just adjust the scale appropriately. A bug-fix release doesn't need a press tour, for example.

UNDERSTANDING CUSTOMERS

To market your product successfully, you'll need to know how your customers make decisions. Thinking about marketing early on, even when you're doing your initial customer development, will help your product enter the market successfully. For example, your customers might expect to buy your product at Best Buy. It can take months for your sales team to set up the relationship so that your product is available in store, which means you can't wait until launch to start the process.

Back in Chapter 3, we introduced the Business Model Canvas and the Value Proposition Canvas. At the time, we used them to help look for a product opportunity. We can use the same tools to understand how to best market our product to the right customers by looking at different parts of the canvas. For reference, Figure 8-1 shows the Business Model Canvas (also shown in Chapter 3 as Figure 3-5).

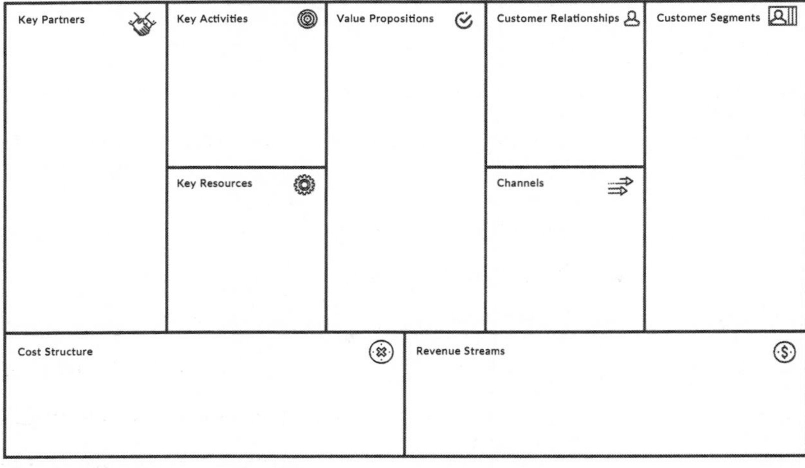

Figure 8-1: The Business Model Canvas, from *http://strategyzer.com*, provides insight for how to market your product.

These are the key areas to focus on from a marketing point of view:

- **Customer segments:** Who are the key personas?
- **Value propositions:** What's the benefit/value each persona will gain from your product?
- **Channels:** How does the company reach each persona?
- **Customer relationships:** What communication level and type does each persona expect?
- **Revenue streams:** How much and how often will the customer pay?

As you do your customer research, you'll want to fill out these blocks and expand your persona to include the marketing side. Here are some specific things to make sure your personas address:

- How the persona would consider your product a success
- How the persona perceives your product/company (if you have an existing product)
- What buying criteria the persona has
- How the persona evaluates products (e.g., does he expect a free trial?)
- How the persona perceives your competition
- What influence this persona has on the buying process

By fleshing out the marketing side of a persona, you'll help the marketing team make successful decisions. For example, your persona might focus on new parents who look for advice online. Then the marketing team will do additional research to determine what parenting websites and blogs the actual customers read, along with where they buy diapers and other supplies. In other words, once you know what your personas are, you and the team can figure out what channels the customers they represent use to learn about and purchase new products. That lets your team make choices, like where to buy advertising, so that the right people find your product.

The Customer Relationship block will help your team determine how to reach these customers, too. With an enterprise product and a high-value customer that purchases a lot of licenses, the customer likely expects her account manager to talk to her personally and maybe even come to her office to give a demo. Again, make sure the choices you make for customer relationships match your customers' expectations.

Sometimes, especially if you're releasing a completely new version of a product, you'll want to call out any customer segments the product isn't ready for yet. For example, when Apple released Final Cut Pro X, which was a completely rewritten version of Final Cut, it left out certain advanced features and waited for customer feedback to determine which to add back in. This also meant that Apple explicitly *didn't* market the product to customers they knew needed those advanced features, as those customers wouldn't have been satisfied with this new version.

Product Messaging

One of the most important things the Business Model Canvas and the Value Proposition Canvas can help you and your team determine is the right product message. Specifically, how do you communicate your product's value to customers and explain why they should care and what problems your product solves? These canvases can help because they specifically ask you to think about your customers' needs, problems, and goals along with what problems your product solves and what benefits it provides to your target customers.

Framing your product in this way—why should the customer care?—helps with everything from how you'll sell the product to what features really matter. It's so important that back in Chapter 5, we recommended including at least a first pass at your product's core message in the PRD. If you don't think about the customers you're trying to reach and why they should care, then it will be much harder to find customers. For example, if you're working on a new version of a student-loan product, your focus will be on getting students and recent graduates to care about and buy your product.

Before you start creating your product's message, make sure you really understand the customer personas you're targeting and how your product fits their life. The Value Proposition Canvas, especially, will help you see those connections. In an ideal world, we'd come up with one universal message that addresses all of your personas, but we'll likely need different messages for each persona.

Using the same message for every persona is like starting every letter you send with "Dear sir," even if the recipient is a woman. And the same way that you wouldn't greet someone in person with "Dear sir," you'll likely have different messages for different mediums, from website to email to video ad. In other words, it won't just be the message language that changes. Different personas will want different value propositions and care about different features/use cases. A stay-at-home dad will likely care more about a car's safety rating than its horsepower, whereas a dad having a midlife crisis will care more about horsepower.

PMs are frequently responsible for the first pass at a product's messages and will have input into the various forms these messages takes. Let's dive into how to craft a great message. We're going create a message by putting some notes together around the elements that go into a message and then putting those notes together into a message.

Key Elements of Your Product's Message

We'll start our notes by thinking about the product's themes, which we talked about in Chapter 2. There are three key questions our theme should answer: Why is this product/company important? Why are you doing this? What's special about your company's mission that will make a customer want your product over a competitor's? Ideally there will be one fundamental theme that answers those three questions. Grab a blank sheet of paper and start writing down what you think your company's core theme is. Revise what you write as needed to make sure that theme applies to all three questions.

Let's write down Moover's theme. Moover's founders created the company because they found planning a move to be overwhelmingly stressful, especially while working full-time. Their core theme is making moving as stress-free as possible so that it's easy for you to get to where you want to live. While we might never explicitly say those words to customers, that theme will guide our product messaging.

Another element to look at is what's fresh and new about the product: What are we building a message for? On your sheet of paper, create a new section where you list what's fresh and new. In Moover's case, it's the chat feature.

Note that the "fresh and new" part might differ for new versus existing customers. With Moover, we can specifically tell existing customers about the messaging feature. But when we try to reach new customers, we likely have to educate them about Moover in general first, and the chat feature will be a bullet point beneath the main message. This is a common problem companies face, and it's just another reason you'll need different messages for different customers.

Rather than telling people about these fresh and new features, though, we want to talk about the benefits they provide to the customer, using the underlying theme and the customer's problems/needs to affect our diction. Next to each new feature you listed, write why the customer should care and how this feature relates to the theme.

Moover's chat feature lets customers communicate with moving companies at the customers' convenience, not only from 9am to 5pm. We could rephrase this to explain why a customer should care by writing, "Never stress about missing a phone call from the movers: talk with them on your schedule."

Continuing with crafting your message, how is your product different and better than what the customer's doing now? This is especially relevant in the messaging for new customers. In another section on your paper, create "Now" and "Future" columns and write out what the customer's doing now and why your product, especially with this new feature, is better.

Right now, Moover's customers, both existing and potential, have to stress about answering phone calls and not missing emails from moving companies, even when they're really busy dealing with life. We could further refine our message by saying, "We're taking the hassle out of talking to movers." This is great because it quickly encompasses all types of communication: "talking" can mean via phone or email. And we're saying why Moover is better: it's hassle-free. This version of our message is also strong because it's positive (the previous message started with the negative "*never*") and it's in the customer's diction ("talking" rather than "communicating" and "hassle" rather than "stress").

Another aspect of your message is to address what someone's first impression of your product might be, and whether you need to influence that impression. Our first impressions have a big effect on our attitudes. For example, the first time you see 3D software like Unity, it will look overwhelming and complex. Unity addresses this on its website by specifically stating, "You can create any 2D or 3D game with Unity. You can make it with ease." As another example, CleverPet is a game console for dogs, and at first glance it looks like it's just the memory game Simon even though it costs $299. CleverPet's website explicitly calls out that it's "One hub. Unlimited games." This wording influences your first impression to know that it's more than just Simon, and it helps justify the $299 price.

In your notes for your product, write down what you feel each persona's first impression of your product will be. If you need to influence that impression, write down how you want to shift the perception.

Finding Your Company's Voice

After you've assembled your notes, you'll want to think about your *voice*. This refers to the diction and tone you will use in your marketing and advertising materials, possibly also even inside the product, such as in alert messages. Basically, do you want to have a very formal tone with your customers, a casual tone, a "hip" tone, or something in between?

Enterprise products traditionally have taken a formal tone to create a "business" feeling and consumer products have adopted a casual tone to create a friendly and accessible feeling. The overriding trend now for both enterprise and consumer products is to have a more casual and authentic tone. However, some B2B products in highly regulated fields like medicine and finance still have to use very formal and specific voices because the wrong language can get you into legal trouble.

Some companies will create formal style guidelines for their brand's voice and require everything, from alert panels in the product to every ad, to conform to those guidelines. This can make it hard to adapt your message for different customers. Instead, we recommend having a general sense of the voice you want your brand to have, but use that as a starting point and not a required approach. Just make sure you stay consistent within each medium/message! It's confusing if you start a letter with "Dear sir" and then switch to "Hey, dude" in the next paragraph.

Using similar diction to your customers can help your customers quickly understand your value proposition. With consumer products, this means not using industry jargon—you'll likely need to cross out and rewrite some of your "why should the customer care?" descriptions. For example, Microsoft describes its Surface devices as "the most productive devices on the planet" and goes on to describe the Surface Book as "the ultimate laptop." Right away, you know if you're looking for a high-end laptop, this is the product you want to look at. If you want something to just browse the web, you also know this isn't the right product. If Microsoft had instead listed each device's CPU specs, most customers wouldn't know which product to look at.

With enterprise software or specific, targeted products, you often want to use certain buzzwords that a customer is looking for. For example, if a head of IT at a hospital is looking to buy a medical records system, he likely cares about compliance with government regulations. Calling out a specific compliance level as part of the message helps him quickly know this product exactly meets his needs.

A simple way to make sure you're using the right diction is to ask how a customer would tell a friend about your product. If their diction is similar to yours, excellent! If it's very different, reconsider your word choice. You want your message to match how your customers see the world. Your message gets bonus points if it really creates images and evokes emotions in a customer's mind.

Putting the Message Pieces Together

If you were following along, you now have a few pages of notes and ideas for how you could tell a customer about your product. That's excellent because, again, there's no one message that works for all personas on all mediums. For example, what you write in a press release will be different from what's on the product's web page, and that will be different from how you advertise the product on TV. As another example, how many websites have you gone to that essentially ask you to pick your persona by choosing between text like "For developers" or "For designers"? The messaging will be different on each page, focusing on the things each of those personas cares about.

While you won't be responsible for creating ads, it's worth looking at ads to understand how other companies express their messages. Spend some time looking at websites and watching ads for products you use, or know about. What is the company saying about each product? Is the message explicit or implicit? What diction or imagery does the company use?

Video advertising is really interesting to analyze because the message is often implicit, and you'll have to think about what the company was trying to say. Then note how it chose to convey it: What personas did it appeal to? How did it make those personas clear? What emotions did the ad create? Watch Apple's classic 1984 ad or Google's Parisian Love ad to see two fantastic examples. 1984 focuses on how Macintosh enables you to stand out and break free of your constraints. Parisian Love examines how search changes your life by giving you the answers you need. It's also worth explicitly noting that these ads don't focus on the product—they focus on your life, the experience you want, and how the product helps you have that experience.

In general, it's good to figure out the shortest possible message that appeals to the most personas. You'll likely use that message a lot, whether as a sound bite during a meeting with the press or as the headline on the product's page. Then, create different, more specific, and more targeted messages as needed, using your notes to guide you.

We highly recommend taking a stab at determining this short message early in the product-development life cycle and then revising it as needed. This will help keep any product decisions focused (do they enhance/detract from the message?) and provide a starting point for discussions about how to bring the product to market.

Just like writing user scenarios for stakeholders is the secret to good PRDs, writing your message as a story can help it become clear and resonate more with customers. You can even use it to give increased value to something new that might not seem exciting. For example, if your new feature is a tutorial section on the website, tell a story about how the customer can use these simple tutorials to become an expert on the product very quickly, leaving their peers in the dust.

Finally, remember that your message is not about what the product *does*, it's about what the product *lets the customer do*. Customers buy your product to make their lives better. Make sure your message clearly highlights how your product will help your customers improve their lives.

CHAPTER EIGHT TIP

This tip comes from an amazing product leader, Kirk Paulsen, SVP for Marketing at DxO. For more than a decade, Kirk directed worldwide product marketing for all photo software and cloud-based services from Apple's headquarters in Cupertino. As an executive for start-ups Sonic and then Spruce, he helped launch the world's first commercially available DVD encoding and authoring systems. Kirk was also one of the first technology experts to introduce the very concept of computer-based audio and video editing systems to the music and film industries.

ASK THE DRI TO WHITEBOARD IT FOR YOU

In my experience at a certain fruit-named company, each of our software application releases typically involved dozens of new features and enhancements. For each launch, it was the PM's job to cull the complete list down to a half dozen or so top-level features (TLF) which represented the story of that particular release. It was the responsibility of the PM to present the TLF to the broader marketing team, which included creative directors, copywriters, graphic designers, etc. It was absolutely essential that the message be clear, concise, and delivered with enthusiasm. Tell the story right, with clarity and passion, and the entire creative team would get engaged to do their very best work to help you showcase the product. Were the message to lack cohesion or come off as uninspired, the creative team could just as easily disengage, performing mediocre work at best, which would invariably result in the industry giving it a collective yawn. The quickest way for a PM to lose the respect of engineering is to make the product sound boring or obscure. Conversely, one of the best ways for a PM to earn kudos from other teams is to tell the story in an articulate, engaging, and insightful manner.

So how exactly do you figure out how to succinctly and effectively communicate the solution that will make the customer awesome? Simple: for each and every TLF ask the engineer or scientist most directly responsible for that particular bit to explain it to you in detail, in layman's terms. The process requires you to search out the directly responsible individual (DRI) for that exact feature or technology. In some cases, particularly with small start-ups, it may the founder. Often it's the product's chief architect who directs the engineering team. In a Fortune 100 company, it might well be a shy but brilliant scientist who works within one tiny team among a vast R&D organization. What I can assure you is, it isn't someone who is somewhat close to the feature but not directly involved. Rather, it must be the DRI, the person who coded, engineered, designed, or directed the work that led to that particular feature. At Sonic Solutions it was Dr. Andy Moorer, at Apple it was usually Randy Ubillos, and at DxO it is often Dr. Frédéric Guichard.

When you take the time to identify the precise DRI for that specific feature or technology, you'll discover that that person, and only that person, is capable of explaining it to you, in depth and with more clarity than you could possibly imagine. Most important, you will have the opportunity to feel firsthand their personal passion for the product, and gain a better understanding of the true benefit of the solution as they originally conceived of it. In my experience this process typically involved either a private one-on-one session, or a very select gathering, but never a large group. And in my experience it always, always involved a whiteboard, because I've never met an engineer or scientist who wasn't keen to express themselves with an erasable marker. After listening carefully to their description of the feature or technology, it's essential for you to try to immediately channel their voice and repeat what you've just learned, as in, "so, would I be correct in describing this as…?" The process, which involves focused listening and detailed note-taking, may well require several interactions before you are in complete harmony with the DRI and are able to perfectly articulate, in layman's terms, the solution. Follow this tip and you as the PM will be properly equipped to tell a great story to the creative marketing team, who will help you share your message with the industry, media, channel partners, and your soon-to-be awesome customers.

GOING TO MARKET

It's tempting to think that once development's done and you've put together an initial product message in the PRD, you can just give the product to marketing/sales and let them do their thing. But what happens if during launch your server crashes and your engineering team is out of the office celebrating? Or worse, what if the marketing team didn't fully understand the product's new features, targeted the wrong PR/advertising outlets, and no one showed up for the launch?

Many companies create launch checklists, preset templates of the information the marketing team needs to launch a product. But the problem is that not every product launch is the same, either in terms of the product you're launching or how people receive information. For example, a big product launch might warrant an event that you live-stream. Five years ago, live streaming wasn't an easy option. In a couple of years, live streaming in virtual reality or some other way we can't imagine now might be the norm. And if you're launching a new version of a small feature, you likely don't need a live stream at all.

A great way to launch a product is to identify a launch owner early on, to form a team with representatives from each key group (Design, Engineering, Product, Support, and Marketing), and to establish clear launch objectives and responsibilities within a go-to-market (GTM) plan. Sometimes the launch owner is the PM, but PMs are often busy enough that someone else from the marketing team will take on this role. Although the launch owner will organize and manage the GTM plan, each department will contribute to it. Each week, the team will meet to make sure everything is on track to ensure a successful launch, and they'll communicate any delays or issues and discuss solutions.

For these meetings, it's helpful to create a launch tracker to organize the launch. Three sheets in a spreadsheet are sufficient. The first sheet will contain the action items. These are specific tasks, assigned to a particular person/team, along with when each task was assigned, when it was due, and any comments/status updates appropriate for the task. The second sheet will contain caution items. These are possible problem issues along with who raised them, when they raised them, when each issue was resolved, and any comments. The last sheet will have key decisions, including who made them, when, and any comments. In the same way the PRD is a living document that acts as the key product resource as you build the product, this launch tracker will be your launch reference.

A lot of the work you've done so far, from identifying your target customers to analyzing the competition to developing product messages for each persona, will inform your overall strategy and influence the decisions you make within the GTM plan. Keep those in mind as you read this section!

At a high level, the GTM plan is subdivided into three sections: prelaunch, launch, and postlaunch. Let's look at each.

Prelaunch Planning

The main things to decide during prelaunch are the key launch goals, how you'll make sure the product is ready for that launch, when and how you'll launch the product, and what assets you need to launch.

Launch Objectives

Launches have different purposes. For some products, like the latest Google Pixel smartphone, the goal is likely to get as many customers as possible upgrading to this phone or new customers buying the phone. For enterprise software like Salesforce, the goal might be getting a subset of customers engaged with a new feature. Sometimes the goal is simply awareness of a new feature so that when customer enter their buying cycle, your product is on their mind.

Identifying your key goals up front will let you make other launch decisions, such as when to aim to launch your product.

Launch Timing

After the launch objective, most launch teams identify when they want to launch the product. Sometimes this is a specific date, but usually it's a date range. For example, consumer product launches tend to happen at the start of the year, in late April/early May for the "dads and grads" window (Father's Day and graduation), or after the summer but before Black Friday.

It's important to pick this launch window as early as possible because it can affect your product's development. If you're selling a consumer product and the development team thinks it will be ready to launch December 26, then you'll have missed the entire window from Black Friday to Christmas, when consumer products sell well. If you want to have the product available for holiday shopping, you'll need to reduce your product's scope to have it ready in time.

Businesses sometimes have buying periods, too, that you might need to time your launch around. Schools often purchase products in the spring and summer, before the start of the next school year. Sometimes companies have extra money in their budget they need to spend before the end of the year, so they'll buy more in December. Understanding your customers and their buying habits will help you identify the best launch window for your product.

For feature releases for existing products, the launch timing depends on the launch type and goal. If it's a big update that will encourage new customers to buy your product, then you'll likely treat it like a new product and align the release with your customers' buying habits. Smaller releases' timing varies a lot. The only rule of thumb for these smaller releases is to release earlier in the week so that if any support issues arise your team doesn't have to work over the weekend to resolve them.

If the feature is a bug fix for a critical security issue, then your launch goal is to get this into as many customers' hands as possible, as soon as possible. If it's a small update designed to improve the product for existing customers, your goal will also be to get as many existing customers as possible to update, but it's not as urgent. If your customer has to explicitly take an inconvenient action to upgrade, like restarting a computer, you'll want to schedule your releases to balance the value of the release with the inconvenience of upgrading. Fortunately, newer tools like the Mac App Store and the Windows Store are making upgrades easier for customers, automatically handling the inconvenient actions like restarting when customers are away from their computers.

A common question is, What does *launch* mean and how do you pick a date when you have an agile team, producing usable products at the end of each sprint or cycle? It depends! For small features and bug fixes, often companies don't even bother with a launch plan, and just deploy the feature when it's ready (just not on Friday). For larger releases, such as an important new feature, the company might choose to deploy the code internally but not release it publicly until a certain date.

Scrum makes this easy because you will pick a sprint whose date aligns with your launch window to be the release sprint. Velocity calculations and story point estimations will give you a good idea about what work will be available on that date. It's always smart to have the prerelease sprint be devoted to any last-minute, launch-related tasks that come up, and during the prelaunch phase you can make sure that each sprint is on track towards release. During each launch team meeting, one discussion point will be, Is everything still on track product-wise? If you find the velocity dropping, you might have to adjust your release plans.

Once you've picked a possible launch date, you'll establish a work-back schedule to determine what tasks you need to do when in preparation for launch—i.e., the week before launch, you'll do press briefings—two weeks before, all video assets need to be ready—and so on.

Testing

As part of getting ready to launch your product, it's important to put a plan together to test it with real customers so that you can make sure the product will deliver on its success metrics. Generally, companies first do an internal release of a product. The goal is to make sure everything works as expected and to catch major bugs before showing the product to any external customers.

Next, companies do a broader beta, where they open up the product to a small group of external customers. This might be via an exclusive invitation to the top contributors on your support forum or via some automatic opt-in.

The former is a better approach for bigger releases, where you have specific new features you want customers to test. Creating a select group of customers to give early access is useful because it gives you a group of people who actively use your product, and they're the most likely to use the new features and to have valuable feedback. Early access also makes these customers feel special, and they'll often want to share that status with the world when your product is released. Specifically, this group often becomes product experts, providing tips and support to other customers and advocating for your product among their peers.

Automatic opt-in is most common with web apps with a large number of users, where you can enable the feature for a short period of time for 1% of your customers and get valuable feedback. Automatic opt-in is fantastic because it gives you real data from real customers, likely exposing the product to far more customers than would manually opt in to a beta test. But it makes it hard to keep the new product a secret, just look at how often people report seeing new Facebook features before there's an official announcement. Automatic opt-in might also generate complaints or a temporary drop in your success metrics, but that data will help you improve the product so it has a successful launch. Many companies have built internal tools to allow for selective feature rollout/testing, and LaunchDarkly has built a general-purpose tool that anyone can use.

The key to planning a beta is thinking about how perfect your launch needs to be. If your product is a mobile app and new customers find it buggy, they're going to delete it and likely never reinstall it. Hardware is even less forgiving because a customer will return your product, and that costs you money to deal with. Web apps tend to be very forgiving, as you can update them multiple times an hour without the customer having to do anything. Of course, if you're strictly adhering to Lean methodology, you will do minimal if any testing and just keep releasing as fast as possible. But as we've mentioned before, most companies take a hybrid approach, which means you'll have some type of beta.

You will either own or be heavily involved in product testing. A few key things will help you run a successful beta test:

- **Make sure your beta group matches your target persona(s).** This will ensure that the people testing are the people you want to reach.

- **Test your product messaging with any outreach you do.** If you email certain customers to invite them to the beta, include the product messaging you think will make them want to use the product. It's also possible to A/B-test messages to the same persona so that you can test which message gets the most people to sign up for the beta.

- **Ensure you have appropriate onboarding.** Onboarding is the first experience a customer has with your product or updated version. In the shipping product and later betas, it's usually where you call out key features and explain why they're useful and relevant. In a beta context, onboarding is extra important because it includes any specific testing instructions, such as what part of the product to specifically test or parts that you know don't work right yet. Sometimes an onboarding experience is as simple as a release-notes email with instructions for installing the beta.

- **Have feedback mechanisms in place.** Make sure you have quantitative analytics tools in place to measure against your success metrics and to capture any crash logs, provide a qualitative feedback mechanism like Qualaroo or UserVoice so that customers can tell you what they think and reach you with any issues, and follow up with customers to see what they think. Special beta forums can provide a great way for beta testers to interact, provide feedback, and help each other out. The key pieces of feedback to look for are the product's discoverability, engagement, repetition (people come back to use it), actual use cases, and any barriers to adoption.

- **Assess your feedback and use it to inform launch decisions.** Beta tests give you a chance to see if your product addresses customers' needs successfully, and help you meet your success metrics with a small group. This gives you useful data about things you'll want to address before launch, like what bugs or other barriers to adoption many customers encountered. Sometimes you'll find a feature isn't discoverable and you need to add a callout to it specifically, or an onboarding experience to walk customers through using it. Sometimes you'll find something doesn't work as expected in the real world, and you'll decide to remove the feature. Occasionally you'll find that the whole product just isn't good and customers don't adopt it, and you'll cancel the launch. The most common result of a beta test is that you use the results to make a few minor changes and bug fixes, and then you do another beta test. After a couple of iterations with larger sample sizes in each, the product will be ready to launch.

When putting together a GTM plan, establish when you want to run each testing phase, what you're aiming to get out of each phase, and who will own it—generally support or the PM will own the tests. Make sure to plan time to react to feedback from the betas before launch.

For some products, you will also want to run stress tests with Engineering during the prelaunch phase to make sure your technical capabilities can handle any demand. For example, some very popular products generate so much interest that their web servers crash because of the sudden spike in visitors. It's quite common to add a launch task for Engineering to scale up your virtual server capacity during a launch window, until traffic has leveled off to a predictable level.

What Kind of Launch?

Think about product launches you've seen before. Sometimes you just notice a new button appear in the UX with a pop-up tip telling you to check out something new. Other times you don't get anything done for a couple hours because you're watching an Apple or Google presentation, large events we call "big-bang launches."

It's important to align the type of launch you do with the product's scope and your capability. If you don't, your product might flop or even become the punchline to a joke. Back in 2011, a mobile app photo-sharing start-up called Color focused on big-bang announcements. It received $41 million in funding right off the bat, which was huge. Then it launched its app with big fanfare, but there was a problem—Color focused on sharing with nearby users, but most people who downloaded Color found they were the only one using the app nearby and stopped using it. Color's poor testing prelaunch failed to discover this problem. Over the next few months, the company made changes to address these problems, but it had lost its momentum and the company shut down in 2012. Put simply, the product wasn't ready, the company did a big-bang launch, people gave the product a shot and were disappointed, and Color never got a second chance.

Alternatively, look at products like Gmail. Google tested it internally and then launched it with an invite-only beta. In addition to giving Google a chance to discover and fix problems before Gmail was huge, it created a feeling of exclusivity and demand for the product.

Now imagine that the new feature you're responsible for is adding a "watch offline" button to YouTube's mobile app. While this could be a great feature, you likely don't need a huge event to launch it. Instead, working with the press to get articles on various tech and media news sites and letting existing users know about the feature either in-app or via direct communication could be sufficient to achieve your launch goals—likely adoption in this case.

Small events can be another great way to effectively launch and reach key influencers. For example, if Sonos were launching a new speaker lineup, it could do the following: rent a mansion, fill it with the Sonos speaker system, cater the event, invite key customers, partners, and members of the tech and audiophile press, and expect these influencers to write for outlets Sonos customers read.

Sometimes, you'll work with a product that a customer really needs to experience to understand, especially if it's an expensive product. Would you buy a car just based on a review, or would you want to test-drive it first? For these products, you'll need a launch strategy that is very hands-on-focused, both for the initial launch and with follow-up events that let customers try the product. The VR/AR (virtual reality/augmented reality) space is a great example. The best way for people to understand why VR/AR is compelling is for them to try it themselves. When HTC released its high-end Vive VR system, it had a traveling roadshow where customers could try the Vive in specially built trailers.

These are the key things to think about for your launch type:

- Which personas care about this feature, and what customers do they map to?
- How will you reach new customers?
- How do you reach existing customers?
- What's your launch objective, beyond reaching the right customers effectively?

If you have a new product or a significant new version of an existing product, you'll want to reach new customers and existing customers, and a large event might be appropriate. If you have a big new feature, a small event or a series of press briefings focused on reaching existing customers and some new customers is likely more appropriate. If it's a small new feature, then reaching existing customers is more important than securing press coverage.

For a small company struggling for attention, successful launches can be hard. You might do everything perfectly, but if customers don't show up, it doesn't matter. One simple approach is to build up an email list of interested customers prelaunch. A "tell me more" landing page for your product is a simple way to capture email addresses. This ensures that you're reaching people who are explicitly interested in your product.

You'll want to make sure your outreach methods match your capability. If you have a sales person who manually sends email and makes calls, will he be able to handle the volume if you want him to reach out to thousands of customers the day your product launches?

Many smaller companies choose to work with a PR agency that has connections at various media outlets to help get coverage in places your target personas look. That's another reason that knowing how your target customers find information—part of the Business Model Canvas—is important: it lets you be efficient!

Once you've picked how you want to launch, you'll align your launch planning on delivering what you need to make that method successful.

Launch Asset Planning

No matter how small of a launch event you're planning, the launch team will always end up creating various assets to accompany the product launch. As the product manager, you'll often have a hand in creating these launch assets, even though other people will handle the details. Specific launch assets to consider include the following:

- **Website updates.** How will the product's page be updated on your website?

- **Support documentation.** What needs to be updated on your product's support page for the new version? Is there new training material to be created ahead of time?

- **Sample video/images.** Do you need to create new screenshots for the App Store or wherever you distribute the product?

- **Blog posts and other social media material.** What material do you want to create for the product's launch on your company's blog/social media channels? These outlets are called *owned media* because you control them, and you want to make sure they support your launch/company goals.

- **Ads.** Do you intend to have any advertising material with your product launch? If so, you'll need to create the media ahead of time.

- **Demo plan.** When company representatives are showing off the product, how will they demo the new product? Or if you're releasing a new version/feature, how does it affect existing demo plans?

- **Distribution review needs.** Application stores like the App Store often require special reviewer logins or video demos so they can make sure your app works as designed. Do you have to create anything for this process?

- **Internal product FAQ.** If you're planning on doing press briefings as part of the launch, it's also handy to create an internal product FAQ with the questions you expect to get about the product from reporters. Having clear, on-message answers to common questions, including any hard questions you might get, helps whomever is doing the press briefings prepare effectively.

- **Support-team training materials.** While the design, engineering, and product teams are likely quite familiar with the product when launch comes around, the support teams might not be as familiar. Create materials for them with the most common problems customers will face, and the solutions. Use what you learned during your testing periods to gauge the most likely problems. During and after launch, update these training materials with any new questions that arise.

- **Sales-team training materials.** As with support, it's important to create materials for the sales team so that the reps clearly understand the value in the product. These materials should focus on understanding the key buyer personas and what the product offers for them. For existing customers, be sure to provide migration information so that the sales team can help ensure smooth migrations.

While not an explicit asset, make sure to work appropriately with any external partners so that they're not caught off guard by your launch. For example, with Moover we'd want to make sure the moving companies have been notified and helped test our messaging feature. We might even choose to launch the updated web console with them quietly before launching the app to support a beta test.

A Helpful Prelaunch Marketing Framework

There is a marketing framework that's very handy for the launch team to keep in mind as they determine how to launch a product. This framework, called the 4Ps Framework, is a guide to making marketing decisions and a reminder of key decisions you have to make when launching a product. The *P*s stand for product, price, promotion, and place. Let's dive into each.

Product includes both the obvious parts of the product (what is it, who's it for, what's the benefit?) along with the non-obvious. Non-obvious elements include the packaging, accessories, support, warranty, and return policy. A helpful way to remember these non-obvious elements is that they're things the customer encounters after purchasing the product. For example, after you buy it, you unbox it. Or you buy an accessory. Or you have a problem and contact support.

Price refers to what you charge for—both normal, everyday transactions and with possible volume and sale discounts. Determining the right price can be quite complex, and it's influenced by your product goals and your desired business model. Social games are often free to play to get as many people as possible downloading them, which enables a better social game. Then, ads help provide a small bit of income from each customer, and in-app purchases help generate revenue from engaged customers while also making the game better for them. Hardware pricing is commonly based on component pricing, but sometimes companies use a razor/blade model and sell the core hardware at a loss, making money on software and accessories. As a product manager, you'll often have input on the pricing strategy, as the price is influenced by your product goals and has an impact on your success metrics and product planning.

The next *P* is *promotion*. This is what we think of traditionally with marketing: What will your press release be like? What ads will you create? How will the sales team reach customers?

Finally, we come to *place*. Where do your customers find your product for sale? Is it only on your website? Is it in specific stores, either virtual or physical? The key here is to make sure the place lines up with where your target customers go to find products. Some customers don't feel safe buying from a no-name start-up's website, for example. They might be interested in your product, but they'll hold off buying it until it's available on Amazon. Or perhaps customers expect your app to be on the Google Play store, and they'll look for it there instead of in the Amazon app store. If you're not selling where your customers are, you'll miss out.

Launch

The nice thing about planning thoroughly before launch is that during launch you're mainly executing on your plan, which is relatively relaxing and even fun!

Product managers are often company spokespeople, and we recommend working with your communication team to make sure you speak well and know the key product messages. And of course, if you're speaking externally, take care to look your best, wash your hands, trim your nails, and present a professional image.

Back in the office, the engineering and support teams will want to watch to ensure everything is functioning correctly and customers are receiving any aid they need. You, as the PM, will also want to work with them to look for any critical bugs you might have missed during your testing phase. Have a plan in place with Engineering ahead of time to asses, fix, and release these bugs as needed. But beyond that, you can take a breath and watch how your customers react to your hard work.

We call the social media posts your customers write, reviews your product receives, and articles the press writes about your product *earned media* because you don't control it nor did you pay for it. Earned media is very valuable because it means people find your product worth writing about. Of course the risk is that they don't like it and the earned media isn't positive. Fortunately, most people, especially professionals, usually choose not to write a review rather than writing something negative.

Postlaunch

In Chapter 9 we'll go into more detail for what you, the PM, will do postlaunch. Most of your work will be internally focused, assessing early results and metrics and planning what's next. The marketing and sales teams will focus on how to promote and sell the new, current version. We'll briefly define some terms you might hear when working with those teams.

The Customer Life Cycle

Just like we think about product funnels with analytics (covered back in Chapter 3), marketing also thinks about funnels. Sort of. Product marketing has become complex enough that many people think about engaging with customers as a loop called the customer life cycle.

Customers often start their journey with the awareness, interest, and engagement phases. This simply means people know about your product and seek to learn more. Marketing teams often pay for display and social ads to get more customers at this part of the funnel. A display ad is the typical visual advertisement we think of, such as an ad in a magazine or a banner ad. A social ad is an ad you pay for on a social network, whether it's a text ad on Twitter or an image on Instagram. What marketers love about online marketing is that it can be very targeted. Unlike a newspaper ad that lots of people see, online ads can be shown only to 31-year-old women who are interested in casual video games. This helps ensure your advertising reaches the right personas!

The next life cycle phase is about getting people to trust your product will deliver on its promise and to buy it—offering money-back guarantees is a common technique here. It often includes seeking out peer opinions and doing research on the product, such as looking for reviews. Affiliate marketing can help move customers through these steps. Affiliate marketing is when a trusted source receives a small payment for encouraging its audience to buy your product. Customers are happy because they now feel they can trust your product, affiliates are happy because they received a payment for their expert advice, and your company's happy because you have a new customer. Sometimes companies provide special deals for their affiliate partners, such as discount codes, which gives new customers even more incentive to purchase your product.

The last phases of the customer life cycle are about customer satisfaction and advocacy. The ultimate goal of the customer life cycle is to have customers advocating for you. Word of mouth is one of the most important factors in why people buy certain products, and it brings new customers into the customer life cycle, making them aware of your product. While the support team will play the largest role in this phase, ensuring customers have a positive experience, the marketing team will often also help with customer retention and loyalty so that they in turn recommend the product again. They might do this by sending swag like T-shirts to customers or by sending special offers to get the customer to make another transaction. If you've ever tried to cancel your cable, phone, or Internet service, you've likely found yourself talking to a person whose job is to do whatever it takes to retain you as a customer, such as offering you a fantastic deal.

As a customer moves through each phase, you'll need to make sure she sees the appropriate messaging and material. You don't need to show a money-back guarantee—which helps the trust phase—when you're trying to just make people aware of your product.

The different messaging is important when working with search engine optimization and marketing (SEO/SEM). This is an entire field, and we're not going to go into it in depth, but SEO refers to how you optimize your site so that when people search for keywords, you're the relevant result. SEM is when you pay to have an ad for your website appear based on certain keywords.

Marketing Cost Measurement Terms

With all of these approaches, there are a few key terms you should be aware of, as they sometimes come up during strategy meetings between product and marketing:

- **Pay per impression (PPI):** You pay for the ad whenever it's shown. *Impression* means "someone saw the ad."
- **Pay per click (PPC):** You pay for the ad only when someone clicks on it.
- **Pay per action (PPA):** You pay only when the user achieves some final action, such as downloading your app.
- **Click-through rate (CTR):** The percentage of people who click on your ad.
- **Cost per impression (CPI)/cost per thousand impressions (CPM):** This is how much you pay to have your ad shown once (CPI)—more commonly listed as the cost to have it shown 1,000 times (CPM).

This can be used to assess how effective a campaign is. It's simply the advertising cost divided by the number of impressions.

- **Cost per click (CPC):** This is the actual price you pay for each click in your PPC advertising. In bid-based systems like on Google and Bing, this might be lower than the price you entered. For example, if you placed the highest bid at $2/click, which means you'd pay at most $2 for each click, the actual amount you'll pay is based on various factors such as the closest competitor's bid and your ad quality. CPC is often used when there's a daily budget for running display and search ads. When you hit your budget, you stop running the ad for the day. As you'd expect, CPC is often CPI divided by CTR.

- **Customer lifetime value (CLV/LTV):** How much money do you expect to make from this customer over the product's lifetime? This is useful for determining how much to spend advertising to this customer. The CLV should be greater than what you spend to acquire the customer. If you have to spend $100 on display and affiliate promotions to acquire a customer but only expect to make $20 on this customer, you'll have lost money.

MOOVER'S GTM PLAN

Here's a first pass at Moover's GTM plan. The launch team will break these tasks down into explicit action items and assign them, and they might raise concerns during launch for issues not listed here. But this should give you an understanding of how to start thinking about launching and marketing a product.

Key message: Moover takes the hassle out of planning a move.

New-feature message: Moover's new chat feature takes the hassle out of talking with movers.

Prelaunch

- *How we will test this internally?* We'll ask for volunteers on various teams to help test the mobile app and web dashboard for 10 minutes each day over the course of two weeks. By using both aspects, they can make sure everything goes through as they expected. Using the product for a few minutes each day is likely the most common use case. We'll also designate one person on the QA team to handle a different fake company in the database so that she can test the "many clients/one response source" system.

- *How will we test this externally?* We will ship it and turn it on for a small group of customers with no special announcement and see how usage changes, if customers have problems, and more. It's tough to create a beta pool for moving customers because people move and then don't do it again for a while. Letting customers try this feature also means we'll have to roll out the web portal to our moving companies earlier, as they'll need to be able to answer messages. We'll need to create training material for these companies and provide support.

- *How will we launch this?* This is not a huge feature, so it doesn't need much fanfare. However, because many people haven't heard of Moover, we want to use this to help generate fresh articles about our product. We'll work with our PR firm to do a small press tour, and we'll make sure the focus is on the core product message more than this specific new feature. We'll need to come up with a sample demo flow for these briefings. Perhaps we can have a fake moving company that automatically sends a series of replies on the back end so that it appears like you're having a real conversation with the company during the press briefing.

- *What assets do we need to create?* We need training and support materials for our moving-company customers, updated screenshots and documentation for the website and app stores, and a blog post describing what's in this update.

- *How will we reach customers?* We don't have frequently recurring customers, so reaching existing customers isn't a big concern. We can continue to promote Moover in general on job boards like LinkedIn (given that after people get a new job, they often move).

Launch

There should be very little to do during launch, aside from updating the website with new product information and releasing the updated app.

We'll want to make sure our website can handle an increased visitor load, but given how infrequently people move, we don't expect a huge uptick in simultaneous active users in the app. Given we see an average of 1,000 users per day, we could start by assuming that each user sends two chats per day to every moving company he has a bid from. There's an average of five bids per user. This means we should be prepared to handle 1000 * 2 * 5, or 10,000 chats per day, which isn't a huge number. We can adjust capacity as needed after things level off.

Postlaunch

We will continue to promote Moover as normal, especially focusing on targeted display and search ads. The general message is still the key message to promote, as our app awareness isn't at the point where it's worth advertising specific features initially.

We'll want to watch how often people use the chat feature to make sure it's sufficiently discoverable and intuitive.

For many in your company, especially the sales, marketing, and support teams, postlaunch is when they really go to work. For you, this is the last major step in the product-development life cycle. Read on to learn how to finish up the life cycle.

CHAPTER NINE

FINISHING THE PRODUCT-DEVELOPMENT LIFE CYCLE

Congratulations! You've successfully shipped your product! Everything's done, right? Well, you need to do three more things during this cycle: PARTY, self-assess the cycle, and create a recommendation for the next iteration. Let's look at these three in detail.

CELEBRATE!

It's really important for team and company morale to celebrate even small wins. For instance, you might celebrate fixing a difficult bug by getting cupcakes (make sure to take dietary requirements like gluten/sugar-free into account.) When you ship a major version of your product, you might take the core team out for a nice dinner. And when you ship something big, you might help organize a companywide celebration.

These celebrations provide a way for individual contributors to get recognized for their work. Product managers are often the most visible representatives for their products, even though they're not the ones designing it or doing the coding. It's important to give credit to the team for doing a great job so that each person feels important and like a part of something bigger. It's also a great way to build respect between you and the team—one of the easiest ways to lose your team's respect is to take credit for the team's work.

If you're organizing a companywide celebration, as a PM you'll likely give a quick speech. This is a great opportunity to recognize the core team, specific others who have gone above and beyond to help get the product launched, and any groups that contributed to it beyond the product's core team. It's also really nice to have positive feedback from internal people (what'd the CEO think?) and external people (press quotes, customer emails) to share. This feedback is extra validation that the team's work is being well received. If a launch wasn't well received, you should still recognize the effort that went into it, as you want the team to have a positive attitude when working on the next iteration of the product.

Organizing small activities and celebrations while building the product can also be very helpful for team morale. When the team hits a key milestone, you might go on an outing to play mini-golf.

It will likely fall to you to organize these celebrations—though your office manager/HR team can help with companywide ones. Make sure to be cognizant of the importance of these celebrations, as it's easy to forget about them with all the other things on a product manager's plate.

ASSESS HOW THINGS WENT

Ultimately what matters most to the company is what your customers think of the product and if you achieve your success metrics, but it's important to look at how you got to the release. If you alienated everyone or made the product extremely hard to build, the people on your team likely won't want to work on the next version and might even look for different jobs. Assessing how things went ensures that you gather feedback, letting people feel their concerns are heard, and think about how to do better in the next cycle.

For some people, assessing how things went during the development cycle is very difficult, personally. This is when you explicitly put yourself out there and ask for feedback, and you will get feedback, both positive and negative.

Discussion with Your Lead

The first part of getting feedback is to see what your lead thought of your work. Was she happy with how you approached everything, or were there things she'd like you to try doing differently? Did she get positive feedback from other teams about you, or were other leads always complaining about you? It's very useful to schedule a one-on-one meeting with your lead, if you don't have regularly scheduled meetings, to check in and make sure everything is good. A way to start the conversation is by asking, "Could you give me feedback on how you feel this cycle went? I want to make sure I'm doing the best job possible." After all, we grow by working on our weak spots.

Team Postmortem

The other part of assessing how things went is to get the team's feedback, and an effective way to do this is with a postmortem meeting. There are a few different ways to run these meetings. We'll walk you through how to run one yourself with the core team. If you feel you had problems working with the team, you might ask someone else to run the postmortem so you can be absent from the room to make the team feel comfortable speaking openly. Some companies have open-door postmortems, where anyone in the company can drop in to hear about the process. You'll just have to pick what feels most appropriate for your situation.

Here's how we like to run postmortems. Find a time where the product's core team and the key stakeholders are available, and schedule a meeting for an hour or so. You'll want to try to create a relaxed and open atmosphere, which can mean anything from booking the meeting room with the comfy chairs to providing food and alcoholic/non-alcoholic drinks for the team—it varies company to company. Just make sure you have a whiteboard or something to write on that everyone can see.

Since this meeting is about feedback, all opinions are valid—make sure you don't put value judgments on what people say, especially if they give you negative feedback. Divide the whiteboard into two columns: things you did well, and things you wish went more smoothly. Start by asking everyone to say what they think went well. After a bit, switch to the other list and ask for things people wish had gone better. Bounce back and forth between the lists until you feel everyone's been heard.

Last, take some time to discuss what you want to do differently and what you want to keep the same during the next cycle. You should write down the postmortem notes somewhere, like on the product's wiki page, including the key things you're committing to doing differently during the next cycle. Periodically refer back to this list to make sure you're alleviating as much of the process pain as you can while keeping the good things.

RECOMMENDING WHAT'S NEXT

After launch, it's time to start another iteration of the product-development life cycle. However, there's a challenge. In an ideal world, you'd have useful data about how what you did during this iteration affected your success metrics and goals. Unfortunately, it usually takes time to gather enough useful data to see whether your changes worked. Your immediate next iteration will be driven by your product roadmap (Chapter 2) and other approaches we covered in Chapter 3. Then, after enough time has passed to gather useful data from this iteration, you'll put this product into one of three high-level buckets. Specifically, you'll recommend moving on to something else because this product/feature is good enough, iterating more on this product, or sunsetting this product.

If you've achieved or surpassed your success-metric goals, then your recommendation will likely be to move on to something else. Automatic crash reporting can be very helpful here for mobile and desktop apps, as you might uncover bugs affecting lots of customers that you want to fix before moving on, even if you hit your success-metric goals.

If you're not hitting your goals, then you need to dig deeper to think about where and how you want to iterate. Running simple A/B tests with tools like Optimizely is a great way to quickly see if you can make any small changes to help you achieve your goals. Sometimes non-core-product changes, like the wording on a website, can make a big difference. The marketing team will likely be running a lot of A/B tests on the marketing website to see what gets the most customers buying/using your product.

Looking at what your customers think is also important. Maybe you hit your revenue goals by switching to a subscription payment model, but if your customers hate it and are looking for alternatives, your long-term success is in question. What's nice about releasing a product into the wild is that you'll see product reviews, social media posts, and support tickets about the new product. Look through these, in addition to reviewing your metrics, to see what customers think.

We'd recommend rereading Chapters 3 and 4, thinking about how to come up with your next opportunity hypothesis for an existing product/feature that's not achieving its goals. Moover, for example, might find that customers love and use the chat feature, but the company still is not hitting its goals. By leveraging the advice in Chapter 3 around asking why, we might conclude we have a platform-growth problem to address next.

You might conclude that no reasonable amount of effort will make the product achieve your success-metric goals. Or maybe your company's priorities have shifted, and this product just doesn't fit with the overall strategy anymore. Or maybe a technological development has made something much better for your customers possible, but creating that "something better" will mean a completely different product and not an upgrade. In this case, your recommendation should be to end-of-life or "sunset" the product.

Sunsetting a product simply means you'll stop doing active development on it, and customers should switch to something else. We won't go into this in depth, but you usually don't just suddenly stop selling a product. It's important to have a window where customer support is still available for the product, time where customer data is still available so that customers can retrieve it for online products, and ideally a migration path to help customers move to an alternative product. While it can be frustrating for loyal customers, sunsetting products isn't a bad thing, and companies do it all the time. The trick is just to make sure you have a reasonable plan in place.

In March 2013 Google announced it was going to discontinue its Reader RSS feed aggregator because fewer and fewer people were using it and the company wanted to focus on other products. Google gave customers four months to retrieve and move their data, and they showed customers how to use Google Takeout to retrieve that data.

In another example, Apple retired its professional photo-management tool, Aperture, in mid-2014. The company provided an update to make sure Aperture worked on the upcoming version of OS X so that customers could continue to use it for at least another year. Apple also worked with its main competitor, Adobe, to ensure Adobe's professional photo-management tool, Lightroom, had an "Import from Aperture" command to help customers migrate their data.

Ultimately, whatever your recommendation is, this final step of the product-development life cycle feeds nicely into the first step we went over in Chapter 3: deciding what you should do next. The key difference is that you start by evaluating whether you're happy with what you just did, whether you need to work on it more, or whether you need to sunset the product so that you can focus on something else. And then you repeat and repeat and repeat.

CHAPTER NINE TIP

Our final tip comes from Carlos González de Villaumbrosia, founder and CEO of Product School. He has dedicated his entire career to bridging the gap between education and employment in tech. Carlos was inspired to create Product School based on his own experience when he had to learn how to break into product management the hard way.

As a good agile PM and lean entrepreneur, Carlos focused on tackling that specific problem and built a very basic MVP to validate his solution. Product School started as a casual recurring meeting between Carlos and seven aspiring product managers in Starbucks around the Financial District in San Francisco. In those meetings, Carlos would share his experience and would even invite other PMs as guest speakers to share theirs. The reaction was so positive that Carlos rented a room in a coworking space, created the first version of the product management curriculum, taught the first 10 cohorts to refine every detail related to delighting his students, and make sure they were equipped with the right tools and knowledge to build products and get PM jobs.

In just two years, Product School became the first tech business school in the world. It currently offers product management courses in San Francisco, Silicon Valley, Los Angeles, and New York. All of its instructors are senior-level PMs at top companies such as Google, Facebook, Snapchat, Airbnb, PayPal, American Express, and Netflix.

This piece of advice comes from the data and experience gained from working with Product School's product management students every day.

HOW TO BREAK INTO PRODUCT MANAGEMENT

I transitioned into product management from software engineering eight years ago, and I founded Product School to teach others aspiring product managers do the same.

The main reason people make a career shift into product management is because they are interested in having more decision-making power on the product strategy of the company. I don't blame them; this is a big shift that will impact your long-term upside since you will stop being a specialist in one part of the process to become a generalist in all the parts involved in the process by leveraging other people's talents. This approach will serve you well professionally and personally.

Throughout my career, I have meet dozens of current product managers, and entrepreneurs and investors who worked as product managers in the past. They all shared the exact same problem about how they didn't have proper training when they started their management careers in tech. Yes, it's true that a lot of them earned MBAs or similar business-related degrees at top universities that provided different skillets and access to networks that helped in the long term. But these business degrees aren't always applicable to product management, nor do they teach you how to be a product manager. In fact, most of today's product managers, whether they have MBAs or computer science degrees, had to learn their craft on the go because there wasn't any product management school that had a holistic view, incorporating business, engineering, and design, Fortunately, Product School fills that gap.

Here are some examples of different career paths to break into product management. Keep in mind that this list isn't complete:

Engineer → Senior engineer →
Technical project or program manager/engineering manager →
Product manager

Startup founder ↔ Product manager

Management consultant/investment banker → Product manager

Customer support →
Business analyst/project manager or program manager →
Product manager

Marketing → Product marketing → Product manager

Design → Product design → Product manager

The one thing all of these career paths have in common is that PMs don't start as PMs. They spend at least a few years in a different role, develop a few key skills, and then transition into product. The three critical skills I think you have to develop in order to get a job as a product manager are technical expertise, domain expertise, and communication expertise. Let's look at these three.

As you've learned from the previous chapters, even if you don't know how to code, it's critical for product managers to understand some of the engineering behind the products they're managing. This knowledge will help you communicate with designers and engineers, assess technical feasibility, and understand what the technical side of implementing a project.

Next, especially for your first product management job, it's important to understand the domain you're working within. As we discussed in Chapter 1, we've found that when you get your first PM job, if you know about the field you're working in, you will be able to spend your time focusing on how to be a product manager rather than learning the nuances, challenges, competitive landscape, and more of your domain.

Finally, something we don't cover in detail in this book is how critical great communication skills are to PMs. PMs have to communicate all the time, whether via email or presentation. In our Product School bootcamps, we spend multiple hours teaching students how to be great public speakers with plenty of practice. If you can't communicate, it doesn't matter how great of a PM you are because no one can understand you.

Beyond Product School, there are a few specific things that will help you transition into product management:

Build something. In class, our students work towards a final capstone project where they pick a company they'd be qualified to work at, determine what feature that company should build next, and create a presentation explaining why the company should build it next and the key requirements. Try doing this on your own! If you know how to code, take a project from start to finish so that you can experience shipping a product and getting feedback from customers.

Attend hackathons. Check out product hackathons such as ProtoHack or StartupWeekend to get hands-on experience building a product in high-pressure environments.

Find a mentor. Reach out to PMs you respect and who you feel could be good mentors to you. Product School has an active Slack community, product-school, which is a great place to find a mentor. A mentor can provide war stories and help you understand best practices.

Network. Check out product events in your city. Websites like Meetup and Eventbrite often feature events. These events can be a great place to find a mentor, too.

Read. The Further Reading list at the back of this book has great resources to help you learn more about being a PM. We'd highly recommend you check out *Cracking the PM Interview* by Gayle Laakmann McDowell or *Decode and Conquer* by Lewis C. Lin to understand what PM interviews involve.

Apply to associate product manager (APM) programs. Some big tech companies such as Google, Yahoo, and Facebook have entry-level APM roles for new college graduates, where they teach you how to be a PM on the job. You might qualify to apply.

One of the most common mistakes in landing your first PM job is setting your expectations too high, either in terms of your title or your company. Just because you are a senior software engineer now does not mean your first PM job will be as a senior product manager. Similarly, your current company might not be your dream company, but if there's an opening for a PM, you likely have a better chance landing that as your first PM job than getting a job elsewhere.

Be realistic! Asses your current expertise and map out realistic career paths inside or outside your current company. Your ideal PM job will likely not be your first PM job, but that's OK. As long as your first PM job is relevant to your career goals and you're surrounded by more senior people that you learn from, it will still be a great job.

NOW GO BUILD AWESOME PRODUCTS!

FURTHER READING

Chapter 1

Balez, Mat. (2014, April 14). *Product Manager You Are…A Janitor, Essentially. https://medium.com/@matbalez/product-manager-you-are-664d83ee702e#.ae25xz72r.*

Elman, Josh. (2013, July 19). A Product Manager's Job. *https://medium.com/@joshelman/a-product-managers-job-63c09a43d0ec#.h6re9qq6r.*

First Round Review. Find, Vet, and Close the Best Product Managers. *http://firstround.com/review/find-vet-and-close-the-best-product-managers-heres-how/.*

Horowitz, Ben, and David Weiden. Good Product Manager Bad Product Manager. *http://www.khoslaventures.com/wp-content/uploads/Good_Product_Manager_Bad_Product_Manager_KV.pdf.*

Laakmann McDowell, Gayle, and Jackie Bavaro. *Cracking the PM Interview: How to Land a Product Manager Job in Technology.* CareerCup, 2013.

Nash, Adam. (2011, December 16). Be a Great Product Leader. *http://blog.adamnash.com/2011/12/16/be-a-great-product-leader/.*

Chapter 2

Cagan, Marty. *Inspired: How to Create Products Customers Love.* SVPG Press, 2008.

Christensen, Clayton. *The Innovator's Dilemma: When New Technologies Cause Great Firms to Fail (Management of Innovation and Change).* Harvard Business Review Press, 2016.

Pichler, Roman. *Strategize: Product Strategy and Product Roadmap Practices for the Digital Age.* Pichler Consulting, 2016.

Reichheld, Frederick F. (2003, December). The One Number You Need to Grow. *https://hbr.org/2003/12/the-one-number-you-need-to-grow.*

Sinek, Simon. *Start with Why: How Great Leaders Inspire Everyone to Take Action.* Penguin Group, 2009.

Sinofsky, Steven. (2013, January 28). Balancing Tradeoffs Across Different Customers. *https://blog.learningbyshipping.com/2013/01/28/balancing-tradeoffs-across-different-customers/.*

Tavel, Sarah. (2016, March 23). The Hierarchy of Engagement. *https://www.linkedin.com/pulse/hierarchy-engagement-sarah-tavel.*

Chapter 3

Blank, Steve. *The Four Steps to the Epiphany: Successful Strategies for Products that Win.* Cafepress.com, 2013.

Eyal, Nir. *Hooked: How to Build Habit-Forming Products.* Portfolio Penguin, 2014.

Olsen, Dan. *The Lean Product Playbook: How to Innovate with Minimum Viable Products and Rapid Customer Feedback.*

Osterwalder, Alexander and Yves Pigneur. *Business Model Generation: A Handbook for Visionaries, Game Changers, and Challengers.* Wiley, 2010.

Osterwalder, Alexander, Yves Pigneur, and Gregory Bernarda. *Value Proposition Design: How to Create Products and Services Customers Want (Strategyzer).* Wiley, 2014.

Ries, Eric. *The Lean Startup: How Today's Entrepreneurs Use Continuous Innovation to Create Radically Successful Businesses.* Viking, 2011.

Segall, Ken. *Insanely Simple: The Obsession That Drives Apple's Success.* Penguin Group, 2012.

Traynor, Des. *Prioritising Features: Who'll Use It & How Often?* Retrieved from *https://blog.intercom.io/prioritising-features-wholl-use-it-how-often/.*

Chapter 4

Alvarez, Cindy. *Lean Customer Development: Building Products Your Customers Will Buy*. O'Reilly, 2014.

Constable, Giff, Frank Rimalovski, and Tom Fishburne. *Talking to Humans: Success Starts with Understanding Your Customers.* Gift Constable, 2014.

Hoekman, Robert Jr. (2016, May 17). UX Reality Check: 14 Hard Truths About Users. *http://www.fastcodesign.com/3059921/ux-reality-check-14-hard-truths-about-users.*

Intercom. *Intercom on Product Management. https://www.intercom.io/books/product-management.*

Nash, Adam. What are the best ways to prioritize a list of product features? Retrieved from *https://www.quora.com/What-are-the-best-ways-to-prioritize-a-list-of-product-features.*

Traynor, Des. *Product Strategy Means Saying No.* https://blog.intercom.io/product-strategy-means-saying-no/.

Chapter 5

Cagan, Martin. How to Write a Good PRD. *http://www.svpg.com/assets/Files/goodprd.pdf.*

McAllister, Ian. What is Amazon's approach to product development and product management? Retrieved from *https://www.quora.com/Amazon-company-What-is-Amazons-approach-to-product-development-and-product-management.*

McKee, Robert. *Story: Style, Structure, Substance, and the Principles of Screenwriting.* HarperCollins, 2010.

Yoskovitz, Ben. (2011, November 14). The Specification Is Dead; Long Live the Specification. *http://www.instigatorblog.com/the-specification-is-dead-long-live-the-specification/2011/11/14/.*

Chapter 6

Derochie, Cole. (2014, June 17). Measure Twice, Cut Once: Introducing Usability Testing into Our Design Process. *http://inside.unbounce.com/product-dev/introducing-usability-testing/.*

Knapp, Jake, John Zeratsky, and Braden Kowitz. *Sprint: How to Solve Big Problems and Test New Ideas in Just Five Days.* Simon & Schuster, 2016.

Krug, Steve. *Don't Make me Think, Revisited: A Common Sense Approach to Web Usability.* New Riders, 2014.

Krug, Steve. *Rocket Surgery Made Easy: The Do-It-Yourself Guide to Finding and Fixing Usability Problems.* New Riders, 2009.

Norman, Don. *The Design of Everyday Things: Revised and Expanded Edition.* Basic Books, 2013.

Zhuo, Julie. (2013, August 15). How to Work with Designers. *https://medium.com/the-year-of-the-looking-glass/how-to-work-with-designers-6c975dede146#.kib1vjbd5.*

Chapter 7

Brooks, Frederick P. Jr. *The Mythical Man-Month: Essays on Software Engineering*. Addison-Wesley Professional, 1995.

Chisa, Ellen. Engineers: So Your PM Sucks? Here's How to Fix It. *http://blog.ellenchisa.com/2014/07/20/engineers-pm-sucks-heres-fix/.*

Fowler, Martin. (2003, October 1). Technical Debt. *http://martinfowler.com/bliki/TechnicalDebt.html.*

Jemilo, Drew. (2011, August 8). Leading the Agile Release Train. https://www.agilealliance.org/wp-content/uploads/2016/01/Leading-the-Agile-Release-Train-Agile2011.pdf.

Lotz, Mary. (2013, July 5). Waterfall vs. Agile: Which is the Right Development Methodology for Your Project? Retrieved from *http://www.seguetech.com/blog/2013/07/05/waterfall-vs-agile-right-development-methodology.*

Pichler, Roman. *Agile Product Management with Scrum: Creating Products That Customers Love.* Addison-Wesley Professional, 2010.

Seibel, Peter. *Coders at Work: Reflections on the Craft of Programming.* Apress, 2009.

Spolsky, Joel. *Joel on Software. http://joelonsoftware.com.*

Zhou, Julie. (2013, August 28). How to Work with Engineers. *https://medium.com/the-year-of-the-looking-glass/how-to-work-with-engineers-a3163ff1eced#.h2lk3tr6v.*

Chapter 8

Jiwa, Bernadette. *Meaningful: The Story of Ideas that Fly*. Perceptive Press, 2015.

Johnson, Steve. (2014, January 23). Is Product Marketing the Same as Marketing? (I Say No). *http://onproductmanagement.net/2014/01/23/is-product-marketing-the-same-as-marketing-i-say-no/.*

Kitcho, Catherine. *High Tech Product Launch*. Pele Publications, 2005.

Ries, Al, Jack Trout, and Philip Kotler. *Positioning: The Battle for Your Mind*. McGraw-Hill Education, 2000.

Lauchengco, Martina. (2012, April 28). Product Marketing Contribution. *http://www.svpg.com/product-marketing-contribution/.*

Segall, Ken. *Insanely Simple*. Penguin Publishing Group, 2012.

Chapter 9

Quora. *https://www.quora.com/profile/Carlos-Gonzalez-de-Villaumbrosia.*

Mixpanel. (2016, February 10). So you want to be a product manager? Make yourself the product. *https://blog.mixpanel.com/2016/02/10/so-you-want-to-be-a-product-manager-make-yourself-the-product/.*

Product School Blog. 3 Common Mistakes by Engineers Transitioning to Product Management. *https://www.productschool.com/blog/get-job/3-common-mistakes-for-engineers-transitioning-to-product-management-2/.*

ACKNOWLEDGEMENTS

Many people imagine that writing a book means you simply sit down, write a lot, and press a magical "Publish" button. That couldn't be further from the truth. It takes a team to create a book, not just an author, and we're fortunate to have worked with a great team for this one.

To the team at Product School, both past and present, thank you for the structure and support you brought this book. Special thanks go to Aaron Filous, Jasmin Lopez, and Stany Yeh for their efforts with this project.

We owe a huge thank-you to Jason Alt for being our first reader and technical editor. His notes made this book orders of magnitude better! Jason, we're glad to call you a friend. Further readers helped refine this material, for which we are grateful. These readers included Richard Fleming and Max Kornblith.

A number of great people contributed pro tips for this book, too, to provide extra perspective and advice. Thank you to Kirk Paulsen, Jeremy Toeman, Beatriz Datangel, Conrad Albrecht-Buehler, Nik Laufer-Edel, Mohammad Musa, and Mike Belsito for their wisdom.

Beyond the text, thank you to the talented Candace Cunningham for once again being a great copy editor and fooling the world into thinking we know more about grammar than we really do. We're also thrilled to have worked with the finishing team at *The Frontispiece* for the first time, and we look forward to working with them again.

JOSH'S ACKNOWLEDGEMENTS

To the team at Product School, thank you for giving me the opportunity to write this book! I owe Product School's CEO, Carlos González de Villaumbrosia, a debt of gratitude for getting me involved in Product School and bringing me this opportunity.

I genuinely appreciate the moral support I received from family and friends, including Ellen Anon, Jack Anon, Seth Anon, Eliot Peper, and Kellie Hudson. Thanks to the product team at Magic Leap, including Jeff Gattis, Sakina Groth, and Cole Shelton for helping me be a better product manager.

Finally, I once again owe thanks to my high school English teacher Claudia Skerlong. However, I did once overhear her say that she thought Donald Trump would win a second term before I wrote a ninth book.